S0-ABD-024

LEAVING STORY AVENUE

Also by Paul LaRosa

Seven Days of Rage:
The Deadly Crime Spree of the Craigslist Killer

Death of a Dream:
The Catherine Woods Story

Tacoma Confidential

Nightmare in Napa:
The Wine Country Murders

LEAVING STORY AVENUE

My journey from the projects to the front page

Paul LaRosa

PARK SLOPE PUBLISHING

Copyright © 2012 Paul LaRosa

All rights reserved. No part of this publication may be repro-
duced, distributed, or transmitted in any form or by any means,
including photocopying, recording, or other electronic or
mechanical methods, without the prior written permission of the
publisher, except in the case of brief quotations embodied in criti-
cal reviews and certain other noncommercial uses permitted by
copyright law. For permission requests, write to the publisher,
addressed "Attention: Permissions Coordinator," at the address
below.

M. Berger
Park Slope Publishing LLC
Brooklyn, NY 11215

Printed in the United States of America

Softcover: ISBN 978-0-9837963-0-5

Kindle: ISBN 978-0-9837963-2-9

ePub: ISBN 978-0-9837963-1-2

FIRST EDITION

Book design by Joel Friedlander
www.TheBookDesigner.com

To my friend Tony
Anthony Charles Rauba
(4/15/52 – 2/17/12)

Table of Contents

LEAVING STORY AVENUE

The Newsroom--1977

The noise is what gets you first: the uproar generated by dozens of angry, desperate, hopeful reporters banging away on ancient manual typewriters, the keys nearly blasting through the inky cloth ribbons, tearing into sheets of innocent paper—all at the same moment. The reporters wrestle their man-sized typewriters into submission, forcing them to cooperate on deadline or else. It's more a battleground than a newsroom. Faces are flushed, mothers are rebuked, and curses fill the air.

Where the fuck is my coffee?

Why the fuck won't he call back?

Get off my fucking back!

And the ever-popular: *Fuck, fuck, fuck*!!!

But it isn't only the sound of grown men (and a very few women) having the temper tantrums of young children. There are also the incessant cries of *copy* at which point a handful of young men rise as one from a strategically placed wooden bench. The quickest among them runs over to the reporter holding a piece of paper, or *copy*, high in the air—

one page of a story the reporter is writing for tomorrow's paper. Someone else yells "Slug it 'murder' and give me two takes."

Sometimes, the high-pitched voice of the withered-armed, skinny copy chief, Chile, pierces the air but he never utters the word "copy." *He* prefers to yell "boy" for *his* needs. That a comely young woman is now rushing toward him makes no difference—in Chile's eyes, she too is "boy." He's obsessed with grammar but unaffected by gender. There is a newspaper to put out and Chile's role is integral, or so he believes. He commandeers the U-shaped copy desk, and jams proof-read sheets of paper into a canvas belt that endlessly circles his desk, carrying the copy down to the 6th-floor composing room, where it is transformed into hot type by dozens of brittle old men sitting at blacker-than-black linotype machines. Nearby are giant, forbidding-looking vats of bubbling molten lead, the raw material for those Dickensian machines.

Here at *The New York Daily News*, information is a chameleon, changing shape before your eyes. Photographs are no exception. They whoosh through pneumatic tubes from the darkroom to the picture desk, and ultimately to the composing room floor where they join with the printed page.

But back to the vast 7th-floor newsroom, this glorious newsroom which has been the inspiration for many a movie. This is the real thing—a diorama of the word *deadline*. Everyone is in a hurry. Doors are banging, people are running, intensity fills the sweat-soaked air. The newsroom is primeval. People chomp at each other and fight over anything, everything, especially chairs, a childish currency of tribal importance. Men mark their seats like warriors, not only with names but with odd-shaped symbols, and there is a price to pay for anyone daring to breach clear signs of occupation.

Get the fuck up!

Get out of my fucking chair!

I said, get up motherfucker!

Grown men grapple, pulling chairs out from under one another. These are men who will tell politicians *go fuck yourself* but are afraid even to venture as far as the nearest rest room, lest they lose that chair.

In the middle of this orgy of bad behavior and even worse manners is the switchboard, and manning that switchboard is me.

I sit here in the highly visible job of city desk assistant, having been promoted from copyboy. Operating the switchboard is a three-man operation. Two of us take the calls and the third opens the reader mail and writes obits. The job pay grade is Group 8, not so far from the reporter's pay grade of Group 10. I make a lot of money on the switchboard, and it is fun in that old-fashioned, bang-your-head-against-the-wall-sort of way.

It is a pressure-filled job and I have to deal with people either on edge or in full-blown panic. I wear a headset and do battle each day with an uncooperative switchboard, a tangle of confusing elastic cords. When someone calls, a small light on the board goes green. It is my cue to plug in one of the cords, and growl in my pseudo-tough guy voice: "City Desk." If it's a reporter out in the field looking for a rewrite man, I take the corresponding cord and slam it into the rewrite man's hole, so to speak. His phone rings and he is connected to the man in the field. Most of the calls, whether from reporters or readers, come through that switchboard. I get to know a lot about people that way. I know the married guys with girlfriends, the ones whose wives never stop calling, and the few who are gay. On this switchboard I am an insider.

The heart of the city room is the four-sided, wooden clock. Under that clock sit the editor and the assistant editor. Here, the world revolves around time—*there are deadlines, damnit!*—and if you don't get *your fucking story* in on deadline, well, there is always the lobster shift, the Queens bureau or, God forbid, the features copy desk. Beneath the clock, the two editors on the city desk read the copy as it's placed before them, and if they don't like what they see, they have thick pencils, rulers, sharp scissors and sticky glue pots at arms reach. Like demented grammar school teachers, they will tear and cut and glue and cross out until the story resembles something *they* like, not the piece of shit you turned in.

All of this only adds to the din exploding all over the room. But, in case you get the wrong idea, this newsroom is fun, happening, exciting, and yes, a little frightening. I am 24 years old and a college graduate, happy to be here. Of course I want to be a reporter. All the copyboys do. That is the goal but it is elusive.

As I am untangling one uncooperative phone cord from another, the head copyboy Carlos appears at my side. In his Colombian accent, he tells me: "Paul, Quinn wants to see you. I'll cover."

E.F. Quinn is in charge of personnel at the *New York Daily News* and he wields a fair amount of power. He does not have as much input into decisions as the editors but he has their ear, and if he likes you, you could get far. If not, well....

I do not think Quinn likes me. For one thing, I'm not Irish, and that counts. Quinn is not unlike Boss Tweed; he likes his own. But Quinn has a grudging respect for me because I aced the writing test. It is the first hurdle in getting promoted to reporter.

Quinn does not like to promise anything, just the opposite. The day I was hired as a copyboy was the day I got the speech:

Don't expect to be a reporter. It happens for one in ten copyboys and it probably won't happen for you.

Editor Jean Joyce lighting up a cigarette in the newsroom

Quinn is the personification of low expectations. I think it's because Quinn has not made it. No one joins a newspaper to work in the personnel department.

I have been as good an employee as anyone, not that it matters when it comes to getting promoted to reporter. Since being hired as a copyboy three years earlier, I have risen to increasingly more important jobs at the paper: caption writer, city desk assistant, and have even filled in as a reporter here and there. There have been no complaints, mostly compliments, and I've bagged a bunch of bylines.

Many of my peers wound up here because they have cousins or fathers who work at the paper. I live in a housing project in the Bronx, paid my own way through Fordham University. If I can get a job where I can make a living as a writer, it will mean more than I could have hoped for.

Quinn knows how much I want the job and he is not what you call generous of spirit. Just the opposite—he seems to revel in lording it over people like me. I am apprehensive as I wait in front of his secretary. He has something I want but will he give it to me?

I know one thing—I can write and write on deadline. It's always come easy to me. Getting people to talk, making contacts, ferreting out the story—that is not so easy. But I am learning.

I make the long walk back to Quinn's office which is removed from the city room. As I do, I pass some of the characters here I've come to know so well: Vinnie, the massive firefighter reporter—400 pounds if an ounce—who has a specially made chair with arms removed so his frame will fit; Cheech, the police reporter, pure Brooklyn Italian, complete with gold chains and a Rat Pack gait that says *fuck you asshole* with every step; Alex, a short man—well under five feet—with an enormous voice. And there are others: the drunk poured over his typewriter, waiting to take rewrite one last time; the disgruntled former prizewinner ignored by the city desk; the aging editor who ducks out to sip some "soup" that is 80 proof; the crack night-side reporter who wears a bad toupee and runs an ethnic newspaper from his desk; the artist who tries nearly every day to slip sketches of penises into the paper; and an entire desk of makeup men—responsible for making sure the pages of the next day's paper are *accurate*—who come in stinking of alcohol and proceed to drink their way through the final edition replate.

I have no idea what Quinn wants as his secretary waves me inside.

"Paul, how are you?"

We shake hands but he does not invite me to take a seat.

"Paul, you know journalism, it's a funny business. Some people make it, some don't. One out of ten copyboys who come into my office gets promoted to reporter. It's hard. You know that."

I nod. I've heard it all before.

"I know you've been writing and filling in and people say you do a good job."

"Thank you Mr. Quinn."

"Well look," he says, losing patience with himself. He puts his hands on my shoulders, more to steady himself than to extend good will, and looks me in the eye. "We're promoting you to reporter in the Brooklyn section."

It's the last thing I expect. I am a little choked up, but I recover in time to put out my hand to shake Quinn's. "Wow, thank you. That's great news. I really appreciate it."

But Quinn isn't finished. "Look, I hope it works out but I don't think it will last very long. Enjoy it while you can."

The magic in the air—there only a moment ago—evaporates. It is the most half-assed promotion ever. My anger floods the room. I want to punch Quinn in his bulbous nose, especially when he gives me that smug little half-smile that signals his hope that I will not make it.

But I don't hit him; instead, I walk out, back into that newsroom that I love so much. The noise is still there, abating only a little. It looks the same but I am different. I have a chance. I hear Quinn's words: *I don't think it will last very long.*

"We'll see about that, asshole," I mutter under my breath as I head back into the madness.

Quinn doesn't know anything about me.

East Harlem

My greatest wish is to be a cowboy and my favorite television show is "The Lone Ranger." I am a Lone Ranger nut and crazy about cowboys. "Hi Yo Silver and Away!" I yell day and night. And in a quieter voice, I whisper, *who was that masked man?*

I want to be that masked man when I become an adult, when I imagine I'll move away from East Harlem. I hear the adults say that we live on *a hun sixth* and there are no cowboys or horses anywhere around here. I did once see a little donkey. An Italian man with a heavy accent was downstairs giving rides to kids for 25 cents and my Dad—Paul is his name, like mine—bought me a ride. Even though the donkey was small and smelly, I was higher up off the ground than anyone. It was a good feeling and, more than ever after that, I decided it was the cowboy life for me.

I bug my parents for cowboy stuff and they do buy me a lot of neat things: plastic models of the Lone Ranger and Tonto (and their horses), a rocking horse, a gun that shoots tiny plastic bullets, a gun belt, a cowboy hat, a cowboy shirt, and my favorite—real metal spurs.

The spurs arrive on Christmas morning which explains why I find myself walking toward St. Lucy's Church on December 25th outfitted in full cowboy regalia. It's taken me a while to get everything just right and when I walk into the church with my mother, the Mass has already started.

My mother pushes open the heavy doors in the back of the church. The church is full and we have the bad luck to enter during a lull when no one is singing any Christmas carols. I take one step and then another down the center aisle looking for an empty seat. With each step, my spurs jingle and jangle just like a real cowboy. It sounds pretty good to me but I notice that everyone has turned their heads and is now watching me. I raise my cowboy hat off my head to a nearby woman and, like I've seen on TV, I say, "Howdy ma'am."

She smiles and whispers "howdy" back but a man on the other side of the aisle hisses at me, "Stop making so much noise, and take off that stupid hat."

Well, I don't much like *that* guy and I pull my six-shooter out of my holster, take aim at his big stomach and pull the trigger. A small gray plastic bullet leaves my gun and hits him square in the belly.

A few people laugh but now he looks extra angry. My mother is trying to grab the gun out of my hand as the angry man jumps out of his pew and heads toward me. "I'm gonna teach you a lesson," he says, and with that, I start to run down the aisle. Every step I take the spurs jingle and jangle and before I know what's happening, I realize that I'm running toward the altar. A couple of other men jump out to try and catch me but I keep slipping by them. I see the priest staring open-mouthed at me as I head toward a side door. I am nearly there when an arm grabs me. It is a mean-looking nun. She has me tight by the arm and is squeezing hard as she escorts me out the side door.

As my mother catches up to us, the nun hisses: "You take those spurs off, go home and don't come back into the Lord's House until you are ready to pray and pay Him some respect."

I think my mother is as scared as I am because we nod our heads yes and leave immediately.

My father works nights so I don't see him a lot, at least not when he's awake. I do see him sleeping a lot. He sleeps almost all day long, and my mother says I cannot wake him no matter what. Once in a while I do and he gets very angry.

I ask him about his job and he tells me he's a maintenance man for Railway Express.

"What does that mean?"

"It means I work on trains?"

"Do you help them go?"

"That's right. I help them go."

Sounds pretty good to me but he's tired a lot and I don't think he likes his job because he's kind of grumpy. My mom tells me he could have had a better job but he was drafted into the Army when he was in high school and fought in World War II. My dad shows me photos of himself in uniform, and I can't believe it's him. He has hair and looks a lot younger, like a teenager. He can really draw cartoon characters, and one weekend, he buys a paint brush and paints Disney people all over my furniture. It makes me wish he could have gotten the job he wanted, a job where he could draw but now, my mom says, he's supporting us.

My mother is home all the time. I also have a brother named Bob who is born when I'm five years old. My brother is kind of a baby. He doesn't talk much. So my mother mainly talks to me and her sister Ann. Mom calls what they do *chewing the rag* but I never see anything in their mouths so I don't understand what she means. All I know is that I'm alone a lot. I don't have any friends, so I make up stories in my head about being a cowboy and riding around on a big horse. Sometimes I imagine shooting a gun and killing bad guys. That would be fun.

I'm only 5 so I don't go to school yet, and so I'm in the house all day long, singing and thinking up games in my head. When my Dad does wake up, he usually eats but then he sits me on his lap, and reads me the comics from his two favorite newspapers, *The Daily News* and *The Mirror*. He buys them both everyday, even though they kind of look alike to me. I like Sundays best of all because the comics are in color.

I sit in Dad's lap as he turns page after page reading me Dick Tracy, Li'l Abner, Brenda Starr, and Smilin' Jack. They're always having great adventures and it makes me a little jealous because their lives are so interesting. I wish I could have an adventure, and fight bad guys. I wish I had a watch like Dick Tracy where I could talk to people blocks away. I wish I were Smiling' Jack and could fly an airplane.

My Dad always sounds out the words and puts my finger on the letters.

"See," he says, "Jack. J-A-C-K. Jack. "

It's my favorite thing to do with my Dad and one day, a miracle happens. I see the letters over Dick Tracy's head snap together as one. I say the word I see: "Stop."

"Stop," I say again, louder this time.

"Yes," my father says, "you can read."

Dad starts bringing home comic books. Superman and Batman are my favorites, and I can't wait until new ones come out. More and more, I find that I can read them on my own, and when I have a question, I ask one of my parents for help.

One night, when I'm watching television, a new program comes on—"The Adventures of Superman." It's like a comic strip on TV. Clark Kent, who they call a mild-mannered reporter, goes into a phone booth, tears off his clothes, and becomes Superman and flies. At the start of every show, an announcer says Superman can leap tall buildings but anybody can see that he's flying, and not leaping. Immediately, this becomes my favorite new program, and I start thinking that maybe I don't want to be a cowboy anymore. Maybe I can be like Superman, or at least Clark. I wonder if I can ever work in a newsroom with pretty girls like Lois, and friends like Jimmy. Even his mean boss Perry White is nice some of the time. It seems pretty exciting, with all the bad guys and criminals, and I think it would be neat to have a job that exciting.

I tell my mother my idea of growing up to be a reporter like Clark, and one day, after sitting down and watching the program with me, she tells me that she's taking me and my baby brother Bob to see Santa Claus in a building in downtown Manhattan. We get all bundled up and take the subway down to Grand Central Station. The train station is huge and there are people everywhere. The streets are just as crowded and we keep walking until my mother finds the right building. She helps us push through some revolving doors into a big lobby. Christmas decorations are everywhere, more than I've ever seen in my life. I feel like I'm inside a Christmas tree and sure enough, Santa is sitting right there in a big chair surrounded by girls wearing green outfits. I walk over toward him but my mother pulls me back.

"What?"

"Wait a minute," she says, "I want to show you something."

"Oh mom, come on."

The famous globe in the lobby of The Daily News *building, 220 East 42d Street in New York City*

I'm hot and tired of all the crowds and really want to tell Santa what I want for Christmas. The spurs were good but this year, I want a rifle.

I start pulling one way and my mom pulls the other way. "Paul, look, look over here," she says.

I'm about to complain some more when I see what she's pointing to—a gigantic globe right there in the lobby. I feel something in my chest, something I can't explain except that it feels good. It's all because of the globe! It looks exactly like the one where Clark Kent works—*The Daily Planet*. Only this one is right there in the lobby, not up on the roof. But it looks exactly the same. I forget all about Santa and run up to the railing. The globe is spinning! It's going slowly but it is definitely spinning. I turn to my mother and she's smiling.

"Mom."

"I know, just like in Superman, right?"

"What is this place?" I ask.

"It's a newspaper building, *The Daily News* building. You know that newspaper your father reads, the one with Dick Tracy? All the people who make that paper work here."

I can't believe it. A newspaper building with a globe like Superman! "Does Clark Kent work here?"

My mother laughs. "Not Clark Kent. He's only in the comics but other reporters work here, sure."

I begin walking around the giant globe. It is huge and on the floor are names of countries. On the back wall are clocks that show different times all over the world. This is the greatest building ever. "*The Daily News* building," I say to myself. "*The Daily News* building."

My baby brother starts to cry. "Come on," mom says, "We came here to see Santa Claus, remember?"

I get on line with her. Santa Claus is sitting on a big chair right there in front of us but I'm not looking at him. I already have my Christmas present. I thought places like this were only on TV but here I am. It's not only make-believe, and the best part is that this building is a subway ride away.

My life is pretty good. School isn't as bad as I expected (I cried my way through a week of kindergarten and my mother agreed to let me stop going) even though I hate my second grade teacher, Sister Mary Loyola who yells all the time. In March, I come home one day to find my parents arguing.

"What's the matter?" I ask.

"Nothing's the matter, we're moving to the Bronx," he says.

"The Bronx? What's that?"

"Another borough," my mother says. "You'll be going to a different school."

"They'll be better schools," my father says. "And it's a better place to live."

My father tells me we are moving to something called a public housing project. My mother's family lives near us now and she says she doesn't want to move so far away but my father insists, saying it's cheap and we can save money. He tells me it's called the James Monroe Houses.

"It's brand new," he says. "We'll be the first people living there."

For the next few weeks, whenever my mom talks about the Bronx, she calls it "God's country," and uses the same type of voice that people on television use when they see Superman fly. I begin to wonder what's up there in the Bronx.

She tells me that, in the projects, they'll be more room for me and my brother to play, and one month later, in April, 1961, we are ready to move. It's near the end of my school year but I don't care. I can't wait to ditch my second grade teacher. She once made me sit in a waste paper basket because I was talking and I almost couldn't get out. I hate her with all my might. I don't even care if it's a sin. The day of the move is almost here and I know today is my last day at St. Lucy's. But I don't tell anyone. It's my secret. By tomorrow, I'll never have to look at Sister Mary's ugly face again. I want to stay out of her clutches on my last day but then, right after lunch, she calls my name.

"Paul, collect the trash please."

Somebody gets this job every day and I guess it's my turn. I go to the front of the room, take the small trash can, and begin walking up and down the aisles. The kids begin tossing it old papers, gum wrappers, whatever they've got. I begin to return the trash can to the front of the room but Sister says, "Paul, you know what to do with the trash. It doesn't belong up here, does it? Do you know where to take it?"

"Yes Sister."

And so I leave the classroom, and go down the stairs to a small alley next to the school. There is a big dumpster there and I empty the papers. It is a warm Spring day, and I look toward the front of the alley where the street is. It's very bright out there, and suddenly I think about taking a walk, leaving, going home. I know I shouldn't do that because I still have half a day of school to go, and we haven't studied religion and math yet. But I'm moving the next day, and I'll never come back to this classroom again. How can I get in trouble? What can Sister do to me if I'm going to be all the way up in God's country? The only bad thing is that I'll have to leave my books, and notebooks, and pencils and everything up in the classroom. I think about it.

I look around. There is no one to stop me, and I know the way home by heart. All I have to do is walk along Second Avenue. I put the basket down next to the dumpster and begin walking to the end of the alley, and go into the bright sunshine, and then I begin walking home like I do at three o'clock. It feels a little weird and I begin to walk faster as soon as I leave the building. I don't want mean old Sister Mary to catch up with me. I don't want to smell her bad breath, and see her yellow teeth. I want to start fresh in the Bronx.

I begin to walk home and it is scary because there are a lot of cars on Second Avenue. Cars are my enemy. I've never been in one and really don't know anything about them. At each corner, I stand and wait until the cars roar by, look both ways and then run over to the other side. Before I know it, I'm on my block and I stop at the candy store to buy a comic book with some change I find in my pocket. Then I head upstairs, knock on my front door.

"What are you doing home so early?" my mom asks.

"Sister let me go early because it's my last day."

"Oh, okay," she says, turning back to my brother.

I turn on the TV, and watch some cartoons. Sometimes, I think, you can make up a story, and it works out. I get exactly what I want, and, as the bad guys say on TV, no one's the wiser. When the commercials come on, I wonder if anyone in that classroom will ever want to take out the trash again. As far as they know, Paul has vanished.

Who was that masked man?

Story Avenue

When I move to Story Avenue in 1961, it is a dirt road. The James Monroe Houses don't look anything like my old building on Second Avenue. This one—1790 Story Avenue—is 14 stories high. It's big and brown and brick but I like it because it's new. And here's the neat part—there are two elevators available to whisk us up to our new apartment—6G—on the sixth floor, way up in the clouds. This apartment is big, and smells of fresh paint, and it has a great view. We can see clear across to the Whitestone Bridge far in the distance, and the cars and people downstairs. Our television is sitting in a corner and that first night, we don't even bother to plug it in. The best program now is outside our windows and we huddle up against each other and watch this strange new world.

We explore the apartment. "Now this is a real apartment," I hear my father say. I agree with him. There is a nice new kitchen with a new stove and refrigerator, there is a separate eating area apart from the living room, and a long hallway with a bathroom and two bedrooms. I will share a bedroom with my brother but that's okay because it is so big. It is our first new apartment and I'm proud and happy that we made the move. I think my father was right. But my mother is not so happy. I hear her telling my father how she feels far from her family. My grandmother has died, and my Aunt Ann still lives down in the old apartment on *a hun sixth*.

One of the 14 story buildings in the James Monroe Housing Project

My parents take my brother and me downstairs. What I notice right away is that there are no big streets like Second Avenue right outside our front door. We are *in* the projects, and instead of cars buzzing by, there are two parks right next to our building, forever to be known to us as the Little Park and Big Park. The Little Park has a sprinkler head, iron monkey bars, and colorful concrete turtles. The big park has a bigger set of iron monkey bars, colorful concrete barrels, and a wide asphalt expanse where kids can play games like tag and touch football. Behind my building are two full-sized baseball fields, a grass one for baseball, and a concrete one for softball.

We also notice the benches—they are everywhere. There are men and women sitting on those benches, and my father joins them, pulling out his ever-present red and white pack of Pall Malls. My mother is alongside him, chatting with the other ladies. Everyone starts telling stories about how they wound up here. "Hey Paul," my father nodding toward some kids in the little park, "Why don't you go play?"

I run out into the Little Park and, even though there is a lot of new playground equipment, I wind up playing with a bunch of other kids on a big pile of dirt. It's there because a lot of the project buildings are not open yet and there is a lot construction going on. I'm rolling down this pile of dirt by myself when another kid says, "Hey Paul, what are you doing here?"

The kid is Mike LaScala who was in my grade at St. Lucy's. "What are you doing here?" I ask.

"We just moved in," he says.

"Me too."

It doesn't take too long to meet all the other kids my age. Everyone is new and everyone is friendly. They don't know anyone else either and they're eager to make friends. For the first time in my life, I have a lot of friends. Frank, John, Tony, Gallo, Eddie, Duffy, Phil, Robert, Fernando, Lefty, Bobby, Joe and the girls Mary, Nancy and a couple of Kathys. The girls are way outnumbered. There are not many blacks living in the projects but Joe, Eddie and Fernando are Hispanic, and there are even a couple of Jewish brothers, Jerry and Sol.

We begin to invent new games, using whatever is in front of us. The projects have put some striped concrete barrels in the Big Park and soon we have invented a game called "off the barrel." Basically, we take up infield positions in the Big Park, while the "batter" bounces a rubber ball off one of the cement barrels. Smash it over the "right field" fence and you've got yourself a home run. But putting the ball over the "left field" fence is too easy so that's an out. The game is great fun and we play for hours and hours. One memorable day, me, Gallo and Mike even hold the other team to no hits and a shutout, making us the champs of off the barrel, at least for that moment.

With brother Bob near the barrels that became the focus of our homemade game 'off the barrel'

We also make the most of the giant buildings we live in, playing a game of tag inside the staircases that we call "chubsy ubsy" because the first boy who is "it" is fat. The number of kids playing the game grows and grows until sometimes there are two dozen wild boys running up and down 14 stories as fast as we can, speeding around concrete corners, taking 10 steps at a time. No one ever gets hurt.

I turn 8 years old that April, and when it's time to go to school, it's too late in the school year to get into the local Catholic school so my parents say they are *forced* to send me to public school. That's fine with me. P.S. 100 is right next to the projects, and brand new. My mother promises I'll go to Catholic school for the third grade, and I can tell she doesn't think much of public school. I don't give it much thought. All I know is that it is different being taught by teachers who are not priests and nuns, and that is okay with me. What's pretty neat is that a lot of my friends from the projects—Mike LaScala, Mary Calamino, Frank Spicciati, Eddie Palaez—are in my class.

One day we're doing Reading when the teacher, Mrs. Posner, tells us to open our books. One by one, someone stands and reads a page aloud. I am thinking of my new friends when the teacher calls my name and asks me to read. I am the new kid, and he says, "Let's see what you can do, where you are compared to your schoolmates."

The book is *Treasure Island*, a book I've already read at home. I am still reading and loving comics but have begun to read actual books. I finish my one page, and begin to sit down.

"Wait a minute Paul, can you please continue?" Mrs. Posner asks.

"OK."

I keep reading out loud for a long while and then stop. The chapter is over. The teacher and the kids are looking at me.

"Do you want me to keep going?" I ask.

"How old are you?" she says.

"I turned 8 last week."

"Where did you learn how to read like that?"

"My father taught me."

"Okay, thank you. You can sit down."

After class, the teacher calls me over. "You know, you read well beyond anyone in this class. I'm guessing you read at a 5th or 6th grade level at least."

"Is that good?"

She laughs. "It's very good. You'd be wasting your time going into third grade next year. In fact, you should probably be in 4th grade right now. I'm going to talk to your parents."

It feels different leaving school that day. Mrs. Posner's words burn in my mind. I feel good. This teacher is the first adult who has ever singled me out, and she's said I am better than all my classmates, at least at reading. I am feeling bigger than when I walked in that day. I like it because it's kind of like having a superpower. Superman can fly, Spiderman can climb up the sides of buildings, and I can read.

Catholic School

Almost as soon as I conquer public school, my parents pull me out.

In September, I start going to Blessed Sacrament up on Beach Avenue. It's a long walk from the projects, near the No. 6 train, the St. Lawrence Avenue subway station. Few of my project friends go to this school. There are some: Phil, Kathy, Bobby and a kid named Andrew. I don't usually play with Andrew. He lives in the building behind mine but his mother does not let him hang out on the benches. Another kid who goes to Blessed Sacrament is Robbie. He lives nearby in the Rosedale co-ops next to the projects. My mother says the co-ops are nicer but they look just like projects to me.

My mother decides that I should walk to school each day with Andrew and Robbie while she takes care of my younger brother. It sounds good except Andrew and Robbie don't cooperate—they run ahead of me that first day. I chase them for a while but then give up. But, as the days wear on, they get tired of running, and become two of my closest friends. Andrew is a natural charmer and has what my mother calls the Irish gift of gab. He's always exaggerating to teachers and girls but they don't seem to notice. Or maybe it's because he's a good looking guy. Either way, I'm envious. I am nowhere near the talker he is. Robbie has a different kind of charm. He's like a Great Dane who sits on your lap. He's big and klutzy but lovable. He is friendly and has a family so large, they're like something out of a circus. His brothers and sisters resemble one another so closely that I cannot tell them apart, no matter how often I meet them.

Blessed Sacrament turns out to be pretty much like St. Lucy's, the school I attended in Manhattan. A lot of the kids have funny-sounding musical names like Rose Ann Liparulo, George Marvulli and Sonia Sotomayor.[1] The priests are revered, the indisputable stars of the parish. Mothers and nuns swoon before them. They do possess an undeniable charm.

Father Dolan, a chubby priest with a funny oversized personality, is the school favorite. He's so good at public speaking that I look forward to his Sunday sermons. And he really cares for us kids. He's forever taking us on weekend outings, and it's because of him that I learn how to ice skate and roller skate, going round and round in circles in far flung places like Paramus, New Jersey. On one memorable trip, he escorts us via subway to Brooklyn and the famous pool in the basement of the St. George Hotel in Brooklyn Heights. Going in, we can see what Father calls "the great Brooklyn Bridge." Later he takes us up to the nearby promenade, a walkway overlooking the East River. The night is cold but the sky is clear, and the city's glittery skyscrapers are so close, they feel oppressive, like they're right on top of me. The excitement of New York City, on the other side of

---

[1] Yes, *that* Sonia Sotomayor, now a U.S. Supreme Court Justice

that majestic bridge, is palpable.

Father Dolan, I decide, is a great priest.

The nuns are another story, secretive and guarded, and prone to whisper to each other in the school hallways. They belong to the Order of the Sisters of Charity and wear clam shell-shaped black habits that cover all their hair, except for the stray grayish wisp that breaks free. Even as a third-grader, I understand that women are not meant to wear this clothing and wonder how they can stand it, especially in hot weather. Maybe it accounts for their pinched person-alities. The nuns harbor grudges against certain students, play favorites, throw chalk and blackboard erasers. They yell and stamp their feet. Their faces are barometers of their moods—they grow dark with anger or bright red with exas-peration.

Luckily for me, that first year at Blessed Sacrament, I have a lay teacher, Miss Hannigan. She's short, fat and old but she understands me, and that's all I care about. Like Mrs. Posner at PS 100, Miss Hannigan tells me right off that she thinks I'm smart. The bad news is that she also tells the rest of the class. One day, when she's particularly upset with my classmates and their lack of attention, she announces that she wishes all of them could be like me.

"You all better get with it because Mr. LaRosa is leav-ing all of you behind," she says. "It's like he's on a train and the rest of you are watching the train pull away from you—fast."

You can imagine what a big hit I am after she says this. Even me and Andrew get into a fistfight in the school yard and I'm very aware that no one is rooting for me to win. But we always make up and, as the years go on, me, Andrew and

Robbie form a tight little bond.

As the years progress, I notice that we spend nearly as much time in church as we do in the classroom, not that I'm complaining. Part of me cannot get enough of the church building—it's almost like going into a secret cave or a macabre funhouse. The place is jam-packed with gruesome paintings, sculptures and stained glass windows. There is a gigantic cross hanging from the rafters showing Christ in the agony of his death. Blood oozes from his hands, feet and stomach. On his head, he wears a crown of thorns which sends droplets of blood dribbling down his forehead. And Christ isn't the only victim here. Saint Lucy is no slouch either. She holds a plate in front of her for all to see and on that plate are her eyeballs!

Surrounding the pews are stained glass windows and murals filled with angry Romans wielding whips. There is a lot of talk about ghosts and people rising from the dead. It's a great place to let one's imagination run wild. I've always been mesmerized by fire and here are hundreds of candles burning around the side altars, giving the building an eerie, other-worldly glow. It's easy to imagine this place being haunted. I spend hours upon hours daydreaming, craning my neck upward to the paintings that decorate the dome high above the altar, wondering how anyone managed to paint up there and how in the world can they change those lightbulbs 80 feet above us?

The rituals of the church are endless even in normal times, but everything is now much more complicated because of the historic changes to the Mass by Pope Paul VI. The Mass, he orders, is translated from Latin to English, and the altar turned around to face the parishioners so as to be more inclusive. The chants of *mea culpa, mea culpa, mea maxima culpa* are replaced by the handshake of peace. The New Mass, as it's called, force us to learn everything all over again—when to stand, when to kneel, stand, sit, pray and how and when to receive the body and blood of Christ. Many of my classmates, including Andrew, become altar boys but I resist. It is my one act of mini-rebellion. I'm pretty compliant but the idea of wearing a frilly white cassock and getting up early to serve Mass has zero appeal. What does appeal to me is Confession.

Confession, without a doubt, is my favorite sacrament. I like the concept—sin all you want, and then have the slate wiped clean by simply telling a priest about it. No wonder there are so many sinners in the world. It's a pretty good deal. You walk into a darkened little chamber the size of a telephone booth where, magically and dramatically, the priest slides open a wooden door, revealing a screen with lots of little holes in it. You can hear each other but neither of you can see who is on the other side of that screen; both are in shadow. The next move is up to you, confessing your innermost thoughts. It can be very comforting—as long as you don't know the priest on the other side of the screen.

By 7th grade, this becomes a problem. We are regulars here, and our sins become more, well, complicated. The priests know us and we know them, even by our voices. I decide I don't want to tell anyone how many times a week I masturbate, especially a priest. Besides, who's keeping score?

But we must confess something because, each Friday, the nuns escort us to the church where three priests are waiting to hear our confessions. Behind Door #1 is Father Dolan.

He's the pushover, the one we all stake out. He's more likely to joke about our sins than judge us, but I'd still like to avoid confessing to someone who will immediately recognize my voice.

Behind Door #2 is the Old Monsignor. He's the craggy-faced head of the parish and is the exact opposite of Father Dolan. The Old Monsignor loves to judge, and is liable to tell us that, if we don't mend our ways, we'll be going straight to hell.

And then there's the South American priest behind Door #3. He barely speaks English which, in this instance, is a good thing. We all head for the South American guy, until the cagey nuns see what's happening, and even out the lines. I wind up with the Old Monsignor.

After saying the confessional prayer ("Bless my father for I have sinned...), I launch into a bevy of the most boring sins I can make up.

"I lied to my brother.

"I envied my friend's lunch.

"I, uh, thought about stealing a quarter from my mother's purse."

I pause. That's all I've got.

"Now son, do you have anything else to confess, anything at all?"

"No Father."

Now it's his turn to hesitate.

"No impure thoughts?"

I decide to tell him nothing but hesitate a split-second too long.

"Well..."

"Yes?" he asks eagerly.

"I did have impure thoughts about one of my class-mates."

"Really? Which one?"

Pardon me? Is this really necessary?

"Son?"

"Well, Monsignor, it's Patricia. I had impure thoughts about Patricia."

"Son, you know what you must do, correct?"

"Three Hail Marys?"

"No, son, you should go up to Patricia and tell her that you had impure thoughts and ask her forgiveness."

Yeah, that's likely to happen, I think but when it comes to priests and nuns, sometimes you gotta humor them. It's for their own good.

"Okay Monsignor, I'll do that."

"Make sure you do now. In the meantime, say three Hail Marys and four Our Fathers. You may go."

I hightail it out of there. Maybe Hell won't be so bad. It can't be any worse than telling Patricia all the times I'd imagined removing her pure white Catholic schoolgirl shirt.

In the Projects

Life in the projects revolves around the benches, especially in the spring and summer. We never make plans. We eat breakfast and head downstairs armed with the knowledge that our friends will either be there or show up soon enough. It's been that way since the day I moved in. Our large group becomes well-established. I am friendlier with some kids than others but it hardly matters. We hang out together on the benches.

My friends become my life. We're always doing something. We go through phases—spinning tops, yo-yos, pocket knives, baseball cards. Even stamp collecting has its day. We scrounge stamps from old letters, buy them through mail order houses, or head down to Gimbel's department store in Herald Square where they have their very own stamp department. The activities we dream up are endless, and sometimes incredibly stupid. For reasons unknown, one day I decide it would be fun to ride on the *outside* of a subway car. As the doors close and the train begins to pull away from the station, I put my feet on the small lip near the doors and hang on. I travel about ten feet—riding on the side of the subway car—before I panic and jump off, falling face first on the platform. I have a few bruises but, all in all, I'm lucky. Stupid but lucky.

Fortunately, most of our activities are far more innocent. My brother and his friends race slot cars, and chase butterflies with dime-store nets. It's always something. Someone gets a bug and the rest of us join in. It is a world without parents. If we want to do something, we do it. Parents are not part of the equation, except to provide money. And who needs money anyway? One day, me, Mike LaScala, and Donald take off on our banana-seat bikes with no money, for a ride to who-knows-where. Soon, we're traveling over the George Washington Bridge into New Jersey where we encounter a giant downhill. We go hurtling down at top speed and only when we get to the bottom do we realize that we need to walk back up the hill to get home. That night, I say nothing to my parents about where I've been.

Adjacent to the projects are what we call the lots, empty fields that look like they've been untouched since prehistoric times. The lots are vast tracts of land filled with every type of junk you can imagine: old cars, kitchen sinks, and the remnants of homemade shacks. And then there are the mysterious tar pits, oozing, bubbling, black holes filled with a strange substance that reminds me of what I've seen in dinosaur books. Sometimes we turn over a rock that's been lying on the edge of a pit and piss on it, and it begins to steam. I have no idea what's in those pits and I don't want to know. But that doesn't mean I'm not fascinated by them. A favorite game is to toss an object into the tar pit to see if it will sink, the bigger the object the better. We start with small rocks but are soon tossing in car batteries and whatever else we can get our hands on. It all disappears within a minute or two. The tar pits demand respect, and we keep our distance. We all live in fear that we'll be running through the lots one day, take a wrong turn, and never be seen again. I imagine my friends staring in open-mouthed horror while my hand sinks below the surface.

The lots also happen to be a breeding ground for a hardy bunch of rabbits and wild pheasants running around in the brush. Because of the rabbits, Frank or Donald or somebody else gets the bright idea that we should buy bows and arrows at our nearby department store, E.J. Korvette's, which has an impressive sporting goods section considering we are living in the middle of New York City. Three or four of us manage to filch enough money from our parents so that we can buy actual archery bows with real metal-tipped arrows. The salesman has no problem selling them to young teens. We plunk down our money and off we go, armed for the lots. We march into those fields with determination. We tell ourselves we are no longer fooling around with tar pits and junked cars—now we are hunting for dinner. We form two clubs, The Archers and The Anti-Archers.

We pretend we'd love to have a meaty rabbit for dinner. At least I pretend, because I know that if I were to show up in my apartment with a dead rabbit and ask my mother to cook it for dinner, she would have what she calls *a conniption*, and order me to take that animal right out to the hallway incinerator chute. Secretly, I am repelled by the idea that I might actually kill either a rabbit or a pheasant. My dinners revolve around hamburgers, pasta and pizza—never small game.

I sit for hours in the lots, watching in the underbrush for

any movement and, when finally a pheasant or rabbit does happen by, I am so slow pulling the bow string back and firing that I never ever come close to scoring one for dinner which is actually a good thing. I never hit anything with those arrows except a tree and, once, a friend's thigh. He merely pulled it out and kept walking.

As new buildings—private, not public—fill in our lots, we put away our bows and reach for fishing rods. We head down to an area known as The Point. It's about a mile away, and there the Bronx gives way to Long Island Sound. There is a beach club down here called Shorehaven and we spy on the girls in their bathing suits through the holes in the fences. Nobody I know ever joins the club. The one time I ask my parents for the $90 admission fee for the summer season, they look at me like I'm crazy. Next subject!!

Exterior of 1790 Story Avenue as it looked in the late 1970s

But who needs Shorehaven when we have the actual shore? And that's where we wind up, playing on giant slippery black rocks that line the shore. It's a cool place to explore and hang out. Nobody is looking out for us and nothing is cordoned off. The Bronx is still a free-for-all. Korvette's provides us with some cheap rods, weights and lures. A local store near The Point sells worms. We all have much better luck than we did on our hunting expedition. Before long, we're pulling in long, black satiny eels with eyes that seem to rear back in their tiny heads. I don't even think about presenting one of these to mother whose idea of a fish dinner revolves around Mrs. Paul or Captain Morton. I decide these poor creatures will be much happier back in the Sound than down the incinerator chute (where I know my mother would deposit them), and so I immediately unhook them, and toss back into the water.

When we get bored of fishing, some of my friends strip to their underwear and go swimming off the rocks. I watch them climb down the slippery rocks and swim into the surf but my fear of water always gets the better of me. Swimming looks so easy but that's because these kids know what they're doing. Not me. I spend weeks each summer bouncing around the surf at Orchard Beach and Rockaway (where we go on family vacations) but I never actually *swim*. What I do is ride the waves, and my iron-clad rule is never to go in water over my head—ever!

We play tons of sports, especially baseball. After one Easter break, a teacher asks if I've been to the Caribbean. I have no idea what he's talking about until he mentions my tan. I have not set foot outside the projects but I have spent the last ten days roaming centerfield in pick-up softball games, with the sun blasting away at my face. No hat, no tanning lotion, no nuthin'. None of us are in the Little League, or anything remotely organized. We choose up games among ourselves. But one day, when I have the misfortune to be catching for my pickup team, baseball great and former Brooklyn Dodger Roy Campanella visits Monroe to give all us project kids a few pointers. Of course, Campanella is in his wheelchair, having been paralyzed in a car accident in his prime. But I can tell you one thing—the accident didn't make him any less ornery. Probably because I'm playing *his* position, he rides my ass and yells at me for 20 minutes straight. Everyone looks on, afraid to interrupt the Hall of Famer's tirade directed at me.

When I'm not playing ball or fishing or shooting arrows, I'm shoplifting record albums. It's a hobby I pursue with gusto. I can afford to buy one or two albums but not all the ones I want. So it's off to Korvette's or sometimes Macy's in Parkchester. Here's what I do: I buy something cheap and large, like a folder—anything that provides an oversize bag—and hit the record aisles. I casually stroll up and down, picking up and looking over song lyrics and cover art and, when no one's looking, I slide an LP into the bag. I'm always amazed that I can then leave the store without anyone stopping me, until the day they do.

As I've done countless times, I have slipped a record into my bag and leave the store but, this time, within seconds, two guards clamp their hands on my shoulders and snatch the bag from me.

You're coming with us, son.

The reality of being caught is much worse than I've imagined and I wonder how I'll explain this to my parents.

The guards walk me around to a side door marked *Employees Only*. Every step is agony and we keep getting closer and closer until I completely freak out. I throw the guards' arms off me, and blast off like an Olympic sprinter. I run at full speed and don't stop for what feels like a mile. I look behind me. No one. But I don't take any chances and continue walking at a brisk pace. It is a hot summer day and I am drenched with sweat.

Finally, I come to a church. Churches are always open, and I slip inside. I need to think and rest. The church is cool and dark with only a couple of women cleaning the altar. I am wearing a blue short sleeve shirt with a white t-shirt underneath, and I'm sure the guards have put out an all-points bulletin with my description. I quickly strip off my blue shirt and sit there in my sweaty t-shirt. All I can think to do is pray so I kneel and begin the desperation prayer. Everyone knows it. It goes like this: *Please God, just let me not be caught and I swear I'll be good for the rest of my life. I'll donate my paycheck to the poor, I'll say 50 Novenas, I'll do anything if you'll not let me be caught.*

I've never prayed so hard but, after an hour or more, I decide to see what God has in store for me. I cautiously exit the church but there are no police cars blocking the entrance. There is no one. I begin to walk home, and the moment I enter my apartment, and realize I'm not going to get caught, I forget all about that desperation prayer.

One day, an older kid in our crowd, who is known only by his last name—Kassof—tells us about a very odd photograph of his grandparents that he has in his apartment.

"It's really old," he says, "And here's the weird thing—if you look at it just right, the eyes follow you."

I don't know about *their* eyes but in *my* eyes, Kassof cannot be telling the truth. I've been a victim of many of my friends' pranks but even good old gullible me doesn't buy what Kassof is selling.

"No fucking way," I say.

"See for yourself."

And so I go into his apartment with a couple of other guys. He points to this really old photograph that's encased in an oval of thick glass. The couple looks ancient. The three of us all look at the photo awhile but nothing happens. "So what?" I say, "I don't see their eyes moving or anything."

"You've got to stare at it for a long," he says.

So we stare and stare until I....see....their....eyes....move.

"Holy shit," I say dropping the glass of water I'm holding.

In a second, Frank is claiming he's seen the eyes move too and Kassof is smirking. "I told ya."

News sweeps through the crowd about Kassof's magic photo. Everyone wants to see it and he could sell tickets to his apartment. But instead, he does something much better—he announces that he will personally conduct a séance to connect us with his dead grandparents. It's the biggest news since The Beach Movie Theater announced a screening of The Beatles' film "A Hard Day's Night." Kassof doesn't even charge for attending the séance which gives it a certain air of legitimacy. One night, when the grownups are out, a dozen of us gather around Kassof's dining room table. He's put a candle in the middle and he sits at the head of the table. He dims the lights and orders us to hold hands and close our eyes. This is so boss. Forget the body and blood of

Christ. This is real!

Kassof implores his grandparents to show us a sign that they are here in this room with us at this very moment. Minutes go by until Kassof cries, "Oh my God" and we open our eyes to see that the candle is no longer lit.

I'm willing to give Kassof the benefit of the doubt but another guy in our crowd, who is savvier than I, calls Kassof out. "You blew that out when our eyes were closed."

"No, I didn't," Kassof says.

"Okay then, let's try it again. Only this time we all keep our eyes open."

Kassof agrees though I think I see a bit of panic cross his face. This time, with our eyes open, Kassof goes through the same routine. "Oh grandfather, grandmother, please give us a sign that you're here in this room. Show these non-believers that you're here among us."

Silence but seconds later, there's a knock on the door. "See?" Kassof says.

"So what?" says the skeptic among us. "Someone knocked. I'll get it."

He goes to the door and we hear an enormous explosion. All of us dive under that table looking for cover. I'm truly afraid. We played with the ghosts of his grandparents one too many times and now they're here for us. I wrap myself around one of my friends and shut my eyes tight. Then we all hear laughing coming from the front door. "Look at this," says the non-believer.

He shows us that someone put a light bulb on the doorknob and when he opened the door and turned the knob, the bulb fell to the ground and shattered in a loud pop. "That wasn't your grandparents—it was a light bulb."

I hustle out of that apartment. Maybe it was a joke but it was enough of a sign for me and I never set foot in Kassof's apartment again.

Our adventures are bonding experiences, and I become close friends with John and Frankie mostly. They are my project sidekicks (as opposed to Andrew and Robbie who are my school sidekicks) or maybe I'm theirs but we generally do things together. We are a group within the group. Frankie's parents are more or less like mine, second-generation Italian-Americans who keep to themselves, but John's parents are *different*. John's mother is named Kitty, and her name alone is interesting. It's a movie name. She reads the New York Times and does the crossword puzzles, a feat that separates her from all the other mothers who seem not to read at all. And she works. I don't know what she does but having a job gives her an aura none of the other mothers possess.

John's father, a post officer worker, is named Eddie and he's a gregarious sort who smokes a pipe and likes to play softball with the men from nearby developments. Our fathers, except for Eddie, never participate. Maybe that's because they're not very good, and Eddie is. He happens to be an excellent softball pitcher. Eddie has personality and is one of the few fathers who talks to the kids. But by far the most interesting thing about Eddie is that he has a car! The projects have their own parking lot but none of my friends' parents has a car except for John. His car is a big white Ford. It's old—it looks nothing like the new snazzy models—but it's a car. I am 13 but I've still never been inside a car. I also don't recall ever having been in a cab so when

John asks me to join his family for a trip to Orchard Beach *in his father's car,* I cannot say yes fast enough. I don't care if we take a spin around the parking lot.

I don't remember anything about the beach that day. All I remember is the car, the absolute wonder of it. It is hot, and smells funny but to me, it's like being in a spaceship. I float around the backseat looking at everything, rolling the windows up and down, opening and closing the ashtrays, even lying on the floor with John to explore what's under the front seats. It's a very basic, apparently stripped-down model but riding in it is blissful, especially when we pass the Story Avenue bus stop where people are awaiting the No. 5 bus, the bus I spend half my life waiting for. I hate the No. 5 bus and I have to take it nearly every day. The projects are about a mile from the closest subway, the No. 6 line. I like the subways but buses are the worst. There is no particular hell like waiting for the No. 5 bus in the freezing cold of a winter's day. You edge out into the traffic again and again hoping for a glimpse but it takes forever to get there, and by the time it arrives you have to take a wicked leak and cannot even enjoy being in the warmth.

But not on this summer's day. I am in a car and proud, and wish the ride would never end. Who cares about the beach? The car is the thing, and all I do is ask endless questions about it until John's father says, "I don't think I'm gonna be keeping it much longer. It's not running so well, and it's old."

And he doesn't. Soon, the car is gone, and I'm back to being one of those people waiting forever for the No. 5 bus.

Family

As I get more and more involved with my friends, I think less and less about my parents having anything to do with my life. Someone once explained it to me this way: my friends and I are involved in a game going on inside the stadium, and my parents are sitting outside in the parking lot. Besides, they have their hands full with a new baby in the house—my sister Karen who is born when I am 12 years old.

I know my mother is overjoyed with the idea of having a baby girl. The day she comes home from the hospital, I open our front door to see my mother standing there with the biggest smile as she holds my new sister in her arms. I have never seen my mother happier than at that moment. But Karen's arrival brings some upheaval. For one thing, we need a bigger apartment so we move from 1790 Story Avenue right across the Little Park to 800 Soundview Avenue. Now we live on the 2nd floor instead of the 6th and have new neighbors, but my friends are all the same.

With the arrival of a third child, my mother grows increasingly cheap. No matter what question I ask her—if the sentence involves money—the answer is almost always 'no.' To my mother, everything is a luxury, even napkins. We never buy napkins but are instructed to take "extras" from the pizza shop. We never buy garbage bags, not when we have a lot of paper grocery bags lying around our house, and an incinerator outside in the hallway.

Having a new baby means showing her off and we spend hours on the subways visiting relatives in far flung parts of New York. My mother's parents died young, making her all the more focused on keeping in touch with her five brothers and one sister, so we're forever trudging from one relative to another. My father, whose mother is still alive, doesn't feel the need to be so family-friendly. His two older sisters have moved to upstate New York and, since there is no subway that can take us there, we almost never visit them. Same goes for my father's brother, who lives in Brooklyn. Brooklyn is so far from the Bronx that visiting him means spending an entire day on the subway. Since my Dad's not inclined and my mother doesn't really care, we rarely visit Uncle Larry and Aunt Mary even though they have three children who are slightly older than me and in my eyes, pretty cool.

The relatives we see the most are my mother's brother, my Uncle Mike, and his wife, my Aunt Betty, who live down on the Bowery with their two children who are the same age as me and my brother. We spend every Thanksgiving at their top-floor apartment and they spend every Christmas with us up in the Bronx. It's a fair tradeoff. I'm sure they're not overjoyed at having to bundle up and travel the subways on Christmas, and I feel the same way about visiting them on Thanksgiving. And if spending Christmas in the projects is not their idea of a good time, well, visiting the Bowery on

Thanksgiving is not exactly high on my list either, though I will say this much—it is unique as Thanksgivings go. And that has mostly to do with where my aunt and uncle live—very near Skid Row, home to nearly every flophouse in the city.

After traveling an hour or more on the No. 6 Lexington Avenue train from the Bronx to lower Manhattan, we exit onto Bleecker Street. The moment we climb out of the subway, we are surrounded by what everyone in my family calls "bums." These are scary-looking alcoholic men—*down on their luck,* my mother says—who live in the flophouses up and down the Bowery. And they are everywhere. We only have to walk a few blocks to get from the subway at Bleecker and Lafayette Street to my uncle's apartment on the Bowery and E. 3rd Street but that means passing dozens of men lying on the sidewalks clutching their bottles of Thunderbird. Their trousers are often stained with piss and they stink but, aside from sometimes having to step over them, they don't bother me all that much. Far scarier are the bums who have not passed out. They stand in doorways and yell at us for money, or approach us with hands outstretched. I can barely understand what they are saying but, whatever it is, they make me sad. I know we have Italian pastries in our bags and it's clear these men have nothing. I know they must be thinking of their families on Thanksgiving. How could they not? Once in a while my father hands one of them a cigarette but otherwise my mother instructs us to keep walking and not say anything.

My Uncle Mike and Aunt Betty are so besieged by the bums that the front door to their apartment building is securely locked. There is no intercom, no door buzzer. It was

removed after the bums buzzed my Aunt and Uncle countless times. So the only way we can let them know that we've
arrived downstairs at their building is to use a payphone.
But that's a problem too. Nearly every payphone around on
the Bowery is broken or has something sticky on the ear or
mouth piece. Some of the phone booths are taken over by
bums who are sleeping on the floor with the door closed so
they can stay warm. On days we cannot find a payphone
(which is nearly every time we visit), my mother brings us
around to the back of their building and instructs me and
my brother to scream at the top of our lungs "Aunt Betty,
Uncle Mike" over and over again until one of them opens
the top floor window to indicate they've heard us and will
soon be down to open the front door.

Inside, we climb what seems like a thousand stairs to get
to the top floor railroad flat that has a kitchen in the back
and a living room in the front. My cousins sleep in the two
interior rooms, and the front door opens into one of those
bedrooms. My aunt and uncle sleep on a Castro Convertible
in the front room. Say what you want about the projects but
at least we have a real three-bedroom apartment in an elevator building. I am not envious of this apartment setup. Usually, all my other relatives have arrived before us, and the
long Thanksgiving dinner is underway. It's presided over by
uncle Carmine—my mother's oldest brother—who loves to
raise a glass to toast this or that relative over and over again.
The dinner lasts hours and much alcohol is consumed. My
Aunt Betty is a great cook but the drinking always threatens
to overtake the food, and the family dramas get messier and
messier as the night wears on. I am used to it and can easily
predict how it will all play out.

The main target is my poor Aunt Ann, the "baby" of the family. Ann is sweet and good-natured but woefully lacking in confidence, and her brothers like to gang up on her because she is not living life as they prefer. She is not married but is living with her boyfriend Frank in what was the familial apartment on *a hun sixth* where my mother and all her brothers grew up. Now the only one left there is Ann and, much to my uncles' chagrin, she has decided *to play house* there with Frank. Ann is approaching 30 years old when she makes this decision. My uncles heap verbal abuse on her and Frank, and, after fortifying herself with a few drinks of her own, she fights back. That's usually when the evening degenerates into chaos. My mother always refers to Frank as "simple," probably with good reason. He was mugged once and stabbed in the chest and, after he recovered, he swore off smoking for life. As he told me *sotto voce*, he was afraid the smoke would leak out of what was the wound in his chest.

On family occasions, he knows better than to get involved with the brothers and sits in the corner trying to pretend he's somewhere else.

My cousins and I retreat to the front room where we watch Jackie Gleason on television, gossip about Ann and Frank, and do what we can to avoid the crazy adults gathered around the dining room table. Most years, the Thanksgiving meal ends in a raucous shouting match that has Carmine storming, or more accurately stumbling, down those thousand stairs. I don't know how he does it but, no matter how much he drinks, he never falls. Soon, my Aunt Ann, who is by now very upset, is also out the door, followed by Frank fumbling with his fedora, leaving the rest of us bruised and thankful for one thing—this "festive" meal will not take place for another year. We wobble down the stairs and file out into the bum-filled streets for the subway and bus long ride back to the Bronx.

Those Boots

In Blessed Sacrament, there is always a lot of talk about the missionaries, and sometimes a priest in a brown cassock (our priests wore black cassocks) comes into class and bores us with stories of the missionary work he is conducting in some remote corner of the globe. It's not that I have anything against the priest or the poor children in Africa; any distraction is a good distraction. It's just that, to me, starving children are unreachable, and unimaginable. My life is filled with screeching subway cars and belching buses. I spend what seems like countless hours waiting for one or the other. I don't understand my own world, never mind one halfway across the globe. I am a 14-year-old, 8th-grade boy, filled with thoughts of my own survival, how to negotiate girls who confound me, and boys who don't like me.

Today is a missionary day. Father Domingo, a very skinny priest with dark skin and an accent, stands in front of the class pouring his heart out about the poor children he sees. Sad but I've heard it all before, many times. You don't get through eight grades in Catholic school without many such talks. After about five minutes, I find myself ignoring Father Domingo, and looking out the window, wondering if there's a new episode of "Lost in Space" on that night.

But our teacher, Sister Jean Marie, knows us all too well, and so today, she has something new cooked up, something perfect to shore up our flagging concentration. She's announced an auction to raise money for Father Domingo's missionary work. We've all been told to bring something from home that we'd like to auction off to the rest of the class. Sister Jean Marie announced it earlier that week but there is nothing in my little room that I think anyone would want. My classmates, however, are much more inventive. I see them one at a time march up to Sister's desk, carrying the possessions up for auction—sweaters, umbrellas, books, and a couple of record albums.

I have a pocketful of change—about three dollars—but nothing looks all that enticing. Then the auction starts, and Sister is nothing if not canny.

The first item up for bid is a record album featuring Nancy Sinatra. I recognize it immediately from my endless shoplifting trips through the record aisles at E. J. Korvette's. This is the record where Nancy sings "These Boots Are Made for Walking." It's not, however, the song that holds me in thrall—it's the photo of sexy Nancy on the cover. She's lying on her side, her very short red mini-skirt hiked up to mid-thigh, wearing black and white tights, and red boots. Her blonde hair is big, her lips alluring, and, to me, she is the personification of sex. I get an immediate boner. I want that record, and I want her in my bedroom where I can stare for hours.

Sister Jean Marie, a Sister of Charity, stands in stark contrast to yummy Nancy. Sister wears a full-length black dress, a black habit, a giant gold cross on her belt, and plain, wire-rimmed glasses. Sister is the opposite of sex; Nancy Sinatra is her evil, devilish twin. I must have that record.

The bidding starts at 25 cents and my hand shoots up immediately.

"Paul is bidding 25 cents. How about 50?" the good Sister asks.

My hand shoots up again. My libido is bidding against myself.

"Very well, Paul, 50 cents. Anyone else?"

My classmates turn toward me. Everyone, not only the boys, knows what's up and why I want that LP. Father Domingo looks amused but pleased, no doubt thinking of how a horny 8th-grader in the Bronx will fetch him three cows and a goat in Africa.

Another hand shoots up on the other side of the class. It's Philip, the hemophiliac. It's well known that Philip, once he starts bleeding, cannot stop. He's like a living saint or something and his status as a non-stop bleeder keeps the boys on edge. No one wants to be the one who bumps into Philip, sends him flying into a corner, and starts the bleeding that can't be stopped. It's spooky and so is he, with his mournful eyes. Normally, I keep my distance, and today his bidding is making me feel bad. Maybe I should let him win.

"75 cents," he says.

Everyone, including Sister Jean Marie, looks at me.

"Paul?" she goads.

"Uh, okay, one dollar."

"A dollar fifty," says Philip.

Now that class is into it and they ooh and ahh. I know they're looking back at me but I'm looking down at my change. I can do $3.25 and that's it.

"Two dollars," I say.

"Two fifty," Philip counters immediately.

Now what? I wait. "Going once," says Sister Jean Marie. "Going twice..."

Everyone is looking at me.

"Three dollars," I yell a little too loudly.

I see Philip counting his money. He looks up smugly. "Three dollars and ten cents."

I don't need to look down at my money. This is it, take it or leave it. "Three dollars and twenty five cents."

Philip looks at his money again. He looks as if he may cry. "That's all I have," he says, holding out his hand. "$3.10."

"Okay," says Sister Jean Marie, taking that in. "Paul has bid $3.25. Anyone else? Going once, going twice. Sold to Paul for $3.25."

I beam, and begin walking to the front of the classroom where Sister is holding the album. Father Domingo is happy. My classmates are clapping. I am the man of the hour. My eyes zero in on the cover photo of Nancy. I am nearly at the front of the room. I hand the money to Sister with one hand and reach for the record with the other, and that's when Sister pulls a fast one. She takes the money all right but holds onto the LP. She whips the record out of its sleeve, and hands me the black vinyl. I don't know what's happening. She is still holding the album cover featuring luscious Nancy in Sister's tiny, pale white fish-like hand.

"This picture has no place in a Catholic home," she announces.

And then she rips the cardboard record sleeve into many little pieces, and dumps them into the waste-basket at her feet. My mouth hangs open. I turn and walk back to my desk, holding the black record, and feeling my neck radiate red.

All I Find

The good feeling my family felt when we moved into the projects doesn't last long. Seven years later, a lot of the original families have moved on, and their replacements are welfare families, many of them black. The original families feel cheated, like the rules of the game they agreed to when they moved here have changed. The whites are not welcoming to these new black families, and there is an inevitable pushing back on their end. There is tension between black and white, each side angling for a feeling of control. I watch the television news and I know about the civil rights movement in the South. Black and white are marching side by side in Alabama and other Southern States, but here in the projects—living side by side—the feelings of racial prejudice are sky high on both sides. Nobody is linking arms.

I feel the change most acutely because of the muggings. The new black kids are tough, and they let the quiet white boys like me know it. Guys with names like Delmont and Bing seem to enjoy going out of their way to pick on us. I am on a first name basis with my muggers.

Typically, the mugging goes like this. I am walking back from what my parents refer to as the Italian-American store to buy a quarter pound of Genoa or hard salami—*sliced thin,* my mother says —when one of these black kids stands in my way.

Hey man, you got any money?

No.

All I find, all I keep?

Without waiting for me to consider this offer, the mugger jams his hand into my pants pocket and takes all the remaining change. It could be a few bucks, or it could be change. It doesn't matter—he takes whatever I have. I feel powerless but I know better than to object. I've tried that. Before learning the rules of this bizarre ritual, I told one of these muggers that I had nothing for him and tried to step around him. Without a word, he punched me hard in the stomach. I doubled over. Then he took whatever I had in my pockets.

Next time, don't lie to me.

I begin to look far ahead when I walk, anticipating the spots where these punks hang out, and I do anything to avoid them. I walk a mile out of my way on these ridiculous circuitous routes just so I can hang onto my money but they still seem to find me.

I lose a fair amount of what little money I have this way. My parents don't yell at me because they know what's going on. They tell me to be careful, to give *them* what *they* want. I resent the muggings, and my feelings about my tormentors harden.

And, as if on cue, the projects begin to change physically. The hallways where we once played with abandon become places to avoid. The grounds seem to have more litter; the playgrounds are not maintained as they once were. Lawns are more brown than green. Maybe it's the inevitable slide due to poor maintenance but because it coincides with the arrival of our new neighbors, we feel they are to blame. I no longer feel safe—there is menace in the air.

One day, a bunch of us are playing basketball. One of my friends is the runt of our litter, smaller and skinnier than the rest of us, and looks weaker.

Playing basketball in the projects has become fraught with tension. The black kids consider it their game, and enjoy showing us how much better they are than us. Today is no different. A group of black kids, slightly older, saunters up to our court, grabs a rebound, and begins playing. There are no niceties here. No one is asking if they can play, and we're not giving them permission. Like the endless muggings, this is a ritual we know well. We are going to play a game of black on white, and we are going to get our asses kicked. I recognize their leader, a tall kid I think of as Big Asshole. He's mugged me a bunch of times so we know each other in the way a mouse knows a cat.

It is a cool spring day and the black guys are wearing jackets. But they do not want to throw them on the ground as we have. Big Asshole has a better idea.

He turns to one of my friends, the smallest kid on the court. "Yo, man, what's your name?"

He tells him.

"So listen Little Man," he says. "I want you to stand right here and I don't want you to move, okay?"

He positions my friend against the chain link fence outside the court boundaries and proceeds to drape his coat over our friend's head. "Yeah, man, that's perfect. Now I want you to stand there exactly like that, and you better not fucking move. If my coat hits the ground, you're a dead man."

Little Man stands there and doesn't move. Big Asshole turns to his friends, "Hey any of you want to hang your coats on my man here?"

With that each of the five black kids drapes their coats over our friend's head, and he continues to stand there. "Okay, let's play," Big Asshole says to the rest of us.

"Play" is not really what we do. They have their fun with us, passing all around us, sometimes shoving us to the ground, but no matter what happens, I feel lucky that I am not my friend who has become a human coat hanger. As the game goes on, I feel worse and worse for him, and can see that he is shaking and probably crying under all those coats. *This sucks*, I think to myself. I decide this is one ritual I'm not going to take part in. Muggings are one thing but this humiliation is too degrading. I can't pretend it's not happening.

After Big Asshole's team scores its next point, I announce I'm done.

"What's the matter, you don't wanna play anymore?"

"Nah, I gotta go home, and so does my friend here," I say, pointing to our friend.

"He ain't goin' nowhere man. He got a job to do."

"Well, he's gotta go eat now. It's getting late."

Big Asshole looks at me, and I know he's not buying my bullshit story for a second. For one thing, it's only 4 o'clock. Without a word, he whips the basketball at my head as hard as he can. I duck and it hits the fence behind me. He comes over to me, "Hey mother fucker, how come you didn't catch my pass?"

"I need to get home."

And with that, I pluck the top coat off my friend's head and try to hand it to Big Asshole. He doesn't take it.

"Did I say you could touch my fuckin' coat?"

"We have to go."

"Fuck you man." He pushes me in the chest and I fall back against the fence. *Now* his coat is on the ground.

I sit there a moment, trying to think of my next move. I know better than to push back; that's all he would need to kick the shit out of me. I stare at him. The moment freezes. My friend still has the coats draped over his head, but I can see him peeking out. Everyone else is staring. I get up and decide I'm going to call Big Asshole's bluff. I'm going to start walking away, and if he comes after me, then I'm going to fight back. I always knew this day was coming; I didn't know when it would arrive.

I get up, pick my coat up off the ground, and start walking. Or at least I try to. By now, I am surrounded by Big Asshole and all his friends. One of them pushes me into one of the other ones, and they begin treating me like a human pin ball. I am about to push back when there is a commotion. All my friends, including the guy under all those jackets, take advantage of the focus on me to grab the ball and coats, and run as fast as they can. It takes a second before I realize what is happening—my own friends are leaving me, running as fast as their legs will take them. *Huh.*

Big Asshole watches them running away, and then looks back at me and laughs. "Man, some friends you got there."

I didn't know what to say. "Yeah," seems like it'll do it.

I'm not really angry, just kind of shocked.

One of the other guys says, "Let's fuck this dude up."

Big Asshole licks his lips and considers the request. "Nah, man."

He eyes me for a few seconds that feel like an eternity. "Your friends are pussies, man. At least you got some balls. Go 'head, get outta here 'fore I change my mind."

I begin to walk in the direction of my friends when I hear Big Asshole say, "Hey man, wait a minute."

Oh shit. I turned around.

"You got any money."

"No."

"All I find all I keep?"

Newspaper Boy

In 8th grade, I become a newspaper delivery boy. It happens by chance when a friend of mine asks if I'd like to take over his route which essentially *is* the Monroe Projects. I agree because, by now, I like the idea of working for a newspaper like *The Daily News*, home to that ever-spinning globe in the lobby, and my favorite comics. I still read them, and tell myself it's out of habit but the truth is I *enjoy* them as much as I ever have. As a delivery boy, I'll be part of the newspaper behind the comics, a very small part, but still. What I don't take into account is how early you have to get up.

Delivering newspapers in a public housing project is not like the suburban ideal of riding a bike through wide streets and tossing newspapers onto manicured lawns from a wire basket. I don't know anything about the suburbs but I see that kind of life when I watch television. Everyone on TV—except for Jackie Gleason in "The Honeymooners"—lives in a big house with a front lawn, and they drive everywhere. There are no programs about what life is like in the projects.

Here, I'm worried about wild dogs, and stray gunshots, and there isn't a lawn in sight. The Monroe Houses have deteriorated, and are far scarier today than when I was younger. There's no telling who might be waiting around a hallway corner. The elevators smell like piss, and the walls are scuffed and in need of paint.

Despite the clear danger of being mugged, I take the job and find myself, bleary-eyed from lack of sleep, kneeling each morning in a darkened stairwell where the newspapers await me. I gamely separate them out into my shopping cart. *The Times* and *Daily News* are the major morning papers. The NY Post is still an afternoon paper so I never deliver that. But there is a strange hybrid called the New York World Journal Tribune. I have no idea what that is, never having seen or heard of it in my life. There are only a few of those each morning, and it doesn't last very long. The headlines in the News and Times are filled with stories about the six-day war in Israel but I am oblivious. Sports is my passion and the big story of the day is that Mickey Mantle is working out at first base. The News is experimenting with color and the first newspaper I ever deliver has a color photograph of The Mick at his new position.

Unlike the rest of the country, I deliver the newspaper vertically from the top to bottom of each high-rise. The actual delivery turns out to be the easy part, at least when it's not Sunday and when I'm not late. During the week, it's a snap and soon I've memorized most of my route and no longer need my little cheat sheet. But on Sundays, I have to put the newspaper sections together before heading out and that takes so much time that it always makes me late. I recruit my brother Bob to help me, and on those days, we both kneel in the darkened stairwell and try to figure out which section goes with which paper. Inevitably, we're late and more than a few people give me shit for delivering the newspaper after 10 a.m. on a Sunday. I mumble "sorry" and keep moving.

The real fun begins on days I have to collect the money. That's done in the late afternoon and early evening when most people are home, or when most people should be home. As it turns out, no one is ever home for someone collecting money. People avoid me. I knock on doors where I can hear people inside. I can hear them shuffling to the door to look through the peephole. I try to look as innocent and non-threatening as possible, and then I hear them shuffle away without opening the door.

I knock again: "Newspaper delivery here to collect."

Nothing, except that is for the sound of tenants watching their televisions, listening to their radios, and preparing their dinners. I can smell the food cooking on the other side of the door but they refuse to open up. There is one mysterious apartment where the door is always slightly ajar and I can see inside. I can see the people moving around their apartment, and still they pretend they are not home.

"Hello," I say. "Hello, newspaper delivery here to collect."

Nothing. They don't even glance my way.

Maybe, I think, I should yell *fire* or better yet, *police*.

And then there are floors and buildings I dread going in because they've already *turned,* according to my folks. These are the sections of the projects filled with the new welfare families. I'm not afraid of the families, only their punk kids who enjoy terrorizing anyone weaker, namely me. I go down hallways where tough kids are hanging out in the hall, sitting around eating food and smoking cigarettes like it's an extension of their living rooms. They refuse to move their legs when I come by and snicker and try to trip me, and sometimes give me a push. But I push on. What truly freaks me are their dogs. Dogs are not allowed in the projects but slowly, more and more families are keeping them, at least for a day or so until they realize it's a commitment. Eventually, the families either tire of the dogs or are forced by project managers to get rid of them. At that point, the dogs are released into the wild, otherwise known as the big parking lot adjacent to the projects. Left to their own devices, the dogs gather into wild packs that go after people walking to their cars. I've seen them attack women with groceries and little kids holding chicken wings. It's enough to make me glad my family does not have a car because those dogs look vicious, and remind me of Uncle Carmine's long-departed dog Leo.

What I can never figure out is why I'm not mugged on the days I'm out collecting money. It would be the perfect time because the families that do pay give me single dollars and loose change. The front and back pockets of my jeans fill up with wads of cash, and I jangle with each step. I become a walking cash register, and yet, at those times, when my pockets are literally bulging with cash, I never hear those dreaded words, *All I find, all I keep.*

I dare not look into my pockets to see how much I've collected until I get home but, when I do, I'm always impressed by the $40 or $50 I've managed to accumulate. The problem is that I'm not collecting anywhere near as much money as I should. And, as the months drag on, more and more people put me on their "must to avoid" list. I in turn start crossing them off my route and that works out fine until the day I realize I have about ten paying customers left. Not what you'd call profitable. I decide to quit and so my first job, where I earn all of $2.50 a week in tips, ends as suddenly as it begins. *The Daily News*, I decide, must carry on without me.

Hayes

For high school, I have my pick. It comes down to either Cardinal Spellman or Cardinal Hayes. Spellman has a better reputation, but Andrew and Robbie are going to Hayes. Each school costs only $200 per year and my parents tell me it's up to me. They can afford either one. I decide to follow Andrew and Robbie to Hayes even though Spellman is co-ed, and Hayes is an all boys' school. The moment I drop my acceptance into the mailbox, I wonder if I've made a terrible mistake.

It is September, 1967, and the second day of the first week of high school. Cardinal Hayes, located on the Grand Concourse, not far from Yankee Stadium, is a gigantic building, and I am late for history class, as are about dozen other of my freshmen classmates. We are all dazed by the size of the school with its endless corridors, and crowded staircases. In grammar school, I sat in one classroom all day with 40 other kids. Now I have to get from a class on one side of this massive three-story building to the next all the way on the other side, at the same time 2,500 other teenage boys are attempting the same feat—in two minutes or less.

So that morning, after leaving homeroom, I hustle to my freshman history class but narrowly miss the two-minute bell. I am perhaps 15 seconds late, and hustle in, along with a small knot of other latecomers. I rush past the teacher, a skinny Diocesan priest who looks very angry, and is pulling at his white, starched priest's collar as though he can't breathe. A vein in his forehead is throbbing, and the word *maniacal* comes to mind. He looks very much like a cartoon creation whose head might blow off, and if this were a cartoon, the pressure gauge would be heavily into the red danger zone. To make matters worse, this particular raging maniac of a priest has a nervous tic that has him constantly pulling at his collar, as though it's a too-tight dog leash. It makes him look like a mad dog and right now, he is frothing at the mouth.

"Hey son," I hear him say.

I am looking down at my books, trying to figure out which notebook is for history when I hear him say again: "Hey son, I'm talking to you."

I look up. He's talking to me, and moving down the aisle in my direction.

"Son, when I talk to you, you stand up."

"Yes Father."

I stand up and he's in my face, like a baseball manager arguing with an umpire. His face is so close to mine that I can smell cigarettes on his breath.

"You're late."

"I'm sorry Father. I…"

"Don't talk back to me son."

"I…"

"I said, don't talk back to me."

And then, without another word, this man of the cloth takes a step back, reaches his arm back as far as it will go, and slaps me as hard he possibly can across my face. I stagger backwards, and grab onto a nearby desk. I am shocked senseless. Now I know what it means to see stars. No one has ever hit me.

There is not a sound in the room, absolutely none. The rest of the room turns black and white; the priest and I are the only ones in color. Everyone else has faded, frozen in place. I have no thoughts except this one: I am scared shitless. The thought of fighting back does not ever cross my mind. It's unthinkable. This is a priest after all. There are no options except to take whatever he dishes out.

"Sit down son."

I do but he continues to stand over me.

"I want to be sure you understand that are never to be late to my class again, is that clear?"

"Yes Father."

And then he takes his fist, puts it under my chin, and begins upper-cutting my chin so hard that my head snaps back several times. Each time he says a word, he delivers a shot under my chin.

Good

I

Want

To

Make

Sure

You

Understand.

And then he turns and begins teaching as though nothing has happened. The first thing I do when the class ends is hurry to the bathroom to look in a mirror but, incredibly, there is not a mark on me. I never tell my parents.

Weeks later, as the class is waiting for the dismissal bell, the priest I now and forever will call Crazy Face looks over at me. "Hey son, you turn white whenever I look in your direction. You have to toughen up son."

I say nothing, but here's what I'm thinking: *You sadistic cocksucker. If I ever see you again outside of this school, I'm going to kick the shit out of you.*

So begin my high school years, and now I know I've made a mistake by passing on the chance to go to Cardinal Spellman.

The priests who run Hayes have a problem. The building is overflowing with teenage testosterone, and there isn't a girl in sight, except for the occasional receptionist and a 60-something-year-old librarian. The priests and brothers decide the best way to handle that kind of crazy male energy is to focus on sports, and to draft a rule for every conceivable infraction, and even ones that are not conceivable. Hayes has a rule for how we must walk *on the way* to school— *no more than four abreast*—so that other people can walk on the street without a gang of unruly boys knocking them over. We joke that the Hayes rule book—constantly evolving—will be the world's thickest book if it is ever committed to paper. But it is not of course—these are unwritten rules created on the spot, anytime a student gets out of line. We are told how to wear our hair and sideburns—to the inch. These are the Sixties when long hair is the fashion everywhere, except at Hayes.

It is not unusual for the Dean of Discipline to line us up, whip out a ruler, and begin measuring. Breaking the rules means detention or a receiving a "jug slip," a little yellow piece of paper that means you stand in a room after school with other misbehaving boys, and stay dead quiet. In reality, the moment the room monitor steps away, one of the regulars regales us with his impersonations of various teachers, and so the room turns into an after-school comedy club. It isn't half-bad but you can never even hint that to the powers-that-be.

Hayes has a strong tradition in New York. Despite its crazy patchwork of rules and discipline, or maybe because of it, it fosters many creative graduates. Its alumni include Martin Scorsese, Regis Philbin, and Don DeLillo. The comedian George Carlin didn't make it past freshman year. He famously got kicked out but even he maintained a soft spot in his heart for the school. There is something about Hayes. There is a weird vibe, akin to brainwashing. Maybe it's the ridiculous Hayes fight song which we are made to sing, or the vaguely vulgar catch phrase that ends every official discussion: "Up Hayes and all its loyal men." Hayes prides itself on taking in slackers and transforming them into upstanding young men, college material. Its graduates tend to remember the school in glowing terms despite the undercurrent of brutality that is part of everyday life there. Hayes can be a vicious place, especially if one is weak of mind or body, or doesn't play football, baseball or basketball.

One time, when a group of us are making too much noise getting in and out of our lockers, a chemistry teacher runs out of his classroom, and begins swinging at us wildly with a rubber hose. He doesn't care who is making the noise, he wants it to stop. His eyes are like spinning saucers, and his hair stands straight up as he swings that hose, slamming it against any body part he can.

Another time, Andrew lights up a cigarette near the school entrance but well after the school day has ended. Without warning, the side door of the building is flung open, and a young priest comes running toward us like an Olympian. He comes up to Andrew, rips the cigarette out of his mouth, grabs him by the ear and drags him back into the building for detention. I stand there speechless. One moment I am talking to my best friend, and the next he is gone, pulled inside the school for "special detention."

That's Hayes.

Even getting to the school from where I live in the Bronx proves to be a challenge. We cannot get there with one bus or one subway. We have to switch and therein lies the problem. The place we switch buses is an area called Simpson Street. You may know it from the Paul Newman film "Fort Apache." In these years, it is one of the toughest neighborhoods in the Bronx and white teenagers wearing sports jackets and ties are red meat for the druggies who make Simpson Street their home.

One day, me and my friends are waiting to make the bus switch and I make the mistake of putting down my bookbag for a moment. It doesn't help that the bag is festooned with the bright colors of Hayes—cardinal and gold. Almost the moment I place the bag down and let go of the handle, a kid whooshes by and grabs it on the run. It's so fast that me, Andrew and Robbie don't realize immediately what happened. The kid actually stops at the corner and waits for us to begin chasing him. He runs into an abandoned building where all the windows are nailed shut with boards. The three of us stop at the entrance. The interior hallway is dark and smells of urine. Should we really go in there for a bookbag? The kid who took the bag is very tall and very creepy looking.

"Forget it," I say.

"No, come on, there's three of us," Andrew says.

"Yeah, but we're not armed."

"Let's go."

And so we do. We walk into the dark hallway, and wait while our eyes adjust to the light and there, at the very far end of the ground-floor hallway, stands my mugger with my bookbag.

"Hey man," I say. "I need that bag back."

"Come closer," he says.

This should have been our cue to turn tail and run like hell but like idiots, the three of us move closer.

"You want your bag?"

"Yeah."

"Here."

He puts the bag down and we hear the nauseating sound of a switchblade opening. He steps over the bookbag and points the blade at my stomach.

"Give me all your money."

I reach into my pocket but I've only got a bus pass. "This is all I have. I don't have any money."

"Shit," he says. "What about you two?"

He sticks the blade in the direction of Andrew and Robbie. Andrew has nothing either but Robbie has a five dollar bill. The mugger grabs it and takes off.

"Shit."

"Hey Robbie," I say. "I'm sorry man. I'll pay you back."

"Don't worry about it. At least we didn't get hurt."

I grab my bag and we head toward the bus stop, just in time to see that we missed our bus.

The "D" Class

Inside this cavernous school, I live a sheltered existence. My grade has more than 600 boys, but my world revolves around only 40 of them. That's because I am in the D classes, the class reserved for the smartest kids in the school. While 560 of the kids in my grade mingle and mix in various classes and get to know one another, the 40 boys in D classes remain segregated. We are told over and over that we are special, and will be held to a higher standard. Go ahead and hate me—everyone else in my grade does. To be in the D class is to wear a target. Most of the time, I'm oblivious to the taunts directed at us but not always. Some days, I hear a few of the kids singing the lyrics to The Beatles' "Nowhere Man" as I pass by. I never challenge these guys because, well, why pick a fight you cannot win?

There's no relief from the teachers either. They see us as a special challenge, and rise to the task. The school has three basic types of teachers and they're more or less color-coded—priests in black robes, brothers in brown robes, and lay teachers in short black robes. I become familiar with all of them. Father Crazy Face chooses violence to force us to pay attention. Another teacher, a Franciscan brother whom I'll call Brother Thomas, chooses another method, one altogether more personal. Brother Thomas has a very long and very hard ruler he has nicknamed "The Enforcer" and, every day, he chooses one of us and forces himself upon us.

A typical encounter goes like this:

"Mister LaRosa, why are you talking?"

"No reason sir."

"You know what happens to talkers in my class, don't you son?"

"Yes Brother."

"Come up here son."

And so I go. I'm familiar with the routine. I walk slowly to the front of the class, and bend at a right angle over the side of his desk, the side of my face resting on his worn, green blotter. My ass is more or less exposed—the way the good Brother likes it—but, to make the whole experience even more humiliating, he lifts the tail of my blue sports coat and flips it onto my back. I'm sure he'd pull down my pants and lapse into a full drool if he thought he'd get away with it, but he takes his pleasure in small doses. Licking his lips (I know because I've see him do this every day to one of us), he stares down at my ass and raises his ruler, winds up and delivers three imposing whacks. It hurts but to make a sound only invites an extra shot so I stay quiet. When he is through, he is flushed and says, "Okay son, you can go back to your desk now."

He can barely gather himself to continue with the class.

The lay teachers seem to be the most normal; they exert their will by piling on the assignments but at least it's not corporal punishment. I still recall my freshman English teacher announcing: "If the rest of your classmates read 20 books this year, you'll read 40. You're better than they are, smarter, or at least that's what they tell me. We'll see about that."

You can imagine how the rest of the grade feels about our "special" status. They bump into us in the hallways, stare us down in the lunchroom, and dominate us in gym class. Being smart is no fun but, as I have my entire school life, I embrace it. The 40 of us form a sturdy bond—us against them. We have each other's backs. And there is the competition among our own. Hayes spits out report cards on what feels like a daily basis. Hayes *loves* report cards and they are always being shoved in our faces.

On the day the report cards are released, Father Robertson, our homeroom teacher, stands at the front of the classroom, and calls us out one by one. There is no privacy here. We are held up to praise or ridicule. The students are ranked by number, 1 through 600, and God forbid any of us falls below 40. That would mean that perhaps we might not be in the smartest class the following year; we might even, gasp, be placed in the dreaded M class, the second smartest, a class that is allowed to mix a bit with the other members of our grade, seeing how they are no longer the elite.

"Mister Alfonsi," Father says. "You are now ranked # 38. You'd better pull yourself up son."

"I'm trying father, what can I say?"

Alfonsi is our renegade. He doesn't quite embrace his vaunted status like the rest of us do. I admire him but from afar. He's like a Bowery boy come to life. One day, after bumbling over the translation of a single Latin sentence for what seems like hours, he shrugs at the teacher and says, "Come on Father, let's try another one. This one's shot."

And then there's our hulking classmate Desi. He's a favorite, not only a brain but also a very talented athlete who makes all of us nerds feel proud that he's one of us. He's on the football team, and proves that we're not all weak-kneed sissies.

The good Father beams at him. "You're # 11. Great job son."

"Mister LaRosa," he says looking at me. "You're ranked # 15 this grading period. Keep up the good work."

When our names are called, we walk to the front of the room and take our report cards. The system works. I feel proud to be No. 15 or whatever, and the goal of course is to be No. 1.

Hayes becomes my world, and I take it dead seriously. At school, I'm a shy kid with few friends so I'm very susceptible to brain-washing and cultism, the pillars upon which Hayes rests. It is very easy to sell me a bill of goods, and I embrace the corny Hayes lifestyle with all my might. Before long, I'm using the Hayes tag phrase *Up Hayes* to the point of being obnoxious. My favorite colors become *cardinal and gold* even though, as one wag suggests, the colors look suspiciously like *red and yellow*. My transformation into *Hayes Boy* is complete when I convince my poor mother to buy me a cardinal and gold-colored winter coat. Incredibly, this woman, who regularly refuses to buy me anything costing more than a few dollars, who has never bought a garbage bag or a napkin in her life, picks this moment to become magnanimous. She agrees to spring for the $75 to buy me the coat, which I later realize is about the most uncool thing on the planet Earth. I refuse to wear it until it's dyed black and then she and I never speak of it again. The following winter I even go without a winter coat because I can no longer stand wearing my mistake. It's a very cold winter but I sacrifice to gain a bit back a bit of dignity. I merely put a sweater on under my sports coat, grab a hat and gloves, and trudge through the snow. No matter how cold it gets, I will not wear that Hayes coat and I know better than to ask my mother for the money to buy a new one. She would rather have a frozen son than spring for another coat when I have *a perfectly good one hanging in the closet.*

Because I am so quiet in and out of class, someone gives me the nickname Yogi, after the Maharishi Yogi who was popular at the time because of the Beatles' foray into Transcendental Meditation. I have no idea if the Maharishi was quiet but the nickname is magic. Kids I don't even know begin calling me Yogi and the nickname pulls me out of my shell. The guys begin to joke around with me, and I discover to my utter shock that I possess a sense of humor. One day, a kid behind me finds a long strand of hair on the shoulder of my jacket, and asks me who it belongs to. "I don't know, is it blonde or brunette?" I ask, and everyone around me roars in approval. It's like discovering some special power. *Is it that easy to be accepted,* I wonder? I guess it's funnier because they don't expect it of me and that's fine. Anything I can do to fit in.

The school leaders emphasize extra-curricular activities, especially athletics, and I long with all my soul to be on the baseball team. I pray to God. *Please make it happen. Please.* At 5-feet, 6 inches and 150 pounds, I'm probably too small but I refuse to believe it. Baseball has always been my passion and so I try out for the freshman team. After a few practices, Coach tells us that the names of those still in the running will be posted that afternoon on the gym bulletin board. After class, I go to the gym to see if I'm good enough. I have a lousy feeling but, as always, am trying to be optimistic. It's the only way I know how to be. *Please God, let my name be on that list.* I run my finger down the names. God must've taken the day off. I'm not on the list. I stand in front of the list and read it again. Nope, still not there.

I feel like shit. And of course, at that exact moment, the freshman baseball coach wanders by.

"What's up LaRosa?" he asks, slapping me on the back.

I know if I even attempt to say anything, I will cry so I say nothing, point to the list, and shrug. "I'm sorry, son," he says.

He can see how upset I am, and I turn to walk away, still silent.

"Hey," he calls out after me. "Look, come to the practice tomorrow, and we'll try you out again, okay?"

I reach out to shake his hand. He takes it and, when we lock eyes, I see that he's nearly as choked up as I am.

The next day at practice, I am more ready than I've ever been for anything in my life. I have nothing to lose so I go all out at my chosen position, first base. Coach orders smash after smash hit my way and I field all of them cleanly, even spectacularly. I've never fielded so well in my life but I know I'm in over my head when the shortstop fires a bullet to me and his throw nearly takes my hand off. Unlike the other guys trying out, I don't have an expensive mitt; I bought my glove with my own money at E.J. Korvette's. After the throw, I rub my hand, and see the shortstop laughing. He knows I'm in the D class and I know he's in the Z class.

I get up to bat, knowing it will be make or break. The pitcher looks huge, so *huge* his head is shaped like an anvil. He throws pitches that are faster than anything I've experienced on the sandlots of the projects where I've learned the game without a hint of adult supervision. The Little Leagues seem to have skipped right over the projects. I manage to make contact with nearly every pitch but mostly I hit grounders and weak fly balls. One ball drops in for a hit. I'm a dreamer but even I know I didn't show enough bat to make the team.

Afterwards, Coach comes to me and says he'd be happy to have me around the team if I'd like to be assistant manager.

"You have talent but they're guys here who are better."

He's right. I cannot argue. For a few seconds, I picture myself carrying towels and water and hanging around all these superior athletes. But I know deep down that it's not for me. I thank him politely but this time, I have words. It's not a total waste. I ride back from the practice field with the guys who made the team. I think they see me in a different light. I may not be as good as they are but I'm pretty sure I'm better than they thought I was, and that's something. Even the shortstop who nearly took my hand off with his 100-mph throw slaps me on the back after we get off. Some of the guys are getting rides back home from fathers. I start walking toward the subway in my sweaty clothes. I feel better about myself and I have Coach to thank for that. That's the crazy thing about Hayes, the thing that keeps legions of boys proud of the school. For every Brother Thomas, there is a guy like Coach.

Wendigo

My freshman year at Hayes is 1967 and, while the psychedelic era is going full tilt outside our doors, inside Hayes, we are told to ignore it. I cannot help but be enthralled by all of it, especially the music: The Beatles, of course, but also The Stones, Bob Dylan, Jimi Hendrix, The Who, The Doors, Creedence Clearwater Revival. My mother even takes me to see a live taping of the Ed Sullivan show where I'm lucky enough to see Eric Burdon and The Animals perform "House of the Rising Sun." There's nothing about rock music I don't like. You name the group and I have either bought their album or shoplifted it.

I am a huge fan and spend hours in my room singing aloud to each and every song. I imagine I have a pretty good voice, but maybe it's like that philosophy question about the tree. Can I really have a good voice if no one is listening? Either way, it works for me. I want to jump into the Sixties. The drugs don't interest me but everything else does. I want to grow my hair long, drive to California, surf, and have sex with hundreds of hippie girls. Revolution is in the air, and so is free love, my favorite part of the trip, as Jim Morrison might say.

But we Hayesmen are at a distinct disadvantage compared to the guys who do not have the, ahem, good fortune to go to Hayes. We are subject to that damn Hayes book of rules and regulations. We are not allowed to wear bell bottoms, cannot have long hair or long sideburns. And facial hair—*you're joking, right, son?* to quote the Dean of Discipline. We look like we are bucking to join the ROTC, or hop on the first plane to Vietnam.

I am especially disadvantaged because of my high forehead, and secretly know—*can anyone else tell?*—I am losing my hair. If I can grow it long, my receding hairline will not be so obvious, or so I think. I am bemoaning my lack of hair, lack of bell bottoms, and lack of ladies to Andrew when he tells me that Hayes is sponsoring a dance that very weekend.

"Only guys from Hayes can go so you'll look about as dorky as everyone else," he says.

I punch his arm but he's got a point.

But wait. "What about girls?"

"They'll be there," he says with his sly smile. "My cousin says that girls from all over the Bronx come to the Hayes dances because they know we're so fucking horny."

I'm getting excited hearing about it, and so that weekend, I attend the first dance of my life. It is in the school gymnasium but, to me, it is pure magic. The rock band is called Wendigo. It's the first band I've ever seen live, and they sound pretty damn good. They even have a strobe light which manages to make even this sad-looking gym appear psychedelic. Of course, because we are good Hayesmen, there is nary a bellbottom in sight. We are required to wear jackets and ties even to the dance. I am wearing my good corduroy jacket with the patches on the elbows, and my brown shoes, and I imagine there is a universe where I am attractive to females. As Andrew's cousin promised, there are girls everywhere. Short, tall, fat, with tight skirts and pants and eye-popping breasts of every description. They have no dress code, other than their own modesty. But their clothes belie their immaturity and insecurity. They look sideways at all the boys, standing nervously on the side of the dance floor, silently beseeching us to ask them to dance with eyes slathered in makeup.

And then I smell it. Not the gym, but something else, something that smells to me like raw sex. Every single teenager in that gym is wearing cologne, perfume, or aftershave, and nearly all of us are wearing far too much. That aroma combined with the release of pheromones creates a jungle-like atmosphere of want. We are all teenagers and bouncing off the walls with desire.

I love everything about this night, and I haven't even danced.

This is the first high school dance for Andrew, too, but he is far more experienced with girls. So is the third member of our group, Robbie. Robbie is kind of awkward at all things, including walking, but he puts out a puppy-dog air that I've seen attract girls before. Both he and Andrew are natural charmers; me, not so much. Andrew, especially, has a certain sexiness that I do not possess, and I can only marvel as he walks up to the girl nearest to him, and calmly escorts her to the dance floor. I don't know where this boy has learned how to do it but Andrew clearly knows how to dance. Suddenly, I realize that I have no idea how to move on a dance floor. I sing to a lot of rock songs, and know the words to all of them but never have I *danced* to a single one. I decide my first dance will be a slow one. When I hear the first strains of "Stand By Me," I look around for the nearest girl.

I don't have to look far. Girls to the right and left are being pulled out onto the dance floor but this tiny girl near me is alone. She has a gorgeous face, and long brown hair, and, in my delirium, I think she looks a lot like Linda Ronstadt. She has a slight body, and is wearing a mini-skirt with a tight blue sweater that definitely gets my attention. Now or never, I think. I tap her on the shoulder, as I've seen Andrew do, and wordlessly lead her out to the dance floor. I think I might be in love.

I place my hands around her waist, and immediately feel how small it is, how fragile she is, and how frightened both of us are. I mean, we are practically shaking. I look around and watch what Andrew is up to—he is pulling his partner closer so that their bodies are pressing against each other. I pull my dance partner in a little closer, and she responds immediately. Soon, our bodies are touching. I have a boner the size of a javelin, and there is no doubt in my mind that my dance partner can feel it rubbing against her hip. Am I crazy, or is she trying to maneuver it toward her you-know-what? My hands begin to slide down her back. I want to place my hand on her ass, if only for a moment, and I'm nearly there when I feel a tap on my shoulder. It is the imposing Father McCormack, the Dean of Discipline himself. He puts one big mitt on each of our shoulders and pulls us slightly apart.

"Make room for the Holy Ghost," he says, giving me a knowing look. I've seen that look before. It usually comes just before he writes some poor sap a jug slip. This time, the poor sap is me but really who cares? I'd do detention for a year, if I could only hold this girl all night.

"That was embarrassing."

I say this to myself, forgetting that I am attached at the hip.

"Don't worry about it," she says.

I don't know why but I'm amazed that this girl is speaking, and speaking to me. She even sounds kind of friendly.

"I'm Joni, like Joni Mitchell," she says.

"I'm Paul."

"So who is that guy?"

"Only the Dean of Discipline."

She frowns. "Will you get in trouble?"

Her concern is touching, and I can't speak. She pulls me back into her, and, like I said, I'm in love.

I say nothing more, but it doesn't matter—our actions speak for themselves. She is interested, and God knows I am. But then the song ends, and the next number is "Please Please Me" by The Beatles. Uh-oh, a fast song, but one that I can sing backwards. I look at her and she looks at me and we're off, dancing for all we're worth. I have no idea what I'm doing. I am so wrapped up in my own attempt to look cool that I do not immediately notice that Joni is wearing a leg brace, a very large metal leg brace. I don't know what's wrong with her but the word *polio* leaps to mind. She is doing her best to keep up but I can see it's not easy. She is kind of hobbling. Still, she looks radiant, and is smiling at me.

I ignore the brace, and keep dancing. What to do? It is moments like these that I wish I had more experience, not only with girls, but in life. I want to say something funny, something to ease the tension, but I am a dumb teenager.

When the song is over, I thank her and move away as fast as I can. I find Andrew and Robbie who have seen the whole thing. They don't say anything and neither do I. The night goes on, and I dance with more girls, but I can't forget Joni. All night long, I see her in my peripheral vision. No one else is asking her to dance. She is shunned because of that leg brace. I'm angry with myself. What's wrong with me? Why won't I ask her to dance again? What am I afraid of? She's beautiful, and I'm not. I should feel lucky that she even agreed to dance with me that first time.

It is nearly 10 p.m. and the dance will end soon. The crowd is thinning out, and the three of us are waiting for the last slow song when, for another four minutes, we can rub our bodies against a willing teenage girl. Wendigo begins to play "Under the Boardwalk." I see Joni across the dance floor, and I know she sees me. I can feel her eyes. I still have not seen her dance with anyone else the entire night. I am a coward and Andrew, who has a cruel streak, can sense it.

"You gonna dance with the gimp again or what?" he says.

I push him away. "Fuck you man."

I cross the dance floor, and walk up to Joni.

"Hi."

"Hey."

"So I think this is probably the last dance. What d'ya think?"

"I think we should dance."

Our bodies are together once more.

I don't know what makes me do it but when I lean in close and smell her hair, I whisper "I'm sorry" into her ear.

She pulls me closer but says nothing. We go round and

round, and when the song ends, she kisses me softly on the lips. I want to freeze time but the opposite happens. Suddenly, everything is moving very fast. The band is thanking us, and the lights come on. The dance floor is transformed into a gymnasium once again. Joni's friends are pulling at her, telling her they have to leave. She looks at me and smiles. And I watch her go, forgetting until I'm back on No. 6 train that I did not ask for her phone number.

I am a dumb teenager.

Rock n Roll

The benches are where we spend the Sixties. We listen and sing along to rock music on transistor radios, and eagerly crowd around to hear the latest single by the Beatles. We argue over which band is best—the Beatles, the Rolling Stones, The Who or the Doors. Once in a while a new group breaks into our rotation. Some of us become devotees of Buffalo Springfield while others drift toward the group Traffic. There is a weird subcategory of guys who swear allegiance to Frank Zappa and the Mothers of Invention, and Captain Beefheart. I become a big fan of Jimi Hendrix and Led Zeppelin, so big that I make their albums a special target of my ongoing shoplifting career. We wait for our favorite songs to be played on WNEW-FM, and then sing along for all we're worth. We know the names and shifts of every DJ, and spend hours deciphering the lyrics to The Beatles' "Sgt. Pepper's Lonely Hearts Club Band," examining the album cover and sleeve, and wondering: Could the Beatles really be taking acid? *Nah.*

Between favorite songs, we sit and bullshit about music

and girls and music. We smoke cigarettes (at least everyone else does—I hate the acrid taste and never do), make fun of each other and engage in weird contests, like who will jump off the highest structure. Phil wins when he jumps off the roof of the community center—at least 15 or 20 feet high—and survives without a scratch. Beer drinking—serious beer drinking, like a case at a time, is in vogue—but I resist not because I'm so holy or anything but because I think of it as a waste of time.

The airwaves are filled with news of an upcoming marathon concert weekend in Woodstock, New York, and I beg my parents to let me go but they brush me off. It's just as well since I have no idea how I'd get there. None of us do. We only want to go. As an alternative, we opt to see Led Zeppelin at the New York State Pavilion in Flushing Meadows Park in Queens. It's one of the buildings leftover from the 1964-65 World's Fair, now used as a concert venue. This time, my parents say okay. It will be the first rock concert I ever attend.

Joining me are Andrew, Robbie, John and Frank. It takes a while to get from the Bronx to Queens by subway but we eventually arrive half-hour before the concert, and buy tickets at the door for $7.50 each. The bill includes Buddy Guy, Larry Coryell and the group Raven. The New York State Pavilion is an open-air venue topped off by a huge stained glass ceiling. It's a hot and sticky August night. There are no seats so people are sitting or lying down on the bare concrete floor. Thousands are packed into the place but we are able to move around with relative ease as long as we stay back from the stage. As usual, we are looking for girls who might want to make out. Of course, there is almost no chance of that happening since we look hopelessly square in this sea of hippies. Almost every guy, except those of us who go to Hayes, has long hair, but I think even with long hair, I'd be a square. I'm afraid of acid, and don't like to get high because I like to keep my wits about me. No one here seems to have such qualms. People are falling all over one another, stumbling around, vomiting, and pretty much looking dazed and confused, like the Led Zeppelin song. It's not unusual to see a beautiful girl, clearly stoned or tripping, fall onto the closest guy for some serious tongue. I live for such an event.

I'm so mesmerized by the scene that I barely pay attention to the opening acts. I'm there for Zeppelin. We spend most of the time in search of action, and we occasionally find it. Hash pipes and joints are being passed in every direction, and one sometimes crosses my path. I think there's even a point where I am passing a joint with one hand and a hash pipe with the other. But I don't take a hit. I'm chicken. Not that it matters. The air is thick as can be with the smell of marijuana and who knows what. I feel myself getting a contact high and eventually sit down not far from the stage to watch Robert Plant and Jimmy Page do their thing. Between the smoke, the girls and the blues, I am in heaven. But then, about three-quarters of the way through the show, the drummer John Bonham collapses (from exhaustion or drugs, I'm not sure), and the band stops playing. Pandemonium takes over since no one knows what to do or what is happening up there on stage. I see the lights of an ambulance and suspect Bonham has been taken away.

The concert ends just like that, and in the crush of people, we get separated from Frank. We search for him for an hour outside but eventually give up, and go home. He turns out to be fine and tells us some story about meeting a girl. I have no idea if he's telling the truth but I wish I'd been that lucky because, of course, the undercurrent of all rock music is sex, and man do I feel its pull. But try as I might, I have no luck. Our crowd is noticeably thin in the girl department. There are Mary, Nancy and two girls named Kathy. I've been flirting with Mary for years with precious little to show for it but I'm certain that's my problem. When we were 13, she and I had a "date" to go to a feast at Holy Cross Church, not far from the projects. It was one of those basement things where the church sets up games and sells food and pulls in a few bucks. Mary and I went together as a couple and, as a young teen, that alone felt risqué to me.

It was fairly mundane until the end when I won her a stuffed animal with literally my last dime. I knocked down three clowns with a baseball, won the stuffed animal and handed it to her feeling as proud as I'd ever felt in my life. I could tell she was on the verge of kissing me but I didn't lean in at the proper moment. I regretted it the whole walk home and, when I said goodnight, I again lost my nerve. I didn't know what was wrong with me but the echoes of that near-kiss ran through my mind all night and then in the morning, as I sat on our stoop waiting for a friend so we could walk to school, Mary appeared and, without a word, walked over and kissed me on the lips. It was the nicest gift I'd ever received.

I know I should follow it up but I always talk myself out of it. Mary is always with us, and I think that's the problem. I'm intimidated by all the boys competing for her interest, especially Duffy, and I don't want to seem foolish or have them make fun of me. Deep down, I wonder if I'm good enough for her. Why would she want me anyway? The other guys are so much better looking.

Mary loves the attention from all the boys and flirts constantly, sometimes dangerously so. One of our favorite haunts in the summer is Orchard Beach, out near City Island. It's a small, crescent-shaped beach and my crowd always meets up in Section 13. Since none of our parents have a car, we take buses, bikes and even walk there. One day Mary is there wearing a bikini and showing plenty of skin when she is surrounded by all the boys in our crowd. She is lying on the beach and the boys are burying her in the sand when things get a bit out of control. All that pent up sexual energy at having a teenage girl wearing very little right there in front of us unleashes *something* in the crowd, and we begin throwing sand on top of her with a little more frenzy and energy than is needed. Mary keeps laughing but Bobby, one of the guys in our crowd, doesn't like what he's seeing.

Bobby feels the sexual tension and tells me later that he felt bad about what was happening and worried it was getting out hand. So he steps up, telling us to cut it out. He begins brushing the sand off Mary as she begins to stand, and in that split second, Bobby's pinky finger catches in Mary's top and her breast pops out. By now, she is standing and she doesn't notice what all of us do—her breast is exposed. No one says anything but we all take a long hard look. And then she looks down and restores order.

But she is very very angry at Bobby, who deserves better. He explains what happened but she doesn't want to hear it. She leaves at once. The good times, at least that day, are over.

The next morning, Mary —as she had that time she kissed me—finds Bobby alone and walks up to him but kissing is the last thing on her mind. With steely determination, she asks "Can I slap you?"

Bobby again begins to explain himself but realizes she is tuning him out. He later says that he hopes by letting her have a whack at him that she'll let bygones be bygones. They've always had a good relationship and, after all, he *was* trying to help her. He says okay.

Mary reaches back and slaps Bobby as hard as she can across his face, turns and walks away. Both of them are flushed.

"I thought, 'okay, now we're even,' but it was never the same between us after that," Bobby later told me.

Chopped Liver

In my junior year at Hayes, Andrew and I decide to check out the job bulletin board. He spots the ad first. It's some deli on the Upper East Side of Manhattan, on Third Avenue, between 67th and 68th Streets, advertising for boys who want to work behind the counter and stock shelves. Since we live way up in the Bronx, this is a very long subway ride but Andrew seems intrigued.

"What d'ya think? Wanna check it out?"

I do but not because it's a job and will earn us money. I have my own agenda. I'm fascinated by "the city," which is what those of us in the outer boroughs call Manhattan. I explore it every chance I get. When I was younger, I traveled there all the time to have what lame adventures I could muster up.

One time, a bunch of us took the elevator to the top of the Empire State Building and walked down the stairs. In the hallways, we found boxes of correspondence from the various businesses. We picked through them, God knows why. It made me feel like a spy, like my idol James Bond. I read all the Ian Fleming books and had seen all the movies. It's partly because of Bond—that international man of mystery—that I make frequent trips to the United Nations. But the true, more lame, reason is that I am a stamp collector, and I have begun collecting UN stamps. But it's not really the stamps that hold my attention. It's the UN itself. I like to wander around the building, look at the foreigners, and visit the General Assembly.

Again, it's all very James Bond-like, and the General Assembly looks like it could be in a Bond flick. I can spend hours walking up and down the halls of the UN, sitting in the chairs in the General Assembly and no one ever bothers me. It's a cheap thrill and it doesn't hurt that the UN is very close to *The Daily News* building, the place I visited Santa Claus all those years ago with my mother. I still walk into that lobby every chance I get, to see the globe and bask in a place where I feel something important must be taking place. Somewhere above me, reporters are calling *sources* and writing up stories that will appear in the paper I buy tomorrow. I imagine the newsroom of the Daily Planet. I wish I could go upstairs but it still feels too far away. I'm sure they'd stop a kid like me at the door.

But the idea that *important things* are taking place here is what really draws me to Manhattan. I never have that feeling in the Bronx. The city is happening, man. The girls look better, and sometimes, when I'm riding the subway on the Upper East Side, I can barely believe how beautiful they are. They are mature and sexy, with cable-knit dresses that cling to their bodies, and I ache being near them. I imagine myself one day living in my cool apartment up on the 60th floor of some skyscraper, with one of these beauties in tow. My fantasies are fueled by Playboy magazine which promotes a way of life that is hip and uninhibited. I long to be one of those men in Playboy, the guys with the sports cars and the scotch. Playboy also happens to be my favorite magazine to shoplift, an activity I work at as diligently as I worked at baseball when I was younger. I have a favorite little store picked out right near the Whitney Museum. I walk in, buy the NY Post, and on my way out, pause near the magazines. I put my Post down on top of a stack of Playboys, and pick up Time, Newsweek or something else serious. I leaf through it, pretend to be reading some important article, and then place it back down. When I retrieve my Post again, I lift a copy of Playboy from the stack right beneath it. It's a neat trick that I'm proud of. I do it every month at this little store, and the guy behind the counter never seems to catch on. It doesn't escape me that I am committing two sins in one—stealing a porn magazine, and if I ever return to the confessional booth, I'm sure that will get the priest's attention.

I spend hours in the Whitney, the Frick, the Met and MOMA. Part of it is because I have a lot of school assignments that require these visits. But it's more than that, something that I admit only to myself. I feel special in these museums, taking notes and studying art. It's that superior feeling again, one where I convince myself that I'm smarter than my dumb-ass classmates who would rather visit a White Castle. I use the great art of great men to counter my own feelings of inadequacy. Pathetic but there it is.

And then there are the Manhattan hotels. I'm fascinated with the hotels, especially the Plaza up on Central Park South. I watch all the rich people climbing the steps and going inside, wondering if I'll ever be able to afford to stay there. I do not realize that anyone can walk inside and sail right through the lobby. I think you have to be a paying guest or the doorman will boot your ass out. But one day it hits me. How can a doorman possibly know all the guests? He can't. So I summon my nerve and nervously walk up those marble steps and go through the gleaming revolving door. The doorman nods at me and I nod back. *Act like you belong*, a voice inside tells me.

It is like entering a cathedral. The traffic noise outside recedes and the lobby fills with a hushed silence. Sophisticated people dressed in their fancy suits and designer dresses check out maps, light cigarettes, and speak to each other in a confident way, a way I've never heard in the projects. And if I think my presence might upset the equilibrium, I am sadly mistaken.

I am invisible, a wall sconce. I walk around the Palm Court twice before I see the Oak Room tucked away in a corner. The bar, which overlooks Central Park South, has a picture perfect view of horses and carriages. For me, this is the epicenter of Manhattan. The Oak Room is all dark wood, and men smoking cigars are talking to women who must be models, or call girls or both. I stare so hard I think my eyes might break. This is the world of Playboy, not only a dream, but a reality right here in New York City. My Wonderland exists, and it is only a subway ride away. I leave the Plaza that day determined to visit it again and again.

So when Andrew asks me if I want to go check out this deli job in *Manhattan*, my answer is an immediate and unqualified "yes." I want as much of "the city" as I can get.

The Third Avenue Deli is small and narrow, and I don't

know about Andrew but I immediately feel self-conscious. As always, Andrew takes the lead.

"Hi, we're here about some jobs that were advertised at our school," he says to a 50-something-year-old man behind the counter wearing a stained white apron.

"What school is that?"

"Cardinal Hayes."

"Ah," he says eyeing us. He sticks out his hand. "My name is Jack."

"I'm Andrew and this is Paul."

"Do you have any deli experience?"

We both answer no and the interview is off and running. Turns out Jack is a Jewish guy who lives in Forest Hills, Queens, and the idea that he is advertising jobs for his Jewish deli in a Catholic high school in the Bronx means only one thing—he is looking for cheap help.

We're hired.

Jack could not have hired someone with less experience. I have never even tasted most of the food he sells here. Salami is my sandwich of choice and my palate is so limited that I've never even tried a salami sandwich *with cheese on it.* Jack's deli turns out to be a pretty good place for food, and a lot of the dishes here are homemade in the small, grease-laden kitchen in the back of store. Within weeks, I am making roast beef, roasted turkey, baked ham, rice pudding, and the biggest joke of all, chopped chicken liver. Actually, the real biggest joke of all is that the chicken salad has no chicken in it. Jack has as many rules about his deli as Hayes has about facial hair. He schools us in his ways, and his way of making chicken salad is to boil a few turkey carcasses. Once they cool off, whatever meat remains is loose, and we pick at it—I mean every tiny crevice of the turkey—until a bowl of the leftover meat appears. Add mayonnaise, celery, salt and pepper and voila—chicken salad, Jack-style.

What's even more amazing is that sophisticated Manhattanites love my cooking! They flock in and compliment me on the baked ham, the rice pudding—dishes I have yet to even taste. Jack's method is so fool-proof that he tells us precisely what ingredients to add, we do it, and it comes out tasting fantastic, or so the customers tell us. And what customers! The rock star Alice Cooper is a regular, as is Eddie Simon, the near twin brother of Paul, of Simon and Garfunkel. Other regulars include on-air television guys and anchor John Roland from WNEW-TV which is right around the corner.

Jack is a great salesman and he wants his workers to be miniature versions of him. He's got a million little sayings he browbeats us with. "A buck's a buck, you gotta eat," he says over and over. To convince us that pushing the goods is the way to go, he says, "It's good for me, it's good for you, it's good for the customer." Over and over I hear Jack's voice, even when he's not talking.

If a customer buys crackers, we are immediately to ask, "Would you like some chopped chicken liver with that?"

Jack drills that into us so often that the word "cracker" conjures up chopped chicken liver every time.

If we don't make the suggestion on our own at once, Jack sidles up next to us, gives us a sharp jab in the ribs, and slips us a note the customer cannot see. It says, "Sell them some chopped chicken liver." I can only guess that the markup on this delicacy is sky-high because a) Jack pushes it like heroin, and b) he has a son not much older than us who got a Triumph Spitfire for his 18th birthday.

But Andrew and I do get into the act, and even compete with one another over who can make the most delicious rice pudding, who can get the roast beef center to look just so, and who is better at charming the customers into buying more than they ever thought they would. The deli turns out to be a regular Dale Carnegie course for me, and dealing with the public helps to bring me out of my public-housing shell. Within a few short months, Jack transforms me into someone I barely recognize, someone who chats with the regulars, and flirts with the stock girls from the Schrafft's Restaurant across the street. The girls come in on their lunch hour, and we always make them the best sandwiches. Rose, Jack's wife, a matchmaker at heart who happens to work at the deli, often expresses consternation that neither Andrew nor I ever do more than flirt with the Schrafft's girls.

"When are you going to ask her out?" she says anytime one of them leaves the store without giving up her phone number.

"Next time, Rose, next time," I promise.

What I'm secretly thinking is: *Hey, I might be selling chopped chicken liver to the customers but I'm still no Casanova.* Flirting is in my repertoire but I have little else.

What is far easier for me is ogling the absolutely gorgeous Manhattan women who pass through the store each day. One day, a scrumptious girl, probably only a few years older than me, comes in and can't find her favorite Häagan-Dazs flavor Rum Raisin. I offer to help, of course, and dive into the ice cream case. Before I know it, she is rooting around next to me and when I look over to say something, I realize that I can see right down her shirt and beyond. She is not wearing a bra. Here's what I discover at that moment: it's difficult to find the correct ice cream flavor when you're staring at a woman's breasts. In fact, such an endeavor can take quite a long time. I look for that ice cream for the better part of 20 minutes until my fingers are turning blue from the cold, and the whole time she is right there next to me, seemingly oblivious to the direction of my eyes. And then, by God, I find the damn thing, right where I knew it would be all along. I hand it to her and she gives me such a smile that it's a wonder the ice cream doesn't melt in my hand.

When she pays, she gives me a wink and says, "Thanks for looking so hard," and it's only then that I realize I've seen exactly what she wants me to see.

I love working in Manhattan.

Ski Trip

One day, an after-school announcement comes over the PA system—a ski trip is being planned, and anyone interested should sign up with Father Edward Pipala who will chaperone the trip. I've never even imagined skiing but Andrew says he's going and soon enough, I find myself putting my name on the signup sheet under his. If I really thought about it, I might have realized that this is not a great idea. I have no skis, no ski clothes, no long-johns nor ski gloves or warm hat and yet I feel oddly prepared. I have seen snow after all. Did I mention I've never seen a chair lift or even a mountain in person?

On Friday, February 13, 1970, I board a school bus with 115 other Hayesmen, and we head for Binghamton, New York. I sit next to Andrew who brings along his boom-box and plays it loud so we can listen to music the whole ride. The only song I remember, and I hate it to this day because of its association with this trip, is Three Dog Night singing about how Jeremiah was a bull frog. It's a very long ride as we break free of the Bronx traffic and make our way north.

Father Pipala, our chaperone, is a favorite at Hayes. He is young, has blond hair and blue eyes, and plays lead guitar and sings in the school's folk group. If he was a student, he'd get all the girls but since he is a priest in an all boys school, all he has are us boys who mostly worship him. He is down to earth, funny, easy to talk to, and has real charisma.

We get to Binghamton at nightfall and check into the Schrafft's Motor Inn. I've never stayed at a motel. (On our family vacations, we travel to the Rockaways where my family rents a room that we share with the son of the home-owner.) Being in a real motel with my classmates makes me anxious. I have no idea how to act. When to go to the bath-room? What to wear to bed? Will I make a misstep that will cause me to become a high school laughingstock? I'm hyper aware that I am traveling in this world without a map, a social skills map. I've been here before; other kids seem to know what to do because they've been exposed to things. I have not. My family lives a solitary day-to-day existence. Maybe my parents are old-fashioned but they do not seem to tell us kids much. We are told to brush our teeth but never made to. We are told to go to bed but never at a par-ticular time. We are not told how to behave in social situ-ations because, in my family, there are no social situations. My mother's biggest rule is this—never eat more than three cookies at a particular sitting. It's something, I guess.

My parents are not social themselves. They sit on the benches but no one enters our apartment. Aside from rela-tives, no one comes over for dinner. No one phones except for family members, and it's mostly my Aunt Ann. It is an existence of isolation in a city of eight million.

So it's no wonder I am tense as we check into the motel. Luckily, as soon we drop off our bags, we head out for dinner to a nearby restaurant. A bank clock says it is minus 10 degrees outside, and I believe it. On that short walk, I am colder than I've ever been in my life, and start to wonder if the jeans and polyester sweater I've brought along will keep me warm enough on the slopes.

But I don't have much time to worry about skiing because our first embarrassing activity is before us—swimming. The motel has a small pool and I pull on my too tight bathing suit, and join the others. In minutes, dozens of us are in this pool meant for a couple of families with small kids. Now it is overrun by rowdy teenage boys. I find myself in the middle of this melee even though I have a lifelong fear of water. I'm pretty sure my fear can be traced to the fact that I cannot swim. I'm no fool and stay firmly planted in the shallow end while my more daring classmates dive, execute cannonballs, and do everything but drink the pool water.

Someone produces a very small football and a simple game is hatched. The ball is thrown in the general direction of a group of boys and whoever comes up with it is immediately submerged by the whole group. I don't notice right at that moment but I'm soon aware that there is no lifeguard watching us. Father Pipala turns out to be a rather lax chaperone. Every once in a while, I see him and two or three other priests looking toward the pool through a hallway window. They never even set foot inside the pool area.

The football game is fun but it's very wild, and I have no desire to ever catch the ball. I talk to Andrew and a couple of other kids in the pool. A senior named Chris, who is so nerdy that he smokes a pipe when he's off the school grounds, tells me he relishes the game. "I want to stay under the longest," he says.

I nod, make a note to myself that he's nuts, and move away. Maybe he's a world champion underwater swimmer. The game goes on and on and indeed sometimes Chris does come up with the ball and is suitably dunked. After a while, I get bored and tell Andrew I'm heading up to our room.

Around 12:30 a.m., Father Pipala and various chaperones come by our room to do a head count. They walk in, and check off who is supposed to be there against there list. "Is there anyone else in this room," one of them asks. "Is anyone hiding in a closet, under a bed, anything? Make sure you tell us now."

But it's only us.

The next morning—Valentine's Day—there's a knock at the door. I'd rather sleep than go skiing but the knock is insistent and I answer it. Father Pipala is standing there with another priest. In the three years I've known Father Pipala, I have never seen him look so upset. In fact, it looks as though he's been crying. The spark in his blue eyes is gone.

"There's been an accident," he says. "Tell everyone to get dressed and come down to the restaurant—right away. This is serious."

Half an hour later, when we're all in the restaurant waiting to eat, Father Pipala delivers the news. The kid I was talking to—Chris—has somehow drowned. He's dead.

No one says a word. There is no music. This *is* serious.

I am trying to grasp how this could have happened. In fact, I want to ask *are you sure* but dare not. A group of large men are standing near Father Pipala. "These men are detectives," he says. "They're here to question you about what happened last night at the pool. Whoever was there should line up and they'll question you one at a time."

Whoa.

I play back my conversation with Chris. *"I want to stay under longer than anyone else."* That's what he said. That is really what he said. It is so bizarre and, yet, I am obliged to tell the detective.

"Are you sure son?"

"Yes."

"Did you see anyone near him?"

"We were all there. I was near him for a while."

"Did you see him go under?"

"Yes, he caught the ball and went under but when I was there, he came back up."

The detective writes everything down, and then leaves me at the table for a moment to talk to Pipala and the other detectives. I see them looking over at me. Then the detective I've been talking to returns, and tells me I can go.

In the lobby, two of Chris' roommates give the police a list of his possessions that they've collected from his room. There are 44 items on the list, and they are mind-numbingly mundane, and yet unbearably heart-breaking: a green tie *with* clasp, a pack of Winston cigarettes, five handkerchiefs, a bar of soap, three pipes, one packet of tobacco, and some pipe cleaners. His effects will be sent with his body to a funeral home on Manhattan's Lower East Side where Chris lived with his parents.

Soon, we get more news. There will be no skiing. We are going home. We pack and board the bus for the return trip. Andrew puts his radio on very low but Father Pipala[2] tells him to turn it off. Along the way, we see a horrible car accident and Father Pipala orders the bus to stop. He gets out and attends to the injured.

I dare not say out loud what I'm thinking, that he is somehow trying to make up for what happened back there at the motel.

That Monday, an announcement is made about Chris' death during the ski trip. A Mass is held at the school in his memory, and that's the last I ever hear of it.

---

[2] In 1993, Father Pipala pleaded guilty to sexually abusing at least 11 boys and engaging in a variety of sex acts with them over a ten year peirod. He was sentenced to 8 years in prison.

Pipala told the court he was a sex addict and had first received psychological treatment in 1977.

Saint Patrick's Day

In New York, St. Patrick's Day is a holy day of obligation. And here's what that means: Catholic high school students, boys and girls, are *obliged* to get stinkin' drunk, and make fools of themselves at the big Irish heritage parade on Fifth Avenue. Puking ones' brains out makes the celebration all the more special. It's a tradition, or at least that's what I've been told.

I'm not a big drinker, don't like to get drunk, and I'm not Irish so clearly I'm hamstrung when it comes to celebrating the big day. But I want to do my part for tradition so in junior year I agree to join a group that includes Andrew and a bunch of other Hayesmen down to the parade. We leave the Bronx at 10 a.m. and someone has brought beer which we inhale as the No. 6 train snakes its way through the Bronx and into Manhattan. The atmosphere in the subway car is full of jittery anticipation, jammed as it is with boys and girls dressed in green and in high spirits. More than a few of the girls wear *Kiss Me, I'm Irish* buttons, green eyeshadow, and have tiny shamrocks painted on their adorable faces. They're giggling with each other, and flirting with the boys but it's way too early for any hanky-panky, and everyone is far too sober to take advantage of the clear message the girls are sending. We need at least another half-hour or two beers, whichever comes first.

The pot of gold at the end of every boy's rainbow on this day is to find that special moment when one of the girls is so drunk that she'll fall into your arms, and give you a mouthful of tongue, no conversation required. The whole thing is very sloppy and yet requires delicate, if not split-second, timing. You must grab hold of her at exactly the right moment. Miss that sweet spot, and you risk the very real possibility that she'll puke all over you, or worse, you might actually have to converse with her.

It's a fine balance I never quite master. But this year, I'm abandoning my cautious approach to drinking. And when the subway arrives at the 86th Street and Lexington Avenue subway stop, I am prepared to celebrate. We exit along with hundreds of other teenagers, and join thousands more heading to Fifth Avenue, the parade route. More beer is produced, and I do my part. The streets are electric. This is Mardi Gras, New York style. There is a competitive spirit in the air as everyone wears their school colors. It's clear who is from Hayes, Spellman, Stepinac and on and on. And the more alcohol we drink, the more we are convinced that ours is the best school ever and, what's more, we're willing to fight to prove it. None of us have any intention of watching the parade.

The small group of about ten boys I'm with joins the throng, and we make it to 84th Street, between Madison and Fifth before the trouble begins.

I am slightly in front of everyone, and when I turn around to see what's up, I witness a sea of hooligans punching one of our friends, a guy named Jerry. In seconds, the group surrounds him so thoroughly that he is using his hands, not to fight back, but to cover his face and head. It's an unfair fight for sure, probably ten to one. I am vaguely aware of Andrew and Robbie and the others on the periphery of the fight, watching the whole thing. *This is not right*, I say to myself. *Jerry is a fellow Hayesman.* That's about as much analysis I put into the situation before I run over. Without saying a word, I grab one of the kids hitting Jerry, spin him around by his shoulder, and punch him right in the face. It is truly a John Wayne moment as my fist connects with his jaw. But the sad news is that it's the very last punch I throw.

Now the hooligan crowd has a new victim—me. There is flurry of punches thrown in my direction and in seconds I am on the asphalt sidewalk, with *my* hands covering *my* face and head. Kids are kicking me from every direction, and I'm aware that I'm getting a real ass-kicking, no pun intended. But the weird thing is that the fight seems to last all of 30 seconds. The boys run from the scene, and I soon understand why. They think they've killed me. My head is spilling rich red blood onto the sidewalk, and there's a lot of it. I can feel my face covered and sticky, and I can taste it. I get to my feet, barely able to see through the blood, and I don't see any friendly faces around. It's a bunch of anonymous drunken high school kids staring; no doubt they're happy they are not me.

I stumble over to the entrance of an apartment building and approach the doorman.

"Do you have any water?"

"No," he says.

He looks disgusted, and not at all helpful.

I don't see anyone I know. I turn away from the apartment building, with a vague idea of trying to get to Central Park when a passing ambulance stops short. A guy in a white coat jumps out.

"Hey you're hurt. Why doncha you come with us?"

"Okay."

The next thing I know I'm riding in the back of this ambulance with another kid who is unconscious. *Is that vomit on his shirt?* The tech is a nice guy and he's wrapping my head in white bandages. I'm happy for his help.

"How bad is it?"

"You have a gash in the top of your head but you'll be all right."

It sounds like he's just said that my head is split open. I'm a little worried but I'm also incredibly exhausted all of a sudden. The adrenaline I used to throw that one punch has evaporated, and I feel like taking a nap. My eyes close.

"Hey now, no sleeping. You could have a concussion. Stay awake."

He slaps my face softly and I come around. He keeps rolling that white gauze around and around my head. The bleeding has stopped. He tells me we're going to Lenox Hill Hospital, a few blocks away.

In the Emergency Room, I see Andrew and the rest of the group. Their eyes open wide when they see me.

"Paul, what happened?"

"Are you all right man?"

I don't even have time to answer because I'm escorted to a cot somewhere in the back. On the way, I pass a mirror and see my reflection. My head is completely covered with white bandages, and I look like some sort of Vietnam war casualty. All that's showing are my eyes, nose and mouth. A nurse takes my name and other information, including my home phone number. She informs me that she is going to call my parents, to have someone pick me up. I sit there in a daze until a doctor comes in and unwraps the gauze.

"Looks like they got you pretty good."

"You shoulda seen the other guy," I say.

It's a stupid line from some movie, but he laughs.

"Ah, I love St. Patrick's Day. It looks like your head is split open right at the very top. We'll have to shave it a little and stitch it up."

"You have to shave it?"

I'm more worried about losing any of my hair than I am about the wound. My slow hair loss is my shameful secret.

"Sorry buddy but that's what we have to do. Lie down here."

Soon I'm lying face down on a cot, and he's shaving the very top of my head. Then, he's putting some type of iodine on the wound, and the orange liquid rolls down my forehead, onto my nose and onto the floor. He tells me he's giving me a local anesthetic. I feel a little pinch but I'm so out of it that I close my eyes and enjoy the feel of liquid rolling down my nose. It feels pleasant. I like the feeling of being taken care of, being in the care of someone who knows what he's doing. I'm also relieved that I don't have to do any more drinking.

Sometime later, my father shows up and asks me what happened. My dad is nothing if not a stoic, and he stays in character, very calm, even reassuring. There is no yelling, or repercussions. Dad doesn't talk much but I have the feeling that he knows this is only a rite of passage. I'm beat up, yes, but there is no real damage, no broken bones. He even tells me I'm lucky because my friend Jerry has broken ribs and a punctured lung and he's going to be in the hospital for a few days. I'm at least going home.

We ride the subway in silence, and even though I am sporting a large white bandage on my head, and even though my shirt is covered in blood, and even though I must look like shit, no one gives me a seat. I feel woozy, and lean into the metal pole. I stand the whole way back to the Bronx because the train is very crowded. But I understand—after all, it is St. Patrick's Day.

College Daze

By senior year at Hayes, all my friends and teachers are talking about college. My parents are the exception—they don't really talk about it much. I assume they know that high school ends after four years but we don't have a lot of deep conversations about the future or much of anything really. They have not gone to college, and don't seem to give the idea of me going all that much thought. I believe that if I tell them I've decided to work full-time in Jack's deli after graduation that would be okay with them. We never talk about potential college expenses, going away to school, or where I might be applying. Nothing. So I do it all myself, following the lead of the guidance counselor and teachers at Hayes. I more or less mimic what my classmates are doing. The SAT's go pretty well so I do have some options. I have even saved what for me is a fair amount of money—a couple of thousand of dollars—from working at Jack's.

I do have my dream schools like everyone else and they have nothing to do with New York. I am utterly taken with California for dumb and trivial reasons. "California Dreamin'" by the Mamas and Papas is my favorite song of all time, and I worship the Beach Boys and the whole surfing culture. But that's not all. I am fascinated by Charlie Manson and his Family. I'm not sure why but I think I believe that if Charlie, that crazy old troll, can attract a Family of beautiful women, then why can't I? I'm certain *cult leader* is not a major at any of the colleges I'm considering but a boy can dream, can't he? There's a lot going on out west and I long to be a part of it. I take the line from the Jan and Dean song *"Two girls for every boy"* to heart. I decide I'm going to do everything in my power to go to college in California, preferably Los Angeles. Without discussing it with my parents, I apply to USC and UCLA. But to be on the safe side, I also apply to NYU in Manhattan and Fordham University in the Bronx. They're my fallback schools.

I get accepted at every school but, in the end, only Fordham offers me money. It is a partial scholarship, half tuition, and I can take out a $500 National Defense Student Loan which means I'll only have to come up with $500 annually to attend. I long for a true college experience with a dorm and female sleepovers but I don't know how to get the money required to attend UCLA or any of the others. I hate the idea of going to Fordham. So many Hayesmen are going that I'm sure it will be like attending another four years of high school. I accept Fordham's scholarship but I don't like it.

Not only am I *not* living in a dorm with beautiful California girls, I'm living in a public housing project with my parents, and have the opposite of privacy. I share a room with my brother Bob, as I have forever, except now I'm 18 and he's 13. My sister is now six and a great kid. That's not the point. I love my brother and sister but this is no way to attend college. Making things even worse, I have to take two buses each way to the school. I want to shoot myself.

After the cocoon of Hayes, where every waking moment is accounted for, Fordham is not only a shock to my system—it's a tsunami.

It is 1971. I no longer need to bend to a dress code. I can wear anything, and have hair down to my knees if I so desire. But nature is not cooperating, my nature. My hair is growing thinner by the day, and I am using some strange over-the-counter hair thickener called "Ego" to make it look slightly more there.

Fordham's campus in the Bronx is called Rose Hill (the Manhattan campus is south of Lincoln Center but it mainly houses the Law and Business Schools, not really a place for me), and it is beautiful. When I think of why I finally caved in and agreed to go here, it's because of the campus which, I believe, is the prettiest in the city. The Gothic buildings also harbor a touch of mystery and while I'm a freshman, a few scenes from "The Exorcist" are filmed on campus. Linda Blair's isn't the only head that's spinning.

My very first class at Fordham is English. I enter the classroom cautiously, sheepishly—scared shitless really. I know not a soul but, on the bright side, there are plenty of girls here, many of them very attractive. It's the first time I've been in a class with females since 8th grade. Some of them are wearing denim mini-skirts, the rest are wearing jeans, and have long hair parted in the middle. But this is still a Catholic School run by Jesuit priests, and the kids are not really rebels. The Abby Hoffmans of the world—people who want real societal change—go to Columbia and NYU.

These kids are mostly Irish and Italian Catholics—exactly the type I do *not* want to hang with—and I can't help but notice that some of the jeans are very neatly pressed. I'm wearing a beat-up pair of jeans and a t-shirt, and can't shake the feeling that a wild-eyed priest with a rubber hose is itching to get in here and beat us all until we wear something *appropriate*.

And then the English professor enters. I'll call him Professor Martin. He's in his early 40s and has long stringy, greasy gray and black hair, and around his forehead is an American-flag handkerchief. He is, to my eyes, the epitome of a slob. I come from a school where even the sloppiest of the lay teachers wore suits.

"Hey guys," he says by way of introduction. "Okay move these desks into a circle, and we'll begin in a couple of minutes."

Professor Martin has a goofy face with big lips and even bigger glasses. He places his chair square in the middle of the circle and looks around in a self-satisfied way. I'm waiting anxiously for my first college lecture when he pulls a brown paper bag out of his knapsack.

"No time for lunch today, sorry," he mumbles.

He is holding one of those tightly-wrapped-in-plastic sandwiches from the cafeteria. It is egg salad, and, as he unwraps the sandwich with his hairy paws, the egg salad drips over the sides of the bread in all its gooey glory. Next, he pulls out a small container of chocolate milk that he has trouble opening. While he tries to find the little opening for the straw, some of egg salad spills onto his pants but he doesn't notice. His concentration is elsewhere. I feel as though I am watching a mental patient. And if this isn't revolting enough, he begins the lecture, talking and eating at the same time. He spews tiny bits of egg salad when he speaks, and sometimes chocolate milk dribbles from his giant lips onto his shirt. I don't hear a word he's saying because I cannot believe what I'm seeing. I think back to my first week in Hayes when I was beaten by Father Crazy Face for being 15 seconds late to class.

An hour after the class ends, I head to Fordham Road to wait for one of the two buses that will carry me back to the Monroe projects. The bus, when it comes, is jammed with dozens of tired working-class people heading home after a hard day. I move to the middle of the bus (of course I'll have to stand nearly the entire way home because of the crowds) when I spot Professor Martin standing there with a short gorgeous woman. He has his hand on her ass, and he's talking a mile a minute.

I always avoid talking to people I know on public transportation. It's one of my *things*. There's something about having a private conversation in public that does not appeal to me. I don't want everyone on the bus to hear what I'm doing this weekend, or how I aced some exam, and I'm pretty sure they don't want to hear it either. I also love to read and escape into my book which I cannot do if I'm talking to someone. I certainly do not want to be in such an enclosed space with this slob of a professor, and I try my best to avoid his gaze. But of course, he recognizes me and greets me in the loudest voice possible. "Hey, weren't you in my English class?"

"Yes sir that was me."

"This is my wife, Sabine. She teaches French at the school."

Sabine says *bon jour*, which I believe might be the first

time that greeting has been uttered on the B-27 bus line. She is as glowingly attractive as he is repellant, an ingénue come to life, a sexy Gallic version of Audrey Hepburn. What is she doing with this overgrown, ham-handed, uncouth bore?

I only have a few moments to think about this because now Professor Martin is asking me what I want to major in, and do post college, blah, blah. All those questions that make every college student want to projectile vomit. I don't know what I want to do other than some vague notion that I love to write and hope to make a living at it. And besides, I've just *started* college!

"I want to be a writer."

"Ah, so you want to be like Ernest Hemingway," he says. "You know most writers need to take other jobs, right, something menial, blue collar, something like working in a post office."

All the working stiffs in the bus, including a couple dressed in postal uniforms, immediately snap their heads in our direction. I notice a little warning on the bus window that reads *in case of emergency, kick out window*, and consider whether that might be appropriate under the circumstances. I want to slink away from this conversation but Professor Martin is immune to embarrassment, and his Frenchy wife seems only to relish every word he utters. She has her hand on his belt as though she cannot wait to give him the hummer of his life. I wonder if I can pretend to fall asleep while he's talking to me. Would that be rude?

The only thing that saves me is that he exits in three stops, but not before he begins discussing with me and his wife the XXX-rated movie "I Am Curious (Yellow)." After they get off, I notice everyone looking at me. I shrug when I catch some guy's eye and he shakes his head. I ride the bus down to Pelham Bay where I'll have to switch to another bus on my daily 3-hour commute. It's a major transfer point in the Bronx, and there are always about a thousand people milling around, also waiting. Next to the line, one of those ubiquitous folk singers is performing for the crowd. He ends one song and then begins singing "California Dreamin.'"

I consider breaking the guitar over his head.

Coeds

There are hundreds of great-looking women here at Fordham, and many are in my classes but I am not equipped to converse with them. I'm just not. I have not been around females very much in my life. I went to tons of high school dances but I did way more dancing than talking. Except for a few high school plays, when girls were imported to the school to fill the female parts, those of the opposite sex were not a part of my high school life. There are four girls my age who live in the projects, Mary, Nancy and the two Kathys. Both Nancy and the two Kathys have steady boyfriends. Mary and I flirt constantly but I am too dumb to do anything, and I mean anything.

Now in college, I'm surrounded by women, a dream situation but it's just as I had feared. The commuter women go to class and quickly leave campus. Those who live on campus have some sort of hidden life in the dorms. I'm nowhere. I cannot find the center of this college life, and I don't believe there is one.

And I realize something else—no one here cares much

what I do. The school is big, there is no homeroom, and if I don't want to go to class, well, no one is going to get all that hot and bothered about it. On one hand the school treats its students as adults, which is good, but for someone like me, coming from a tightly-wound Catholic high school, it is too much freedom. I am adrift.

There is a social chasm between the commuters and those who live on campus, and the two sides seem not to meet. There is very little to pull any of us together, except dumb football and basketball games. We come and go in the student center, crossing each other's paths but not communicating. I don't know what I am doing here except, get this, majoring in communications. Paging Dr. Freud! Between classes, I pal around with the guys who went to Hayes but all they want to do is get drunk at the bar just off campus. I decide I'll try to make believe I live on campus by spending as much time there as possible. I schedule my classes with three and four hour gaps in between even though I don't have to. That way, I'll have plenty of time to hang out at the student center and meet girls, or so I hope. And I can put the daily three-hour commute out of my mind as much as possible.

In my spare time on campus, I become a stalker but in the nicest possible way. I latch onto a few girls who seem nice and non-threatening and note their schedules in my notebook. I know, for instance, Candy's schedule as well as I know my own but, more than that, I know which direction she's liable to come from so I can oh so casually run into her. Yes, I know—the word *pathetic* is still too good for me. I do everything I can to pop up outside of classrooms these women are waiting to enter, or try to bump into them in the student center. As usual, the schoolwork comes easily to me; most of my time is spent in pursuit of morsels of conversation.

Over the months, my strategy works and that's how I meet Deb. Deb is easy to stalk because I can spot her from a distance by the cape she's so fond of wearing. We're in a couple of classes together, and like me, she's a commuter, only she lives on the lower East Side. After bumping into her *accidentally* a few dozen times, we actually begin to converse. She's open, easy to talk to but not perfect. Almost from the moment we begin speaking, she casually drops the information that her boyfriend has a black belt in karate. I think she's kidding but then I meet him and learn he's captain of the school's karate club. So I'm more or less forced to become friends only with Deb but I like her. She's kooky and enjoys drinking, and soon we're buddies. Hanging out with her gives me a bit of confidence and I begin to meet other coeds, breaking out of my iron cocoon.

I begin dating one or two, meeting up in quiet corners of the school to do something other than homework. It's a start but I still find college rough going because of the damned four-bus-a-day commute. It's much easier to take subways than buses in New York because they run faster and are immune to weather and traffic. Buses are always late and seemingly immobile, and I have to take two a day going from one end of the Bronx to the other. Most of my schoolwork is done standing in the back of a bus. When I need to write a paper, I go to the cozy school library where, for a quarter every half-hour, I rent one of three ancient black manual typewriters. I slide quarter after quarter into those slots, banging away on papers long into the night. I never want to go home.

College becomes a grind, but I hate the time off between semesters even more because then it's back to the deli and living at home with no outlet. The whole thing makes me morose, and I wonder what I'm doing there. No one in my extended family ever has graduated from college. I wonder if I should stick with it, or junk the whole thing and move to California.

But that ain't happening because the backdrop to my college years is the Vietnam War, and, as a college student, I have a deferment. The moment I leave, I'll be drafted. My Dad served in the Army in World War II but it's unimaginable to me to join the Armed Forces. Of course, I'm against the war like 99 percent of my fellow students but it's not out of outrage as much as stone cold fear. The idea of being part of something as restrictive as the Army makes me break out into a sweat. I never even get as far as imagining myself shooting a gun; the cult-like nature of the military is enough to send me over the edge. So opting out of college is out.

I'm the most depressed I've ever been in my short life. My parents do seem to notice though because, at the end of my freshman year, for my 19th birthday which falls in April, my father, who does not have a driver's license, tells me they're buying me a used car.

Driving

I'd learned to drive my last year at Hayes. As a senior in high school, I took a driver's education course, where I was packed into a Dodge Dart with three classmates. The first day of Driver's Ed was only the *third* time I had ever been *inside* a car. I did not know where the gas or brake pedals were, how to signal for a turn, hell, I didn't even know how to tune the radio. It was like teaching a tribal member from a remote South American village how to ride a two-wheeler. I'm not sure he would have done any worse. That first day, I made my classmates sick by slamming down too hard, first on the gas, then on the brake pedal. The classes were an hour long but, since there were four of us, I only learned in 15 minute increments. I was so fearful when I was behind the wheel that my shirt was covered with sweat, and I needed the other 45 minutes to dry off. My favorite part of Driver's Ed was sitting in the back seat listening to the AM radio which, that year, was featuring "Bridge Over Troubled Water" and "Maybe I'm Amazed."

I was amazed the Driver's Ed teacher allowed me to practice in live traffic. When I signed up, I was sure we'd be off somewhere in the far reaches of the Korvette's parking lot but there we were, out in traffic on busy White Plains Road. It's a wonder any of us survived when I was behind the wheel.

About a month after the Driver's Ed course ended, I decided for some odd notion that I was good enough to take the state driving test. I had high hopes of getting my license because I had improved some during Driver's Ed. Of course, I was starting from such a low base, that wasn't saying much. So I signed up for a couple of private lessons and hired the car and Driving School teacher to accompany me for my test.

The test was given on White Plains Road, across from Korvette's. A line of cars formed at the designated spot, and we lined up at the curb, one behind the other. The driving inspectors walked up to each car, looked over our papers, and then walked away, making us wait our turn. My driving instructor Ted (*I'm Ted and I teach Driver's Ed* was his motto) had driven the car to the test site, and had parked pretty close to the car in front of me, a car carrying a young muscular Puerto Rican guy. Ted had driven many nervous students to the test so he wasn't feeling anything but I was anxious as hell. I sat there eyeing the driving inspectors get closer and closer. Soon, it would be my turn. Ted was standing off to the side, and I was behind the wheel. The door opened and the driving inspector slid into the seat next to me.

"Okay," he said, "Pull out."

Very tricky, Mr. Driving Inspector, I thought, *but I know this one!* I put on my left directional signal, looked over my shoulder to make sure no one was coming, tapped on the gas pedal, and promptly hit the car in front of me. It's not really a bang, more of a soft, hard landing but there's no denying my bumper hit his bumper. I'm fucked.

The driving inspector looked at me over his reading glasses with a look that said: *Are you fucking with me?*

Or maybe it was, *Am I on Candid Camera?*

Nope, it was all mortifyingly true. The muscular Puerto Rican guy had not yet pulled away from the curb, and I had failed to register that tiny detail. He jumped out of his car to look at the potential damage. So did his driving inspector, as did Ted and my driving instructor. I got out and thought about running away. Everyone alternately was looking at the car and then over at me. I had turned into the story they would all tell their wives, girlfriends and buddies later. *You won't believe it, honey, but this yahoo actually hit a car on his driving test.*

After everyone agreed there was no real damage, the driving inspector walked over to me. "I think you should make another appointment," he said, handing me the receipt that noted that, yes, I had failed in case I'd had any doubts.

Miraculously, I do pass the test on my second try, after about one hundred driving lessons, and so off we go to used car lots where we might as well have "sucker" stamped on our foreheads. Learning how to drive seems easy compared to dealing with used car salesmen when neither of us has an iota of experience.

Ultimately, we decide to let the price dictate the car and, for $600, I wind up with a 1966 blue Chevy Impala with a powerful eight-cylinder engine. Not bad really. The car has one quirk—the speedometer. I can never tell how fast I'm going because the speedometer is in kilometers. If I'm going 50 mph, the speedometer says I'm going close to 100. It takes me a while to adjust to this, but otherwise this is a good and powerful car. I blast the radio and zoom up and down the Bronx River Parkway, barely missing other cars and constantly hearing horns blaring wherever I go. But it's still better than the bus.

As soon as I get my car, my mother, who has always been more than willing to take buses and subways everywhere she goes—in fact, she has insisted on it—decides that the car is a good idea and we should go for some "family drives."

Because I'm eager to drive pretty much anywhere, I agree.

"So where do you want to go, mom?"

"Anywhere, let's take a drive."

I have lived in New York City my entire life but I have no conception of the roads or the traffic. I barely know how to drive from Monroe to Fordham, and both are in the Bronx, 20 minutes from each other. Beyond that, my knowledge of the roads is limited. I don't know that I-95 runs into Connecticut or that "the Hutch" will take me to Westchester or even which three boroughs are linked together by the Triborough Bridge. I am the driving equivalent of a typist who never learned how to touch type. My experience on the highways in and around New York is classic hunt and peck. My method of driving from place to place involves looking briefly at a map, trying to remember whether to go north or south, east or west, and then merging with traffic. If I get lost, so be it. No one driving with me—my mother, father, brother and sister—can help me navigate because they've never driven themselves and the maps might as well be in Swahili. We're all lost together.

So a typical Sunday drive—my mother always wants to drive on a Sunday because she once read an article in Reader's Digest about families taking "Sunday drives"—means piling into this old beat up Chevy and heading toward one of the New York suburbs. We never have a plan about where we're going, and don't know anybody there. Oh sure, my mother remembers that a cousin, whose name she cannot remember, has moved to Patterson, New Jersey but that doesn't help much. Still, I get the feeling that she really believes if we drive around Patterson for, oh, 20 minutes or so, we'll run into said cousin.

My mother always insists on these Sunday drives that we'll know where to exit and find some interesting attraction. This pretty much never happens although we do look at a bunch of model homes that we know we'll never buy. Mostly, we never know when to exit the road to find *something good*. We drive until we need gas or we see the sign of a town we've vaguely heard of. This is why we spent entire Sundays driving up to places like New Haven only to be bitterly disappointed by how deserted and lonesome downtown New Haven is on a Sunday. Or we get off an exit in a residential area and find ourselves more or less stalking entire communities, going round and round—five bickering Bronxites—lost on quaint little suburban streets and cul-de-sacs trying to figure out why people love this life so much.

"People live here?" my mother asks.

And I have to agree with her. These quiet suburban streets seem kind of boring compared to the varied activities and characters we come face to face with every day. True, many of my colorful experiences involve getting ripped off but it is usually interesting. Once in a great while, we get *lucky* and find a mall. One of our favorite jaunts (because I actually remember how to get there from one time to another) becomes the Cross County Mall in Westchester. We spend a lot of Sundays there, eating ice cream and walking around to look at the many stores. We don't have the money to buy much but we're indoors, it's air-conditioned and there are a lot of people around and that's really all my mother wants anyway. I must admit that I enjoy these malls too. They are like Disneyland to my family because, as un-exotic as they are, they simply do not exist in the Bronx. Oh sure, we've heard of them but never have seen one in person. We are *taken*. It's fun, certainly better than wandering around deserted New Haven.

One Sunday, I decide it would be fun to go to an airport. None of us have ever been to an airport, and I decide if we're going, it might as well be to the largest one in New York—JFK.

We find our way to the famed TWA terminal, the one that looks like an eagle. I think I've read something about it in the newspaper and so we park near there. The moment we step inside, I get the same feeling I do on all those trips to Manhattan. The people here are sophisticated and vastly different than my family or my project neighbors. Men and women, dressed in suits and stockings, uniforms and sleek attire, walk this way and that. They have places to go, meetings to attend, families to visit. We are way underdressed and out of place. We're not getting on any of those flights listed on the overhead signs. I see people sipping cocktails at a bar, overhear men in suits talking about business, and watch women dressed like models move rapidly down long corridors, the sound of their high heels clicking in our ears.

We stand off to the side so we're not in the way of these important people who appear to be a different species. It's hard to shake the feeling that my family and I are immigrants huddled in rags, present in a place we're not supposed to be. I don't want to *these people* to see us, preferring to stay invisible.

"Let's get a soda," my father says.

It's something I love about my father. He is, at heart, an optimist. No matter what the situation, he thinks it's manageable if he can have a smoke and take us kids for a soda or ice cream. At the oddest moments, like after a big fight with my mother or even with one of us, he'll cock his head and out of the blue, say; "Let's take a walk." Those words become music to my ears because, with those words, we usually find a way to forget our troubles.

So at the airport, when he points to some chairs and tells us to sit down, that he's gonna spring for a soda, we do what he says. We nod and take in the scene, watching the people as though we're sitting in a movie theater waiting for our dad to come back from the refreshment stand.

A woman in a uniform notices us and stops. I see the little TWA logo on her blazer and figure she's a stewardess. Thanks to Playboy, I have many pornographic fantasies involving *stews* but have never seen one in person. Here she is, not too different than the way I imagined except, you know, she's clothed. She looks very middle-American and non-ethnic with her blonde hair and blue eyes. Her uniform is as tight as I could hope for; I fantasize about what she looks like naked when I realize she is speaking to me.

"Can I help y'all find anything? Are you trying to find your gate?"

"Uh, no," I say, "We're kind of visiting the airport."

"Visiting?"

"Yeah, we've never really seen one so…"

"Really?" she says.

She looks a bit skeptical but recovers quickly: "Well, if you want to see the planes take off, go and sit over there. It's a better view."

"Thanks," I say. "We will. Thanks so much."

She smiles and then clicks away. We all look after her but I'm sure I'm the only one staring at her ass. Just then, my father comes back with some sodas for all of us.

"Why don't we go over there Dad?" I say. "We can see the planes."

And so we spend our Sunday afternoon, watching the planes take off and sipping sodas. It's the best family drive ever, and I'm so happy I have a car and we can go places like this.

The Projects Redux

Having a car opens up the world a lot, but when I come home I am still in the projects, and they are not what they once were. In the old days, management kept tight control on the environment with a crew of mostly genial Housing Cops. We nicknamed one of them Maury Wills because we convince ourselves he looks exactly like the Dodger base-stealer. Maury would chide us for breaking the project rules, like crossing the small chain link fences and walking on the grass. For more serious offenses, like carving your name on a bench or writing your name on a staircase wall, there were fines that ranged from $5 to $25. No one wanted to get a fine. All it took was for Maury Wills to catch and fine one of us and the others would behave, at least for a while.

But somewhere along the line Maury Wills moved on and those old days evaporated seemingly overnight. Now, even the simple task of entering a building has become a chore. It used to be, anyone could walk into the lobby but then crime and muggings began to skyrocket, and management decided the buildings were a little too open. They "fixed" that by screening the lobby off from outsiders by a locked door, and an intercom system. Those of us who live there get a key of course but, if you don't live in the building, you must call upstairs and have someone buzz you in. The reality is that the security door lock is broken again and again, and everyone still has free access, at least most days.

So a new plan is hatched. It is decided that, in the evenings, a group of volunteers, calling themselves the Tenant Patrol, will set up a table and chairs in the lobby. Each night, they play cards, kibbutz, drink a lot of coffee, and keep a wary eye on that front door and everyone who comes and goes. They wear blue windbreakers with the words "Tenant Patrol" stamped in large yellow letters on their backs. I consider them a joke even though they are looking out for tenants like me, tenants at an increased risk of being mugged. And the truth is that their very presence probably does cut down on the crime.

The project residents are now mostly minorities, and the most powerful of the Bronx gangs—the Black Spades—has taken control. People are afraid of them and for good reason—they don't take only pocket change. They deliver real beatings and use real drugs and really kill people. Tenants are so jumpy that, one night, when I am out late, my father and brother hear a commotion in the lobby, and assume it's me getting beaten. They run down the stairs and appear before the Tenant Patrol with hockey sticks drawn, ready to save my ass. Turns out there was a commotion but it was not violent and did not involve me.

Co-op City, a newly-opened development in the Northern Bronx built on the grounds of what used to be the Freedomland Amusement Park, is drawing white families by the hundreds. Each day another family moves out of Monroe. The whites who stay are scared and tensions between whites and blacks are very high. What's more, the apartment we moved into when my sister was born is on the second floor, and in the warm weather, large groups congregate on the benches that are practically under my window, and they play loud music all night long. We complain and the Housing cops come and chase them away but they keep coming back night after night.

Strange things begin to happen, and the projects—once so idyllic—begin to take on an apocalyptic air.

An upstairs neighbor has a stroke, and grows so depressed that he can no longer make jewelry—his trade—that, one morning, he climbs to the 14th floor roof, jumps, and lands right under my second floor bedroom window, face down in a puddle of mud. Just before I hear the thud, I am listening to the album "Silver Morning" by Kenny Rankin. I never think of that beautiful record in quite the same way. Luckily the ground is soft so my neighbor's body does not break. He looks strangely at rest with his face in a shallow puddle of water and mud. In a moment, people begin screaming and pointing and a crowd gathers while I call the housing cops. It doesn't help that I know this man's daughter quite well. The family has been down on its luck. Everyone knew her father was upset but no one could see this coming. Soon, an ambulance takes his body away.

Because I live on the second floor, there is no reason ever to take the unreliable elevators either up or down. I simply take the stairs even though one of my neighbors, a 6 foot, 4 inch transvestite has made the stairway his personal dressing room. More times than not, he's in there changing into women's clothing—dresses, pantyhose, size 14 high-heels, makeup—the works. It's so unsettling on so many levels that I avert my eyes and rumble past. We never speak.

The packs of wild dogs roaming the parking lot now affect me directly because I have a car. In the mornings, the dogs are especially hungry. They don't care who they go after, they just want someone. Going to my car is a sick joke. I tiptoe into the lot and try to pinpoint the pack. If they are far enough away, I race them to my car door and usually manage to get the door closed as they reach the car. They yip and yammer as I slip the key into the ignition and back up. God help me if the car ever refuses to start. On days they are too close to my car, I wait them out. There's always another victim.

Striped-down car in one of Monroe's parking lots, same lot where I was chased by packs of wild dogs

Accidents keep happening all around me. A wild kid who lives in my building takes to riding on the top of the elevators. It's a game he likes to play until the day his face gets caught in the cables wires, and tears the flesh on one side down, on the other side up. He comes home from the hospital looking like a horror movie come to life. He's still wild and now he's angry too, but at least he no longer plays on top of the elevators.

I fear the feral atmosphere is affecting me. After a big snow storm, I wander up to the shopping area near Korvette's. The parking lot is so filled with snow that no cars can get through, not even police cars. Everyone seems to realize this at the same moment. I watch as one teenager, then three, and then a mob attacks the stores with hands, bricks and anything that can be found. Security gates are pulled and pulled until kids can step over then. Windows are broken, alarms go off but no one pays any mind. The crowd pours into the stores and loots everything in sight.

Almost in a daze, I find myself caught up in the crowd lust and inch closer and closer until I can stand it no longer. I step through a broken front door into a men's clothing store. Without looking, I grab a few shirts and pants and dart out into the snow. *Am I really doing this? Looting?* It's insane but here I am with an armful of stolen goods. I stumble through the deep snow and bright sun toward home, wondering how I'm going to explain these new clothes to my mother who safeguards every cent that comes into the family. She'll know something is up. But then the problem takes care of itself. A thug, a big, tough-looking kid approaches. "Give me those," he says.

I hand them over. What am I going to say, *No I stole*

them, they're mine? I'm secretly relieved. He saved me the chore of explaining the clothes to my mother.

These are strange days in the projects but nothing affects me more than the loneliness I experience the following summer when I am between my first and second year of college. I come downstairs, as I have my whole life, and wait but no one joins me. Everyone is gone. Over the winter, my friends and their families have moved out one by one until none of them are here any longer. I sit on those benches alone that first morning wondering where everyone has gone. Everyone but me. No more softball or 'off the barrel' or Ringolevio or touch football or listening to music or flirting with girls or playing tops or carving our names in the benches. No more hanging out, period. The old days are over.

I have no summer plans except to work a few extra days a week in the deli, and that's what I do—spending more and more time in Manhattan. When I'm home, I read constantly, lift weights in my room, and run laps and play tennis in Pelham Bay Park. Anything to get away from the desolation I now feel in the projects.

I promise myself this will not happen again next summer.

California Days

In the summer of 1973, I organize a trip to California with Andrew. I'm not going to sit around for another summer with nothing to do but read erotic paperbacks—informative and fun as that is. This time, I'm going to see the country by driving across it, all the way to Los Angeles, the place I imagine is some sort of Promised Land. A few of us have used cars, largely clunkers, with Andrew's Ford Fury being the best of the lot. We toy and tinker with it until we feel that it has a fighting chance of getting us to California and back. Despite never having had a car growing up, I've become quite handy making repairs. In fact, I'm something of a grease monkey savant. Changing oil is a snap but I do major repairs as well, and one time, Robbie and I manage to change my drive shaft. Miraculously, the car keeps running.

To help defray the cost of gas—between 43 and 47 cents a gallon—we enlist others to join us on the ride west. Andrew asks Jerry, the Hayes classmate who got beat up along with me on St. Patrick's Day, and Jerry asks if his girlfriend Mary Ellen can come along. She's got a summer job in Yosemite

National Park in Northern California. We hatch a plan to drop her off first, and then head down the coast to see Los Angeles before going back east. The final person to sign up on his merry adventure is John, my good friend from the projects whose father took me for my first car ride. John doesn't have a girlfriend but asks if he can bring his guitar.

On June 3, 1973 at 6 a.m., we all head out, in a 1968 Ford Fury with less-than-reliable tires—four guys, one gal, and a guitar jammed into the car. Our first stop is Pathmark where Andrew buys a pack of cigarettes. On the way out, he decides to take a shortcut and rides over a cement divider. Nothing happens to the car which we consider an auspicious beginning.

It doesn't take long to realize that this 3,000 mile ride would have been far more comfortable with fewer people. It is very cozy in that car, too cozy. But we remain giddy and wildly naïve. None of us has a credit card. We agree that if each of us carries $400 in cash, we should be fine. Based on my calculations, the month-long trip will cost us $300 for gas and food, and another $75 for rooms, leaving each of us with a margin of error of $25.

The idea is to make as much time as we can without stopping so as not to spend too much on hotel rooms. We hope to make it to Chicago the first day. But as we drive and drive, I come to realize that the US of A is one big fucking country. I am sure that once we pass Ohio, we'll be in Illinois and am taken aback by the presence of Indiana. That geographic discovery brings us to the realization that we'll need to stop much earlier that first night, and, when we come across a place named Mary-Joes which has five dollar a night rooms, we stop. As my head hits the pillow, I am feeling more and more confident about my estimate of $75 for all the rooms combined.

It's not long before the tension of being in a car with too many people who have disparate personalities builds to an uncomfortable level. Andrew and Jerry gang up on John constantly, and it's hard for me to take his side since he's so obstinate about everything. He contradicts every suggestion, which earns him the witty nickname of "Mr. Contradiction." Making matters worse is his clumsiness. He cannot seem to open a can of soda without spraying everyone in the car, and after he does that two times in a row, I begin to wonder how much I'd hate myself if I drove off when he's in the gas station bathroom. Not that Jerry and Mary Ellen are much better. There is only so much lovey-dovey stuff one can take before it makes you want to vomit and, by the second day, we've reached that point. It doesn't help matters that they take their sweet time every morning when we're itching to go; what they're doing in their room is left to our imaginations.

The *adventure* of driving cross-country quickly wears thin. We experience miles and miles of highway with nothing to do but play cards, sing songs and tell jokes. John and Jerry pass the time playing chess. I know Jerry thinks he can beat John easily but what he fails to understand is that John's social awkwardness masks a razor-sharp intelligence and he winds up beating Jerry which only makes Jerry dislike him more.

The highlight of each day is bargaining down the cost of that night's room but it turns out $5 per night is impossible to beat. We usually get rooms at motels with names like the "Hi-Ho" for about $25 to $30 and split that three ways. Jerry and Mary Ellen are on their own. By the time we hit Boulder, Colorado, we make an important discovery that keeps our budget in line—Kampgrounds of America or KOA's—where we pay three bucks for a patch of dirt on which we can pitch our tent. The problem is, although we did remember to bring a tent, we forgot all about the poles. So we have no choice but to throw our sleeping bags onto our little patch of paradise and sleep under the stars. I'm afraid of coyotes and lizards and the like but I forget how afraid I am when I look up and see the sky. There are more stars than I've ever seen in my life, more even than the Hayden Planetarium.

At least the KOAs have showers and grills where we cook the cheapest food we can find. My bizarre eating tastes begin to garner some unwanted attention. I have the only Italian-American mother in the United States who is not a good cook (In fairness to my mother, she has told me her entire life that she's an American, not an Italian, and I've concluded that her cooking is her way of proving to me that what she says is true.) Because of dear old mom, I eat mainly—exclusively really—hamburgers, pasta and pizza. In the first 19 years of my life, I somehow have managed never to have tasted chicken, have never opened a can of tuna. Did I mention that I also almost never eat vegetables? But on this trip, I'm forced to since vegetables tend to be pretty cheap. Jerry and Mary Ellen even cook up some concoction involving chopped meat, carrots, zucchini, onions, peppers and tomato sauce. What can I say? The chopped meat tastes pretty good; the rest I can barely get down.

We're doing OK on finances. Gas prices are cheaper the further west we go and the Fury is getting 16 miles to the gallon so we're doing pretty well.

Staying in KOAs gives us the opportunity to interact with our fellow travelers. I am taken aback by the accents and sometimes wonder if they're putting us on but they seem to honestly want to help us out, especially when they hear we've come all the way from the Bronx, New York. As I say, mostly they're helpful but somewhere around Estes National Park in Colorado, we come across a situation that is right out of the movie "Easy Rider." We pull into a little isolated strip mall and, as soon as we get out of our car, there is trouble. We are surrounded by a pack of young guys wearing black cowboy hats. I almost want to laugh at how tough they are trying to look. They eye us up and down. Andrew lights a cigarette as we look back at them and then the leader looks down at our New York plates and says in the thickest Western accent I've ever heard, "This here's a family place. We don't allow no long-hairs or hippies. Y'all better get in your car and keep on going."

If there's one thing I'm not, it's a long hair but Andrew and John do qualify. I cannot believe these kids in hats are serious. For a few seconds, it's a standoff. We are from the Bronx after all and though we're surrounded, I'm pretty sure we'd put a beating on them. But there are more of them, and we don't want to risk getting arrested so we compromise. We tell them we're going inside for a soda and then we'll leave. They look at us. I wait outside to watch the car and make sure no one takes a knife to our tires while the others go inside. The black hats move closer to me but I put my back against the driver's side door and stand my ground. Hey, I've been mugged by 12-year-olds who are tougher than these assholes. I am not worried but I'm still relieved when my guys come out of the little general store, sodas in hand. I spit at the feet of the black hats. They do exactly nothing, and watch us in that mean sort of way as we drive off. We laugh all the way to California about the many ways we would have kicked their redneck asses.

Eventually, we make our way to Yosemite National Park, about four hours north of San Francisco where Mary Ellen has secured a summer job. Yosemite is a revelation. From the moment I set foot outside the car and look around, I'm hooked. This is the opposite of the projects. Everything here is natural, like a woodland cathedral. Before this, Central Park was my idea of nature. Yosemite, as anyone who's ever been there knows, is one of the most beautiful spots on earth. If you had to imagine what the Garden of Eden might look like, you could do a lot worse than the view from Inspiration Point. Waterfalls are everywhere, majestic mountains surround the Valley floor, and there is a smell there I cannot make out but it turns out to be a wonderful combination of pine and earth. We are surrounded by the most wondrous scenery imaginable, so beautiful that the photographer Ansel Adams made a career out of it. Ansel Adams himself is teaching photography courses in the center here that bears his name.

We hang out with Jerry's girlfriend Mary Ellen as she settles into her new job. On her off-day, one of her co-workers, a girl named Jeanne, promises to take us to a special spot. We all hike into the woods, the five of us with a small group of California guys and gals. We get to a place where a small waterfall creates a natural water slide into a catch pond. *Looks good*, I think. I begin to take off my shorts; I have on my bathing suit underneath. But then I see every one of the

California group strip down to nothing! Nothing! I've never seen a naked woman before but now I'm next to about five of them, one more beautiful than the next. I want to join them but I am inhibited. Will Andrew and Jerry really take off their bathing suits? Will Mary Ellen? I wait to see what happens and sure enough, the New York group is way too Catholic to strip. We swim in our bathing suits while the California people go naked. We are so unhip.

On one of my California trips, late 70s

Lying on the rocks to dry off, I close my eyes and think about the trip so far. It's been tense but I've learned a lot about myself, and how I get along with people when my parents are not around, when I'm completely out of my element. There was nothing stopping me from stripping down to nothing but I didn't do it. I wish I had. The sun feels good on my face, but it's so quiet. I open my eyes, and the first thing I see is a giant black bear sniffing my feet. Even if I wanted to run, I can't. I'm in shock. This trip has been one first after another—chicken, tuna, naked women, and now a bear!

I move my eyes and see that everyone is across the water. I'm alone in the bear hors d'oeuvre department. I decide rather quickly that I do not want to get eaten by a bear. I see the California guys across the way, putting their fingers to their mouths to tell me to stay still and be quiet. No problem. I decide the best thing to do is to close my eyes, and hope he'll go away. When I open them again, he's gone. I sit up and paddle over to the other side where everyone else is.

Of course, they're all laughing.

We stay in Yosemite for a long weekend which I never want to end. We know we must keep heading south but I vow I'll be back.

The rest of the trip—even the visit to my own promised land of Los Angeles—is anticlimatic. We wander around the Haight-Ashbury district of San Francisco, drive down U.S. 1 to Los Angeles, and visit the old Universal Studios. Without money, we cannot seem to find the right things to do, and spend a lot of time on the beach at Santa Monica trying to pick up girls with no luck. Finally, Andrew's uncle, who is living in Los Angeles, gives him an extra $100 and we drift back to New York. We nearly make it too, except that the car's water pump breaks in Pennsylvania, and John wires his parents for some money.

Now that I have a taste of California, I want more. The summer between my junior and senior years—1974—I decide to apply for a job in Yosemite and talk Andrew and Robbie into doing the same. When the park concession company accepts us, I panic. It's one thing to spend a few weeks driving around but do I really want to spend my whole summer away from home and everything that I know? It takes me about a minute to decide that, yes I do. Andrew's mother will not allow him to go. It's only going to be me and Robbie but I'm game. We decide to fly out instead of drive. It will be the first airplane ride of my life.

I have no idea what to expect or how to prepare at the airport or on the plane. No one in my family ever has been on a plane, but they are excited. Even though only Robbie and I are traveling, we have about 12 people in tow to see us off. At the airport, we are bumpkins among sophisticates, so out of place that, when a businessman sees Robbie's sweet but somewhat disheveled mother holding a Tupperware container, he puts a quarter on top, assuming that she is panhandling. Robbie and I buy tickets for a cheap flight that leaves New York around midnight and makes at least two stops on its way west. Of course, the fare is very reasonable, and we pay in cash—bills, loose change, and even pennies. I spend most of the flight in the bathroom, terribly air-sick, and am more than thankful when we finally land in San Francisco after what feels like weeks in the air.

A couple of very long bus rides later, we are in Yosemite ready to work and play. Robbie is assigned a job handing out towels and soap to visitors wishing to use the public showers. I am sent to the Valley Deli because I have experience behind the counter back in New York. It's not often that they get an honest-to-goodness New York deli man to work here, and the truth is, I do know how to make a mean sandwich. The job is a delight because I interact with tourists, and wear a little name tag telling everyone I'm from New York

City. It's a lot of fun waiting on people who are so happy to be in this beautiful place. I make friends with everyone I work with, including the baker who feeds us freshly-made, intensely sweet bear-claw pastries each morning.

Robbie and I are assigned to employee housing which means we will live in a tent that has a wooden floor, electricity, two beds, and a chest of drawers. Everyone around us is also an employee of the Curry Company, the family that has run the concessions in the park for decades. We are surrounded by California girls, and I make some headway but am nowhere near as quick as Robbie who, within days, is sleeping in our tent with the girl who turns out to be his summer-long girlfriend.

Each day that I wake up and see where I am, I remain astounded by the beauty of the place. If I walk to work, bluebirds and deer are my companions. If I take the trolley, I stare out the window open-mouthed at the waterfalls booming at full force or the granite cliffs surrounding me. How, I wonder, did I pull this off, traveling from a Bronx housing project, the most urban of environments, to this incredible natural beauty? Robbie and I take full advantage of where we are. During the week, we hike the valley floor and chat with tourists and other workers, sometimes going down to the Merced River to swim or float off inside inner tubes. On our off days, we fill our packs with food and head out into the Yosemite wilderness. It's said that most tourists, or *turkeys* as we smugly call them, never venture past the Valley floor. We're not turkeys and set out to prove it by taking overnight hikes to every corner of the park—Tuolumne Meadows, Upper Yosemite Falls, Cloud's Rest, even the back of Half-Dome. Of course, being dyed-in-the-wool New Yorkers, we're hopelessly naïve about camping. We don't have hiking boots, only sneakers, and our backpacks, which should be light, are incredibly heavy because we carry cans of food, instead of freeze-dried packs. Not that it matters. The bears find whatever we bring and eat the contents pretty much every time we do an overnight. One night, on our way to an area known as Cloud's Rest, we overnight in Little Yosemite Valley, and only after we settle in do we learn from other campers that the area has a nickname—Little Bear Valley.

At Yosemite National Park

Ah, but we know, or rather, we've heard what to do. We pick a tree with a narrow branch and hoist our backpacks up there so they are hanging from the narrow branch, high enough off the ground so the bears cannot reach it. Then we settle in for the night. We watch at twilight as the bears magically appear in the half-light. They're all around us, sniffing for food. They come right up to our tent but we've been careful to put all our food in those backpacks, keeping not even a candy bar with us. It takes one of the bears about five minutes to spot our backpacks up in the tree.

"Don't worry," I whisper to Robbie. "There's no way he can climb out onto the branch. It'll never support his weight."

It turns out that I'm right…and wrong. The bear in question simply reaches out and snaps the narrow branch off the tree. It is *too* narrow and willowy for him to climb on but fragile enough for him to break with one swat. We are forced to watch as he and his fellow bears enjoy our food, tearing open our cans with their claws and altogether having a great time. Examining the damage after they leave, we see there is not a hint of food left, but we resolve to push on to Cloud's Rest anyway. We go hungry that day, surviving on the water running through the mountain streams.

One weekend, a friend of ours named Gary, who's worked in the park before, invites us up to a section of Yosemite he calls "Devil's Bathtub."

"I never saw that on a map," I tell Gary.

He smiles. "Yeah, it's a secret we like to keep from the turkeys but you'll love it, don't worry."

The next day we follow Gary on a short climb that opens up to large, granite outcropping hidden from the trails.

"Why do they call this 'Devil's Bathtub?'" I ask as we round the bend.

Gary grimaces. It's a subject we've been over before. He thinks as New Yorkers, we ask too many questions, and should *go with the flow* more. I shut up and keep walking.

And then I see why going with the flow is sometimes a

good idea. There are about 30 people in front of us, and all of them are stark naked, including many of the girls I work with. They are sunning themselves or soaking in shallow pools of rainwater warmed by the sun. Gary smiles, and leads the way over to a spot where he strips naked. Unlike last year, when all of us New Yorkers were too uptight to strip, this time I have no problem. Outside of gym class at Hayes, I've never taken off my clothes in front of so many people before but I do it now without hesitation. Robbie follows.

We nod to a few of our fellow workers, take a dip in one of the pools and lay our backs against the warm granite. This feels and looks like I imagine Heaven. One of the girls I work with—Grace—comes over and begins chatting. Grace is petite, blonde, and has a face that belongs in a "Moonshadow" commercial; she is the epitome of a California girl. And her body, my God. I feel the way I did when I first laid eyes on Inspiration Point, only I didn't want to fuck Inspiration Point. She seemingly is oblivious to her nakedness. Because she is so tan nearly everywhere else, her white breasts stand out in stark contrast, and her nipples are almost too beautiful to behold. She regales me with stories of park gossip. I admire her ability to be so unselfconscious but not nearly as much as I admire her stupendous body. She is standing right over me as she speaks, and I try to lock eyes with her, difficult as that is. I don't want her to get the wrong idea about me, not that it actually would be wrong at all but I don't want her to think of me that way, and, besides, drooling is so unattractive. I focus on what she's saying and squeeze out a word now and again when suddenly Grace slips on the rock and falls right on top of me, our naked bodies sealed together for a few moments.

"Oh hey, I'm sorry," she says, lifting herself off.

I notice that it seems to take her a little longer than I think necessary but I'm not about to argue. Then she smiles at me and whispers, "Can you help me with something?"

"Sure."

She takes my hand and leads me off the outcropping to a spot in the brush. "I need a little help with something," she says. "It's right over here."

"Sure whatever you need," I say dumbly.

And then she pushes me down and lies on top of me, her mouth on mine. I briefly consider telling her that I'm a virgin, but what good would that do? Besides, she seems to know only too well what she's doing.

Later that night, I write these words in my journal: *Yosemite is Heaven.*

Leaving Heaven

It is true what they say, at least for me. You can take the boy out of the Bronx but you can't take the Bronx out of the boy. Here's the thing—there lurks a thief somewhere in my soul. I know because, when I shoplifted records, I never had a pang of guilt until I was caught. It's not that I thought I was doing anything noble, or rationalizing to myself that I was stealing from the rich—Korvette's—to give to the poor—me. I enjoyed the thrill that came from stealing, and having something I otherwise could not.

Letting me and Robbie—two Bronx boys—loose in a place like Yosemite is no doubt a mistake for the Curry Company. We are good employees but the company is very lax with the cash pouring into the operation every day, so lax that it's impossible not to notice. In the deli, there is a drawer where the large bills are dumped until it's counted at day's end. The drawer is about a foot and a half deep and it's a jumble of $20's, $50's and even $100's. Nothing is stacked or catalogued; it's a mess and no one knows how much is there until it's counted at day's end.

I see the cash every time it's my turn to dump bills into the drawer, but I avoid looking for too long. The temptation to slip a handful into my pocket is great but I resist because I love this job and the place and don't want to do anything to screw things up. But then Robbie gets an idea. He decides we should start *saving* money so we can chip in for a used car in August and drive back to New York. We have opened up savings accounts for our paychecks in the Valley branch of the Wells Fargo bank. I love my western passbook with its little stage coach drawing. We do manage to save most of our paychecks each week because I can eat for free in the deli and manage to sneak out enough food to keep Robbie feeling full. I'm feeling flush as I watch my passbook savings grow each week but I know it'll never be enough to buy a car.

"How are we going to save enough to buy a used car?" I ask.

He smiles that sly Robbie smile. I've told him about the cash drawer and he tells me about some scam he's been thinking about. His job requires him to supply towels and soap to tourists at one of Yosemite's campsites. Instead of ringing up each sale, he figures he can skim at least $20 a day off the top by not accounting for every sale, and pocketing the money.

And because I've stupidly told him about that cash drawer, he challenges me: "All you have to do is reach into that drawer and pull out a $20 bill here and there."

He's right but I don't want to. This place is perfect and stealing here seems so very wrong.

"I don't know, Robbie."

"Think about it."

So I do, and each day that goes by the temptation gets worse. Thanks to Robbie, I now have this thought in my brain that I can't shake.

It seems Robbie and me are not the only one to notice the easy pickings. In the deli, a few workers are entrusted with the combination to the floor safe so they can handle the cash receipts at the start and end of each day. One of them is a co-worker of mine named George, a skinny older guy who likes his weed. Something tells me he's not on the up and up and I'm proved right when, one morning, he is arrested by the park police, allegedly for dipping into the till. One moment George is there and the next he's not and I never see him again. I hear he's in the park lockup, and I do not want that to happen to me. Getting caught shoplifting is one thing. You don't go to jail for that but stealing money is something else all together. I hear George is facing major criminal charges.

But the human mind is a funny thing. Somehow, incredibly—and I can't explain why, not even to myself—I put what's happened to George out of my mind, and begin stealing money from the cash drawer. You'd think I'd know better because of the lessons of right and wrong that have been drilled into me by nuns and priests, but a part of me is very reckless. And so it begins. Sometimes, when I empty a big haul of cash into the drawer, I slide a $20 bill into my pocket. I tell Robbie nothing but one day he sees my bank book and smiles. He knows what's going on.

"Looks like we might have enough for a car," he says.

I won't talk about it. I am worried and know that I'm being an idiot but can't stop myself. It's not a death wish exactly but something like it—a *do harm to myself* wish. I examine my motives and blame it all on the Catholic Church. I tell myself that I am so sick of being a goody two shoes for the Church and God that I am rebelling. It is self-destructive and delusional but I cannot stop myself. I can analyze my crime but am incapable of putting an end to it. My mind is reeling. Before this mini-crime spree, I have thought about staying in Yosemite and California and never going back to the Bronx. A couple of girls I'm friendly with are going to stay, and I wonder what the park will look like in the snowy winter. I've seen the photos and they are breathtaking. But I am nothing if not practical. The following year will be my last at Fordham, and if I go back I'll graduate the following June. Then maybe I can come back here.

In the meantime, Robbie is doing all he can to skim the shower money off the top. He even confronts a dozen Hells Angels who ride their hogs right into the shower area and coolly march by Robbie without paying. Robbie goes after them and tells them in no uncertain terms to pay up. They do. Robbie tells me about a co-worker who's always bragging that he takes in more than Robbie because he's such a dedicated worker. It's all Robbie can do not to break out laughing. One day, he picks up a ride into the nearest town and finds a used puke-yellow Toyota Corolla for $650. Pooling our money, we can afford it, and make plans to leave Yosemite at the start of August. Sick about what I've done, I give Robbie the money he needs and tell him he does not need to pay me back. *Take it, I say. Take whatever you need and buy the stupid car. Let's get out of here.*

Before we leave, the friends we've made take us to the Ahwahnee Hotel restaurant for a goodbye meal. The Ahwahnee is a very big deal. It is where the rich people stay when they come to Yosemite, those who want to see the beauty but do not want to camp. The Ahwahnee restaurant is a giant hall that looks like it could be the setting for a medieval meal, and, in fact, hosts this amazing Christmas pageant every year called the Bracebridge Dinner. On this night, the night before Robbie and I are leaving Yosemite, everyone is all gussied up. The girls look so different, so grown up. I marvel at how beautiful they are in their simple dresses, and even how handsome our male co-workers look in collared shirts, and the jackets provided by the Ahwahnee staff.

Our deli boss—the guy I've been indirectly stealing from—is paying for the whole thing which causes me no end of guilt. I push it out of my mind yet again. I want to make a clean escape the following morning, get out of the park, and never think about the money again. That night, we make toasts all around and swear we'll stay in touch and return for a reunion. Grace is there, and I give her a kiss late that night before turning in. I have only had sex with her that one time but that's all right. I'm grateful beyond all words. It's been a fabulous summer. She has made this Bronx boy very happy.

We head out early the next day. I am still pleased that I had the nerve to come out here, overjoyed I am no longer a virgin, but desperately sorry the way everything ended. The ride back is hell on my nerves and I suspect we're jinxed. In Grand Island, Nebraska our alternator dies along with all our lights in the middle of the night but we stay on the Interstate determined to make good time. I hop into the back seat with a flashlight so the approaching truckers will know they're coming up fast on a broken down car. An 18-wheeler bears down on us, looking like it's hell-bent on going right through us. I scream at Robbie that we should jump out of the car and save our lives but he convinces me not to. At the last moment, the trucker driving the 18-wheeler veers away. We're so burnt out that we pull over blindly and fall asleep in the car. We don't notice until the morning that we've chosen to block the garage of a volunteer hook and ladder company. The company driver hits the siren to wake us up and we push the car out of the way, all the way to a gas station where the friendly owner rebuilds our alternator for a nominal charge.

The rest of the way I am very quiet. We play our static-filled AM radio a lot, and somewhere in the middle of the country, at a gas station, we hear that Richard Nixon has resigned as president. I feel as dirty as he must.

Back Home

It is my last year at Fordham and that is good and bad. Fordham is about to end and that's very good news. I never quite got over the feeling of being adrift, in a place where no one cared if I was there from one minute to the next. But leaving Fordham is also bad news because I know I've blown my college years on this much-too-Catholic commuter school in the same borough where I live. Talk about adventure. This was the anti-adventure, and the best times I had were when I was working in the deli, ogling actresses, call girls and models over a frozen food case. Sad. Topping things off is my rapidly approaching graduation. Now what am I going to do? My major is communications and creative writing and I'm not sure it's qualified me to earn a living. I have some vague idea—as I had on that very first day—that I will make money by writing but where?

To make matters even worse, Jack of The Third Avenue Deli tells me I cannot have my old job back. He's tired of the way I abandoned him the past two summers to go off to California and he's got steady help now. He tells me thanks but no thanks. I'm left to cobble jobs together and this is the moment where I begin my strangest career move. I get a day-time job on the weekends selling pipes and clocks in the old B. Altman's Department Store on 34th Street, and, by night, I get a job as a singing and dancing waiter at a Greenwich Village tourist dive called "Your Father's Mustache."

I'm not sure which job is more bizarre. B. Altman's is an elegant old dinosaur of a department store and part of me loves it. It speaks to the type of New Yorker who would never set foot in a place like E.J. Korvette's and that's fine with me. It appeals to the snob buried deep inside me. The cash register is massive and ancient and one about needs two hands to press down each numbered key. I am trained and the store puts me behind a counter in the pipe and clock section. Why there, I have no idea because, while it is true that I can tell time, I know less than nothing about pipes. It would seem to be a pretty placid place to work except for the old guy I'm assigned to work with. He's worked behind this counter since Truman was president and he makes it very clear that this is his territory and I am to do one thing and one thing only—butt out. If he so much as hears me clear my throat in anticipation of talking to a customer, he elbows me out of the way. Generous of spirit he is not. By the time I leave at 5 p.m. to go to my second job as a dancing waiter, I'm fairly banged up.

You might think one needs talent to be a singing and dancing waiter in Greenwich Village—either that or, at the very least, be gay—but I am neither gay nor talented. I can carry a tune but singing and dancing to entertain people?!! Of course, the place is only looking for warm bodies, and it's almost impossible to be *not talented enough* to work here.

One of my friends at Fordham is a waiter here and, with his recommendation, I am hired on the spot.

The restaurant caters to tourists with a very limited command of the English language. They all want separate checks which is a pain in the ass when you are dealing with 50 Germans who speak virtually no English in a dark, loud club. My job is to take their orders and lend to the merriment of the place. It's kind of hard to be merry when I'm so pissed off at my customers but I do what I can. There are two big show-stoppers each night. One of them has all of the waiters standing on the bar singing "How you gonna keep them down on the farm after they've seen New York?" Now mind you, I do not know the tune or the lyrics of this song is, but I find myself yelling "blah, blah, blah," and doing a chorus-line style high-kick with my fellow waiters, all to the enthusiastic applause of these bewildered international tourists who have heard somewhere that New York is the entertainment capital of the world. No one ever challenges our ability although I do notice that the tips are better if the tourists leave *before* we perform.

I can fake that one song but the other big number requires a fair amount of arm-strength. I am supposed to run around the restaurant carrying an empty (thank you God) metal keg of beer over my head. Now I'll let you in on a secret—even empty metal kegs of beer are enormous and very heavy. One night, as I'm running around like my foot is on fire, trying not to slip on all the empty peanut shells all over the floor, I find myself losing my grip on said beer keg as I'm at the head of a table of Belgian tourists, all of whom of course want separate checks. The keg, delicately balanced over my head, begins to slip forward toward the table. The Belgians, who know a thing or two about beer kegs, realize what's about to happen and recoil in horror. And as I'm about to drop the keg square on the table, I pull it back with all my might, and avoid an international incident. It does have one benefit—their tour leader tells me to bring one check, immediately. Yes sir!

I work the two jobs for about a month until fate—in the form of a postcard tacked to a jobs bulletin board at Fordham—intervenes for the second time in my life. The local TV station WPIX Channel 11 is looking for a college student to work five nights a week compiling program logs. The hours are 6 to 11 p.m. Monday through Friday. I am interested for a couple of reasons: 1) WPIX is situated in the Daily News building and I've never lost my fascination for that globe, and 2) the television station is owned by the Tribune Company, which also publishes *The Daily News*. I have no idea if there's a way to make the jump from PIX to *The Daily News* but it is an intriguing possibility. I take down the phone number and wonder how I can possibly work five nights a week. I decide there's no way. I can't do it. I decide not to even apply. But then I tell my mother about the job, and she tells me to go for it, that working five nights a week my last year in college is no big deal. It turns out to be the most valuable piece of advice she ever gives me.

I call the number and go downtown for an interview. I pause in the lobby next to the globe and think about the first time I visited Santa Claus there. Yes, I decide, it would be pretty cool to work in this building, no matter the job. Who cares about working five nights a week? I have no social life anyway. I go upstairs and some guy wearing a cheap polyester suit explains the job. I can see he wants to hire me almost immediately because he tells me three times that he graduated from Fordham himself. I know he's trying to make me feel better even though the idea that I might wind up like him makes me want to dive out the nearest window, and/or enroll in pharmacy school. But I do the mature thing and stay.

He explains that each night, a computer spits out the program and advertising logs for the next 24 hours of airtime. The logs are printed in a separate room that houses an incredibly noisy printer that is quite deafening, sort of like an electronic gattling gun. It stands about four feet high and has perforated paper that must fit correctly into the side sprockets. Once the paper is loaded, I only have to wait a few hours until it's finished, and then distribute the logs to various desks. It's easy as long as I don't go deaf.

"It's pretty simple," this guy says. "So are you interested?"

"Absolutely."

"Then the job is yours."

I wonder if I should have played a little more hard to get. Should I have told him about my budding dual career as a clock and pipe salesman by day, and dancing waiter by night?

I soon quit those jobs—hard as that is—and begin my first meaningful job, meaning that I hope it will lead to something beyond a paycheck. I get to PIX around 6 each night as all the daytime workers are packing up. I become friendly with this one girl named Janet who, at 25, is a much older woman. She's an out-of-towner and seems kind of lonely. She always makes it a point to talk with me before she leaves for the day. I get the impression that, some nights, she doesn't want to leave and would be happy to hang out with me. If she's interested in me beyond conversation, I am too slow to do anything about it but I do accompany her one night to Central Park West where workers are blowing up balloons for the following day's Thanksgiving Day parade. We buy a couple of beers and watch the goings-on, trying to ignore the temperature which is steadily dropping.

"I'm freezing," she says, moving closer.

"Me too, and I need to take a leak."

She smiles. "Wanna see my apartment? It's around the corner and you can use the bathroom."

We head upstairs where Janet shows me her studio apartment that faces the inside courtyard of her building. I can see she's tried to dress it up with photos of her family and some artwork but it still kind of depresses me. She introduces me to her cat Dusty who hisses at me. "He's not used to me having company," she says. "Anyway, there's the bathroom."

When I come out, she's sitting on her sofa drinking her beer and staring out the window. She looks very sad, as though she's about to cry, and right at that moment, she does. I freeze.

"I'm sorry," she says.

"What is it? Do you want me to leave?"

"Oh no, it isn't you. It's this fucked up city. I'm lonely Paul. I can't seem to meet anyone here. You must think I'm pathetic."

"No, no, I don't think you're pathetic."

I sit next to her on the couch and she readjusts herself so that her head is in my lap. She's still crying but very softly. I'm not really sure what to do but I settle for smoothing down her hair. "It's okay, it's okay," I say over and over.

I know I'm doing this wrong. She's a woman, not a cat for Christ sakes. I look around for that cat and see it on the other side of the room. Dusty is staring daggers at me. I stare back and continue to pat Janet's head. I'm afraid to move. I can't leave now, not unless I want Janet to kill herself, and I'm afraid to move too much because her cat looks like he's about to pounce. So I do nothing but stare out the window and sip my beer. After about a half hour, I hear her breathing change and whisper her name. Nothing. She must be sleeping. Now I'm stuck. I have no desire to wake her and remind her of her shitty life so I sit there staring at her cat and listening to the time click away on her big noisy clock.

It's early morning when I next open my eyes. At first, I have no idea where I am, and then suddenly remember. I sit up, having fallen asleep on the couch. Janet is nowhere to be found and neither is her cat. She has left me a note on her door. "Happy Thanksgiving. Thanks for everything. See you Monday."

We never speak of this night again.

I make one other friend at work, a guy named Marty from Brooklyn. Marty is a very funny guy, and we're the same age but he hasn't gone to college. He has a job similar to mine in another department at PIX, and he lives with his mother in Brooklyn. I like Marty and we often hang out together while I'm waiting for the log to print out, listening to WNEW radio while he smokes cigarette after cigarette. It's a habit I never took up, after coughing my brains out when I tried a cigarette at the age of 14.

I'm sailing through my last year at Fordham; it's as boring as the three that came before. I'm also mindlessly going to work when one night, while waiting for the elevators in The News lobby, I run into Sal. He and I attended Cardinal Hayes together though we were never very good friends. I tell Sal why I'm in the building and ask what he's doing there.

"I work at *The Daily News* as a copyboy," he says.

"Really? I've always wanted to work there."

"Why don't you come up? I'll show you around."

This time, instead of getting off on the 10th floor where PIX is located, I get off at 7, home to *The Daily News* city room. Sal walks in like he owns the place, and gives me a little tour. It looks just as I always knew it would. Newspapers are strewn everywhere. Guys with cigarettes dangling from their mouths are pounding on typewriters, and mumbling "fuck" or "shit" to themselves. The place is filthy. Sal goes up to a desk where he meets the head copyboy who tells Sal to go sit at the copy desk. Sal nonchalantly puts a pencil behind his ear and heads over, chatting me up along the way, telling me how the copy desk works. "They fix the grammar, write the headlines, and make sure the stories read correctly, and then they go downstairs where these pages get set into type," he says.

Sal takes a seat at the copy desk where he is at the beck and call of about ten men who look very serious and very disheveled. All of them are drinking coffee and smoking, while they look down hard at the copy before them. Every once in a while, they cross something out with their pencils or write something new in the margins. "This fucking guy can't write for shit," one of them says out loud. "Listen to this..."

All work on the desk stops as his buddies listen to one particularly awkward sentence, and they all guffaw. The guy doing the talking suddenly notices me watching him and says, "Who the fuck are you?"

"I, er, I, er…"

"He's with me," Sal says, rescuing me. "We went to high school together and I'm only showing him around."

"Okay Sal," he says. "If he's your friend, okay."

And then everyone goes back to work. Sal whispers, "Maybe you'd better go. You never know. He's got a temper and he's been drinking all night."

Sal leads me out of the newsroom. "So what did you think?"

"Any openings?"

"Apply when you graduate and tell them you work at PIX. I'll put in a good word for you."

"Thanks Sal."

I head upstairs but the work no longer seems as pointless as it did before. *The Daily News* is one step closer.

Graduation

In 1975, I graduate from Fordham University. I am working diligently at WPIX-TV, and have submitted a job application and resume to work as a copyboy at *The Daily News* as Sal suggested. But I have no idea if or when that job will come through and things on the home front are bleak. A few years before, my father was laid off by the Railway Express before it went out of business. Thanks to Robbie or, more accurately, Robbie's father, my dad was offered a union job running the freight elevator at an office building in Manhattan. It's a good job but my father's health is not. A lifelong smoker, he has his first heart attack at the age of 50, around the same time he was laid off. Almost worse than the heart attack, which was relatively mild, are the state of his knees which are shot through with arthritis, making it painful for him to walk or stand for long periods which is what he must do at work.

And now, as I am graduating, his doctor orders him into the hospital for a hernia operation. It's not all that serious but seeing my father lying in a hospital bed right around the time of my graduation spooks me. What if something happens to him? My mother has only worked at part-time banking jobs and has no way of making enough money to support a family, and my brother and sister are both younger. I realize that I need to be the family provider in case something else happens to my dad.

Before I can find a job, I need a suit so I go up to old reliable, the Cross County Mall, and visit a discount men's clothing store—it might have been Robert Hall—where I pluck a lime green, polyester suit off the rack. It fits so I buy it, oblivious to the color and material. As usual, I'm stumbling through my life like a blind man inside Grand Central Station at rush hour, bumping into people and things and hoping against hope that I find a track—any track—that will put me on the correct train.

First stop, the classified want ads. I look under "editorial" and "writer" but they rarely lead me to actual employers. Instead, I find myself visiting tiny, ugly offices in and around midtown where a variety of bored employment agency managers interview me for jobs they refuse to accurately describe. I do have one thing going for me. In these turbulent years of social revolution, long hair and rebellion, I am a conformist, at least on the surface. In my cheap lime green suit, with my receding hairline, and my serious demeanor, more than one employment manager thinks I'd be a perfect fit for this or that job. They assure me they will talk to the actual employer and get back to me quickly.

But when I don't hear from them, I am not surprised. Nineteen-seventy-five is a very bad year for New York City. The city is going bankrupt, thousands were being laid off and the federal government wants no part of any of it. It's the year *The Daily News* carries the immortal headline "Ford to City: Drop Dead." My future does not look so great but I can't think of anything better to do than show up day after day at these strange little offices with their strange little men.

The summer stretches into July and I'm still working at PIX-TV when I get a call from Ed Quinn at *The Daily News*. I put on my lime green suit and stop at the seventh floor newsroom. I am ushered into Quinn's office.

"So Mister LaRosa, tell me why you want to work here?"

"Well, sir, I want to be a reporter. I've always been a good writer, and I've worked on the school newspaper in high school and college…"

That's as far as I get. Quinn is not a patient man, and looks bemused, like he's heard my little speech thousands of times which he probably has. He puts his hand up to stop me in mid-sentence.

"You realize, you're applying for a copyboy position, right?"

"Yes sir."

"And do you realize how few copyboys become reporters?"

"No sir."

"About one in ten. It's a long shot that you'll be promoted to reporter. I want you to know that going in—not that you even have the job—but let's be realistic."

"Yes sir."

"Now, do you know what a copyboy does?"

"Well, not really sir except that he runs copy from place to place in the newsroom."

Quinn raises his bushy eyebrows. I've picked up this information from Sal who's allowed me to visit him a few times while I've worked at PIX. "That's right but you know what else a copy boy does? He gets coffee, fetches clips from the morgue—the library—and does what the editors and reporters need him to do. He's a gopher. How do you feel about that, about getting coffee?"

"I'll do whatever it takes sir. I've always wanted to work here at the News. I was a newspaper delivery boy and ..."

Again, Quinn puts up his hand to stop me. He's not interested in my history, only my bleak—in his eyes—future. "You're a college graduate," he says, looking down at my resume. "Fordham's a good school. Do you know what kind of salary you'll be making here as a copyboy?"

I shake my head no.

"The job pays $127 a week and that's before taxes," he says, nearly spitting at me.

"I'll take it."

"I'm not offering it to you," he says immediately.

"We have a lot of competition for these jobs. *The Daily News* is the largest circulating paper in the country. I'll tell you one thing though. There are a lot of changes coming. If you get this job, you'll see a transition from hot type to cold type, from typewriters to computers. This place, and this business, is changing fast. People your age will be the last ones to see hot type and linotype machines. You don't even know what I'm talking about do you?"

"Not really but I've read about computers and used them a little at WPIX."

"Well, they're coming, faster than any of us realize."

He hesitates. "You can go now. One way or another, we'll let you know."

I shake his hand. "Thank you sir. If you hire me, you won't be sorry, I can promise you that. I'm a hard worker."

Quinn looks me up and down, as though seeing me for the first time. "Where the hell did you get that suit?"

"Robert Hall, sir."

"Nice color."

I'm about to smile to let him know that I'm in on the joke. By now, just about everyone I've run across while wearing this suit has told me how hideous it is. But Quinn doesn't smile, and I wonder if maybe he actually likes the color. Maybe, in his eyes, I've done at least one thing right.

On June 27, 1975, two weeks after my interview with Quinn, I find an envelope in the mail with *The Daily News* speed graphic camera logo in the upper left hand corner. I hold my breath and open it.

Dear Mr. La Rosa:

If you are interested in a part-time position as copy boy, please call me early next week.

Thank you.

Very truly yours,

Edward F. Quinn

Where the Action Is

I've been in this newsroom before but I was invisible, not settling into a job where everyone will get to know me. I am shown around. Even before entering the newsroom, I am introduced to two Daily News institutions: Thyrza, a sweet if slightly absent-minded receptionist, and the giant wooden punch clock where I am to sign my name and pull a lever that registers when I report for work each day. I feel like some kind of factory worker. A lot of this first day and the ones that follow are a blur of faces and information. There are wooden copyboy benches placed strategically around the city room, and this is where I am to sit—here and nowhere else—until someone yells "copy."

Miltie Hacker is the genial old boss of the copyboys and his second-in-command is Carlos, a Colombian guy with a nearly-impenetrable accent that he uses to great effect to keep us *boys* in line. His voice, booming across the vast room, is unmistakable, as I learn when I sit in a chair for one moment when all the benches are filled. Carlos' voice is like a Colombian air raid siren that goes off immediately—

"LaRosa, on da bench."

On da bench is where I live. The benches are beautiful in their simplicity and remind me of the pews at church, minus the kneeling pads, although, given the tasks we're asked to perform, that wouldn't be completely out of line. Each of the benches can hold three, maybe four, boys. And that's what everyone calls us. It doesn't matter that I have a college degree or that I work alongside female copykids. We are equal. We are all *boys*. We need to be visible and on the bench so reporters can keep track of us when they have *needs*, and boy do they have needs. The word "copy" is almost always in the air, and when we hear it, we hustle over. Walking slowly is not acceptable. This is a newsroom. Good manners are absent.

If a reporter on *deadline* is not happy with how fast you hop to it when he yells copy, he is perfectly within his rights to scream, *"Come on move your ass, will ya! I don't have all fuckin' day. I'm on deadline."* This is not a place for someone with feelings easily bruised. The skinny copy editor Chile, who has one good arm and an irritating and distinct high voice, insists on yelling *boy* when he needs something. And if his *boy*—there is one always assigned to his copy desk on deadline—is not nearby, he'll scream, *"Where's my boy?"* He is oblivious and does not apologize or have even the hint of shame when a woman or a black guy hustles over. Chile sees no distinctions. He does not care. We are all *boys*.

Well, that's not true. One night, he's really on a tear, angry about some slight from a news editor when he explodes in his usual rant: *"Boy, boy, where's my boy?"* At that moment, it so happens that a copygirl named Barbara is assigned to the desk. For once, Chile notices. He does a double take as Barbara runs to his call and says, *"You're not a boy."*

Chile presides over a cast of characters on the copy desk who look like they lost out—barely—as the cast of crazies from the film "One Flew Over the Cuckoo's Nest." There is the oenophile who begins his shift with a couple of good bottles of wine followed by a couple of shots of Jack Daniels. There is the bald editor who has some sort of incredible green scaly growth on his head. As the tension mounts around deadline, the guy picks and picks at those green scaly things until they begin dropping into his coffee cup. He never notices and drinks cup after cup with gusto. And then there is the usual assortment of odd body types—massively fat, incredibly skinny, and everything in between.

At its most basic, a copyboy's job is to run copy—each page of a typewritten story—from the reporter who writes it to the editors sitting, waiting and sometimes fuming, at the city desk. But that's only a small part of the job, really. On any day, we may be asked to go get coffee, a sandwich, a beer. At the end of every day, Suburban Editor Sal Gerage celebrates his pages being sent to the composing room by calling *copy* and asking us to fetch him a tall Schaeffer from the 4th floor cafeteria. "For the Blessed Mother," he nods, smiling. I have no idea what that means but I take his dollar bill and scurry off.

That fourth floor cafeteria is okay for beer or a soda but unthinkable for anything else. The hot food is encased in an ancient steam table, home to grease-soaked meatballs and nutrition-free vegetables. Having worked in an Upper East Side deli, I have standards which prevent me from even considering eating here, but others do and seemingly survive although a lot of people spend an awful lot of time in the rest rooms. The rest room stalls are packed! At first I think it's because of the cafeteria food but then I realize it is because men like to use stalls as reading rooms, and what better place to breeze through *every page* of the first edition—including the Jumble word game—than in the john! When they're done, the men simply drop the newspapers on the floor. The floors of the john are littered with newspapers, thrown down in a rush to get back to work and left with pages spread wide. You could walk the entire length of the rest room and your feet might never touch the tiles.

One night, a copyboy named Danny walks into that rest room right after two very beefy reporters walk out. Danny immediately comes out and puts a sign on the door, "Out of Order."

Carlos demands to know what he's doing. Danny tells him about the two rather large reporters who've spent *a lot* of time in there. "Good job, Danny," Carlos says.

Most of the copy calls that take us outside the building are for coffee and a buttered roll from Charles & Co. or sometimes a sandwich from the nearby deli J & A. But other times, we are sent out to help a reporter or editor get through his day. One dayside reporter named Stitch is famous for his early-morning needs. The first order of his day—and this is at 8 in the morning—is to send a boy down to the local watering hole for a double Screwdriver *"and make sure they put it in a coffee cup pally."* Some mornings, Stitch manages to get his favorite drink himself, asking the overnight reporter to cover for him while he goes *to St. Agnes for the early Mass.* This goes on for months until someone clues in the overnight guy—there is no early morning Mass at St. Agnes.

He's down in Louie's getting shitfaced. Go get 'em.

But it isn't all coffee and alcohol. Occasionally, we are sent outside the building to pick up a government report, or the fashion editor might have us take dresses back to Macy's or Lord & Taylor. These runs especially piss me off. One day, I'm charged with carrying a very large box filled with designer dresses. It is quite heavy and it is summer in the city where the asphalt feels like it's melting beneath your feet. Everyone, including me, has that look on their face like they've stepped in shit. It is not a pretty sight. The last block or so, I am so sweaty and pissed off that I decide to drag the box. I don't notice until I'm inside the cool air conditioning of Lord & Taylor's that the box has worn through and a couple of dresses are torn to shreds. I am sure I'll be fired but I move the dresses around, stuff them in a different way so that no one can see the damage, and pray. Miraculously, no one says a word.

And then there are the runs that are pure favors. Executive Editor Mike O'Neill sends me to fetch a sympathy card for a close relative. This is the first sympathy card I've ever bought so O'Neill, in my mind, is taking his chances. I pick out three cards that seem the most harmless and non-threatening. I don't go over the top religious or smaltzy. I bring them back to O'Neill. He inspects the cards through his thick glasses and then peers over them at me.

"Are you Italian?"

"Yes sir."

"I thought so. Didn't they have any cards without birds, something a little less florid?"

I head back to the card store. This time, I'm going with

the top religious card and O'Neil, well, he can go to hell.

The favors never end. Reporter Joe Martin appears to be a grumpy old guy but in hushed tones I am told he once won a Pulitzer so he gets respect, meaning that we must fetch Joe's wife's cats their favorite food from a nearby store called Fabulous Felines. Joe always gives us a tip which to me means even more than his Pulitzer. I consider him not such a bad old guy after all. Besides, I never forget one thing—I am here to serve.

We're also sent to other sections of the newspaper—advertising, the composing room, the presses, the trucks. *The Daily News* is located entirely within this building. It is not only where reporters work; the paper is *manufactured* here. If you tore off the exterior wall of the building, you would see that clearly. Below the 7th floor newsroom is the 6th floor composing room. As deadline approaches, there is almost a constant stream of traffic between the two floors with editors running up and down that back staircase. It is the job of the so-called makeup men to see to it that the typewritten pages and mocked up headlines are set in type correctly so they will appear in tomorrow's paper exactly as intended by the news editors. After the stories are approved by editors for grammar and common sense, the pages are sent to the composing room where they are set in lead type on ancient Linotype machines, operated by equally ancient Linotype operators.

The 6th floor is the domain of the printers union, burly, rough-hewed men who wear stiff aprons to protect their clothing from the lead that's in the air and everywhere else. It sometimes seems as though half the printers have other jobs—contractors, sanitation men and the most common second job of all, bookies. It is not only the paper that is produced down here; this harshly-lit, dirty place is home to an underground economy. Bets are placed and paid off with astonishing regularity right under the noses of the biggest editors at the paper. The printers try to get away with anything they can. One of the copy editors warns me to steer clear of them and their shenanigans, and tells me that the first time he wandered down there to ask a question, the printer pulled him aside, produced some steak knives from one of the pockets of his apron and asked if the copy editor would be interested in buying some silverware—cheap!

At deadline, the composing room is a packed, noisy place redolent with the smells of cigarettes, sweat and lead. The way the newspaper is produced has not changed much in the last 100 years. Large vats of molten lead sit waiting, ready to feed the Linotype machines that never stop moving on deadline. Each word of every story is set in lead type, and then those thousands of lines of lead type are placed in a page mold by printers following the direction of the makeup men who, in turn, are following the wishes of the news editors whose job it is to decide what stories go on which pages and the way each of those pages will look, how big the headline, if there is a sub-head etc.

Because of all the people involved, it's inevitable that early editions of the newspaper have a lot of typos. And here's the most astonishing thing of all. Because of the way the page is eventually placed on the printing press, everything on these leaded pages—the words, headlines and photographs—is backwards! In order to read the page and look for the inevitable typos, printers—when they are finished making up the page—run a heavy ink brush over it, place a blank piece of butcher paper on top and then tap the paper with a piece of wood so that the paper picks up the inked type. When the printers lift those page proofs up, everything is as it would appear in tomorrow's paper. The page proofs are rushed upstairs to the newsroom by copyboys and delivered to copy editors who are waiting to look for typographical errors. Sometimes, corrections can be made before they appear in the finished product but oftentimes not.

The deadlines demand that, when a page is finished being typeset, it be taken to the another floor of the building where a mold is made that is then fit onto gargantuan printing presses. When a makeup man or editor gives his approval to the leaded page, the printer yells out "Boy with a truck" or "boy with a double truck" for the centerfold. A larger, more burly version of a copyboy—there is one kid nicknamed "Bluto"—appears pushing a heavy metal rolling cart with a flat, metal top. Very carefully, the leaded page is slid onto that flat table and wheeled away by the "boy with a truck." God forbid a mistake is made and the leaded page falls to the floor. The letters will fall out of the mold and the page will have to be made up all over again and a deadline will be blown. The only thing worse is when anyone other than a member of the printers union touches a typeset page—a union violation and not to be taken lightly. A call goes out and all work on the entire floor comes to a dead stop. I live in fear that I will forget that rule and accidentally reach out and touch a page out of curiosity.

After the leaded page is rolled away, a mold is made and it travels onto the next step, the printing press. The presses are so huge they take up the 5th, 4th, 3rd and 2nd floors of the building, and when they begin to spin and spit out the pages, the great roar begins and reporters can feel the power of those presses all the way upstairs in the newsroom. First you feel it in your feet, then your butt as the presses spin faster and faster. It is a constant, physical reminder that the day's work has produced a tangible result. You can relax but only for a time. The printing of tomorrow's paper has begun but there are still several editions to go, more chances to get your story in the front of the book or perhaps even the wood—the front page.

Finally, on the first floor of *The Daily News* building—on the opposite side of the lobby which is home to the great globe—the printed newspaper is spit out of the presses, bundled and loaded onto impressively solid trucks driven by pugnacious men who spit, curse and drink hard liquor. It is a wonderfully busy, happening place. And it goes on every night, at least five times for each edition. There is *nothing* when the reporters arrive each morning but by day's end, they have created this very entertaining, hard-charging tabloid newspaper that you can hold in your hands and read. And millions will. The paper brags that it has more circulation than any newspaper in America with over 2 million papers sold each day. How many others will read it is beyond calculation; it will be in subways and barbershops and homes, spread across the city.

And now I am a part of it. Everyday, sometimes several times a day, I pass the globe in the lobby and when I do, I remind myself just how lucky I am.

Editors and Reporters

My life revolves around the rhythms of the city room. Those first few days, I feel as though I'm in a fog. I make out shapes and job titles—reporter, editor, and photographer—not identities. There is too much here *here*. But days pass and distinct personalities, names and faces make themselves known. What was unknowable becomes familiar. The city room is large and editorial—the staff responsible for creating the content in the next day's paper—takes up the entire seventh floor of this landmark building. There are few offices in the city room itself, just row upon row of desks with men of all ages sitting in front of large manual Olympic or Royal typewriters. Female reporters—Marcia Kramer, Beth Fallon, Cass Vanzi—are in the minority. I can't imagine what it's like to be one of them in such a male-dominated world.

Early in the day, the clacking of the typewriters is muted. Everyone is in the beginning stages of reporting for the next day's paper. Some of the men are talking on their phones, some to each other. A lot of them are smoking, and many are laughing. It's a time to gossip and carry on. Someone says, *Hey look at this...* while reading the *Post* or the *Times.* Someone else yells *hey fuck face, what d'ya got today?* There is a fight for attention and the currency is funny stories and nuggets of information that can be turned into exclusives. Played right, they become front page news.

The beating heart of the city room is the city desk and there sits City Editor Dick Oliver. Oliver carries himself with the brio of a man who does not suffer fools lightly. I am not introduced to him. I'm far too unimportant for that. But I must, I am told, know who he is for my own survival. He's pointed out from afar, as in *that's Oliver, the city editor.* Watching him bark out orders, with his ever-present cigar sticking out of the corner of his mouth, his giant glasses, his ruddy complexion is to see a man at the height of his power. Dick Oliver = City Editor. Friends call him "Oli." I am not his friend.

He entertains at his desk, holds court and reporters suck up to him, do his bidding. They're afraid, maybe more than me. Oliver has the power to send them to Siberia—the lobster shift (midnight to 8 a.m.) or the newspaper's Long Island bureau. No one wants to be there. Everyone wants to be here, in this room, where tensions are high but careers are made. Oliver is the man who makes and breaks those careers. When he rises from the city desk to walk around the newsroom, he changes the temperature of the entire room. He's a jaguar of a man and he's been caged all morning. Now he's free, and everyone is apprehensive. Where will he pounce, who will he chew up? Oliver has the carriage of an overweight boxer with the pugnacious personality to match. He spends large amounts of time talking to reporter Vinnie

Lee, the 400-pound gentle giant who covers the fire department. But Vinnie is not at all like Oliver. He's got a more youthful, open face, and is a friend to the copyboys. Vinnie also has a slight speech impediment. It takes him forever to spit out what he's saying. But you don't mind because Vinnie is a good guy, someone who goes out of his way to look out for you. Vinnie is also in charge of "contracts" at the paper.

A contract, I soon learn, is code for "one hand washes the other." You do me a favor, I'll do one for you. If a Public Relations guy wants the paper to feature a "nice" story about his client the politician, the immediate question is, "What's in it for me?" Usually, the PR guy or the "flack" as he's universally called (because he catches the "flack" for his client) also represents a restaurant in addition to the politician. So, the paper writes a nice story about said politician and the reporter takes his lady love out to a fancy restaurant he could never afford on his salary. Contract fulfilled. As Vinnie is fond of saying, "A press card is better than an American Express Card because you never get the bill."

Vinnie and Oliver are friends and often laugh so hard at each other's jokes that both of them wind up red and coughing. But Oliver can turn in an instant. The coughing turns into a rebuke and before long, he is yelling at Vinnie about some story that didn't turn out right. It's a minstrel show and they both play their roles. In fact, they seem to relish it. Everyone remembers the time Oliver sent Vinnie to cover the opening of the Ringling Brothers circus when the elephants are paraded through the city streets as they arrive in town. The circus will do virtually anything for publicity and agrees to let Vinnie—all 400 pounds of him—ride atop an elephant. The next day, the news runs a photograph of Vinnie atop the elephant and also one of them standing side by side. Oliver is rumored to have written the caption himself which says: "Elephant (left) and reporter Vincent Lee (right)."

This newsroom possesses a raucous atmosphere and I am more than a little intimidated, yes I am. Nobody holds back, and I'm in the same room, a dirty, sweaty foul locker room. It is a cage match. The simmering tension is part joke, part anger. Everyone is looking to get something over on someone else, to have a story or a good laugh at your expense. Oli's second in command is an assistant city editor whose nickname is Cheech. It is Cheech's job to walk around the newsroom and check on how the stories slated for that day's paper are coming along. He's the in-house enforcer and it's perfect typecasting because nobody fucks with Cheech. Unlike a lot of guys at The News who like to pretend they're related to mobsters, Cheech is actually connected. Any problems? Something not panning out? He wants to know about it sooner than later. He is charming, your buddy, and your *paisan*. He walks around calling everyone "My Troop" or "Troupie," as in *"Hey Troupie, how ya doin?"* It's a term of endearment, meaning you're on Cheech's team.

Cheech is all Brooklyn and even owns a deli there to his great delight. Being a former reporter and now an editor is something to cherish, but the deli, that's what brings in the extra income. He tells me about it often, maybe because I told him I logged a few years in a deli and am something of an expert. I get the sense that Cheech is looking out for me, mainly because I'm Italian-American. He does not feel the same way about a recent hire, and when he finds out the guy graduated from Yale University, he lets the new guy know that he, the Great Cheech, is not impressed: *"Well boola*

boola ah fangoola. ”

While I am bewildered by a lot of what's going on around me and only understand about ten percent of all the complex relationships reporters and editors have with one another, I can't say it isn't fun. It is. Great fun. There are almost no rules for how to behave. Nothing is off-limits. People play pranks. Drink beers at their desks. Swear at the top of their lungs. Howl like animals. I am in a jungle. I must adapt, figure out how to become one of them.

I slowly come to realize that not all reporters are created equal. There are legmen and rewrite men. Legmen, like Vinnie, are reporters with great sources whose fingers never touch a keyboard. They're adept at getting information, cozying up to the blue-collar cops and firefighters but these legmen are definitely not writers so they "dump" their notes to rewrite men who know how to fashion a story in that quick-paced staccato tabloid style. General assignment reporter Don Singleton has a reputation for knowing how to write while Vinnie does not, so the two of them form the perfect team. Singleton is another of the friendly guys and a buddy of Vinnie's even though physically, he could not be more different. Singleton is skinny with longish hair and signature mutton-chop sideburns, a nod to the Sixties, the decade when he came of age.

I watch the reporters work and try to figure out what they do, how they unearth their stories, and how they carry themselves. Some have more time for copykids than others. The ones I'm most aware of are those who sit near the main copyboy bench. That's where Carlos the copyboy chief sits and fiddles with paperwork all day long. Carlos, with his pencil thin mustache, freckles, and fair complexion, seems eternally agitated. He is beleaguered. Someone always wants a favor from him, a favor he can't possibly deliver, at least not without getting an upset stomach in the process. I'm not a big fan but the desk where he sits is where the action is. A host of reporters work nearby and, as part of my education, I always try to place myself on that copy bench as opposed to one somewhere in the far reaches of the room. It would be easy enough to plop myself down there and read the newspaper until someone yells out "copy" but I wouldn't learn much. So near Carlos I sit.

Across from that copyboy bench sits one of the newspaper's star reporters, a 20-something-year-old guy named Sam Roberts. Sam sits sideways to the bench and whenever he writes, he cocks his head to the right and stares off into the middle distance just above our heads. At first I think he's looking at me or communicating some secret signal but no, Sam is just thinking. Sam is a political junkie and one of the new breed of reporters who are beginning to arrive at *The Daily News*. A lot of the older guys, like Vinnie Lee, are blue collar types, and you could picture them collecting garbage or driving a subway car just as easily as being a reporter. They are not deep thinkers. Somewhere along the line, they seem to have figured out that being a reporter is easier on the back than the Sanitation Department and so here they are. Not Sam. Sam is college-educated and more of a journalist than a reporter. I always hear him mumbling into his phone about Mayor Abe Beame or Governor Nelson Rockefeller. Sam has connections.

Sam is also not a big drinker. He's always working sources and then, when he gets what he wants, he positions his fingers on that huge manual typewriter, plasters a little smile on his face, and gets that faraway look in his eyes.

The whole newsroom is a mixture of the old and new, the blue collar types—the reporters who've been here since the Fifties and Sixties—and the college-educated journalists who are more serious and definitely more in control of their emotions.

Guys like Pete Coutros, a sweet, though hot-headed reporter who is one of the paper's featured writers, represent the old school of reporters. He doesn't cover a predetermined beat like politics or education. He covers life in New York and all its oddities. He's always trying to find the quirky little angle. Coutros is a legend, known for his sharp wit and equally sharp tongue that, coupled with his loud mouth, is a weapon unto itself. When Coutros was a caption writer, the photo of mobster Albert Anastasia, who was shot to death at a barber shop, landed on his desk. In minutes, he had the perfect caption—*"He finally got the chair."* And so, Coutros passed into legend.

With his a large head, impressive mane of black hair and coke-bottle black-rimmed glasses, Coutros looks a little like a Greek version of Dean Martin, but only if someone pressed down on Martin's head and made him a foot shorter. But, looks aside, Coutros's most distinguishing feature is his explosive temper. He's not an especially hard drinker, just someone driven by inner demons. He can be scary. One night in a bar, while Coutros and a couple of reporters were drinking and cursing at the speed of light, a patron politely asked if they'd tone it down because he and his friend were with their wives. Coutros jumped on the poor schmuck and literally tore off his shirt. The other reporters carried Coutros away and convinced him to apologize before the police were summoned.

On any given day, Coutros is liable to storm into the newsroom upset about some slight or a story that went awry and take it out on everyone around him. He screams curses, kicks over garbage cans, manhandles chairs and, on one very bad day, he takes a giant wooden window pole, gets a running start, and flings it like a javelin out an open 7th floor window down onto 41st Street between Second and Third Avenue. It's beyond a miracle no one is killed but Coutros never even receives a reprimand. Once he looks out the window and realizes there is no blood, he gets a little smile on his face and everyone around him explodes into laughter and expletives.

You fuckin' asshole.

Holy shit.

Coutros, are you out of your fuckin' mind?

He appears mildly sheepish at his display and calms down. And then everyone goes back to their desks. No one goes out to fetch the window pole.

Sitting near Coutros trying to survive all these shenanigans is another Greek-American reporter, a woman with unfortunate first name of Kiki. She is a handsome, serious woman, but looks like she's in a permanent state of shock given the shenanigans going on around her all the time. How she found herself in this newsroom is a mystery. She couldn't be more miscast in this crew of misfits. She is the newspaper's "society reporter" and when she yells out "copy" it is in a very distinguished voice that carries a hint of an upper crust New York accent. Behind her back, Coutros makes fun of her for no other reason than that she is more couth than nearly anyone else. Reporter Dan O'Grady comes up with the perfect line: "She doesn't cum," he says. "She arrives."

Everywhere in the newsroom, there are characters. And there are nicknames to go with this colorful cast. Gypsy, whose real first name is Eugene, is a composing room printer with a knack for hanging colorful nicknames on some of the newsroom regulars. "The Hat" is a copyboy who appears to have a knit cap permanently affixed to his head. "Captain Corpuscle" is Nightside City Editor Dick Blood for obvious reasons. "Quincy" is a rather effeminate copyboy. "Monique the Cruel" is a brassy copygirl who looks like she works part-time as a dominatrix. And on it goes.

Nearly every bizarre personality quirk is tolerated and most times celebrated, even when it gets close to the edge. There is a caption writer, a very large man, who drops hints now and again that is besotted by young boys. He even sends out a Christmas card of himself posing with a kid, and it becomes a running joke up until the day he doesn't come to work because he's been arrested for trafficking in child pornography. Turns out, *he* wasn't joking.

But he's not the only one here overindulging, far from it. No one has more of a fondness for prostitutes than Phil Mackey, a great rewrite who loves *his girls*. Mackey can be a great reporter but he has a decided weakness for chicks who charge. He has left standing orders that, if he dies suddenly of a heart attack, the city desk is to clean out his desk before letting his wife and family anywhere near it. Physically, Mackey has very little going for him. He's balding, wears glasses, is a bit older than everyone else, and has a body shaped like an egg. That he sometimes favors brown leather pants only adds to the general sense of perversity surrounding him. He is a rewrite man so he rarely leaves the office, at least not to report. But he does leave the office at lunchtime nearly every day to pursue his passion—hookers. As lunchtime approaches, he spreads the Village Voice open in front of him, takes a large magnifying glass out of his desk drawer, and carefully peruses the ads in the back of the newspapers for erotic massages and prostitutes. He is extremely fond of Asian women.

"Hey, here's a new one," I hear him say.

There is not a hint of shame attached to what he's doing; he is embarrassingly upfront --he's going out for a blowjob on his lunch hour. And everyone knows it. He disappears for an hour or so and comes back to regale everyone around him—even me—with stories of how that day's encounter went.

That was a very clean place.

You shoulda seen her.

She really knew what she was doing.

Mackey has a bit of W.C. Fields in him and his voice often is dripping with sarcasm and asides. Returning from his exploits one day when the weather is brutal outside, he approaches the reception desk where the ditzy Thyrza tells him, "It's so windy outside, I just got blown down the street."

Mackey does not even slow down. "That's funny, I just got blown around the corner."

It's that kind of place. Bad behavior is on display—proudly. A makeup man calls in sick from the wire room, just feet from the sports desk where he works, and spends the day sleeping off a hangover amid the click-clacking wire service machines. After the actor Freddie Prinze shoots himself in the head in a suicide attempt, a prominent news editor struts around cruelly repeating Prinze's stock phrase "Looking good" adding "not anymore." He does this over and over until someone tells him to shut the fuck up. That editor is particularly disliked by the copyboys because of his imperious attitude and one copyboy makes him pay. Every time he's forced to fetch coffee for this editor, the copyboy goes into the bathroom, spills out half and pisses in the rest. The editor never complains. Another copykid pees in his plant every single night, and listens with glee as the editor gets on the phone and complains to his wife about how, no matter what he does, his plants keep dying.

Arguments that nearly erupt into fistfights are routine. Joe Kovach, a news editor from Kentucky, is one of the nicest guys most of the time but he can be provoked when he's tired or feeling slighted. One night, someone changes one of Kovach's headlines, a fact he discovers when he's downstairs on the composing room floor. Given the deadline pressure, there is not much he can do, at least not at the moment but when he gets back to the city room, he demands to know who changed *his* headline.

Chile, the manic copydesk editor who never backs down, marches up to Kovach and tells him, "I did Joe." He goes on to tell Kovach exactly why his original headline sucked. Kovach is incredulous. Everyone in the newsroom has stopped what he or she is doing. Kovach outweighs Chile by about 100 pounds and one good arm. He could break Chile in half. But with everyone in the newsroom poised to call for an ambulance, Kovach gets a twinkle in his eye, looks at Chile and in his best Southern drawl, says: ""Goddammit Chile, I don't know what to do with you. You're too little to hit and too big to piss on."

Laughs cut the tension, at least until the next edition.

Coffee is the fuel that runs through the veins of every newsman. I never much liked coffee but, working here, I begin to drink buckets of it. Sometimes it tastes so sour not even the die-hard guys in the news room can stand another cup. That's what happens one night to Bill Umstead, a managing editor with a high-pitched voice and a lot of little boy in him. After taking one sip out of a bad cup of coffee, Umstead tells underling Joe Kovach that he's sick and tired of the swill he's drinking. "Why don't we try some hot chocolate tonight, Joe?"

Kovach looks like he'd rather get his teeth drilled but since Umstead is his boss, he agrees. Both of them retire to Umstead's office where the big boss painstakingly creates his hot chocolate.

Kovach emerges first with a cup of the stuff. He takes a sip and announces to one and all, "Ugh, this tastes like cow piss."

But then Umstead emerges with a shit-eating grin on his face, declaring, "Mm-um, I love this hot chocolate, Joe."

Kovach doesn't miss a beat. "Bill, I was just saying the same damn thing myself."

The copykids do a lot of work with the photographers because they're always out in the field. Reporters can simply phone in their notes to a rewrite man but not photographers. Their film has to be run back to the city room quickly so it can be processed in the darkroom. A lot of these runs are perfunctory. We're told to go to the East Side Bus Terminal or to some railroad track at Penn Station to meet a driver or conductor who has, for a $10 tip, carried some film back from Long Island to the city. The encounters have an air of mystery around them because we never know what conductors or drivers we're looking for. We mill about and more often than not, they find us.

You the kid from the News?

Yeah.

Here.

Those are the ordinary runs but the sports runs are far more fun. Many is the night I am sent to Madison Square Garden where I enter through the Press Gate, flash a temporary press card and head straight to courtside. I feel like a total big shot whenever I do this. I head down to the court itself, sidle up next to a photographer in the middle of shooting the game, and watch the Knicks run up and down the court. It is an otherworldly experience. Before I started working here, I never attended a professional basketball game in person. Now here I am watching the Knicks from the perspective of the players on the bench. They are gargantuan men and the sweat is flying and I am so close I can feel it hitting me. During a timeout, the photographer flips his most recent roll of film out of his camera, hands it to me with a few other rolls he's already shot, pulls out a paper envelope, writes something on the outside and gives me very specific instructions. *This is for the next edition so don't stop for a beer or a blowjob.*

I like the photographers because they're often a bit more friendly than the reporters and seem to have less on their minds. They also love to give advice. One day, I'm driving out to an assignment with Nicky, a seasoned veteran. He takes me to a diner where he brags that he always gets a free meal and schools me in his own brand of journalism. "The first rule? Never and I mean never leave the scene of a job without getting something for free," he says.

"Never?" I ask innocently.

"What did I just say?"

And then he gives me an example.

"One day, I was stumped. I had a job at a gas station, taking a shot of the owner for some cockamamie story. It killed me because I had just filled up my car with gas so I didn't know what I could get. Then it hit me. My doors were a little squeaky so I asked him to grease them up for me.

"See," he says proudly, "You always gotta be thinking."

And so I resolve to *always be thinking* and, the truth is, there is a lot to think about, a lot to see. The newspaper is filled with the names of the famous, people I've been reading or watching all my life. The venerable Dick Young is the chief sports columnist, Ed Sullivan—*the* Ed Sullivan (you know, the guy who introduced The Beatles to America?)—still writes an entertainment column and, though I rarely see the man himself (though Sal claims to have seen Sullivan walking the halls at 3 a.m.), he still has an office in a section of the feature department known as "Dream Street," named after yet another famous column. Bill Gallo, whose sports cartoons I've been reading for almost as long as I remember, is on hand with a cigar in his mouth and his heart on his sleeve. Gallo is a great guy who takes time to talk to everyone, even lowly, starstruck copykids like me. He's the best.

And then there are the newspaper's in-house legends, guys unknown outside the paper but infamous for what they've managed to pull off over the years. Guys like the painfully thin sports copy editor Eddie. These days, he's a marathoner but in his day, everyone whispers that he was an out of control alcoholic who, during one particularly inspired bender, scaled the globe in the lobby. *That* was so out of control that even Eddie realized it; he swore off alcohol, turned his life around and replaced booze with running.

And then there is Pat Doyle a.k.a. "The Inspector." Doyle works at Police Headquarters, and has since it was called the Police Shack. In fact, guys like Vinnie Lee and Cheech still call it that, as in, *Get me Doyle at the shack*. I had no idea what they were talking about until someone explained the old Police Headquarters on Centre Street would allow reporters to work out of an adjoining dumpy building called The Shack. The police have long since moved into their new headquarters just south of the Brooklyn Bridge, and have even agreed to accommodate reporters in offices on the second floor, but old-timers like Vinnie and Cheech never lost their fondness for calling even the new place The Shack.

No matter what the story, Doyle always has a quote from someone at the scene who says something like, "The gun shots sounded just like firecrackers." After the 50th witness said the exact same thing, everyone caught onto the fact that Doyle is what is known in the trade as "a pipe artist." He "pipes" the quotes out of thin air—makes them up. Not that Doyle makes up everything. He is an enterprising soul who travels to crime scenes outfitted in his trademark fedora and trench coat, clothes that make him look very much like a detective. Folklore has it that one day, after arriving on the scene, he told a cop he was "Doyle from Downtown," which technically he was. But the cop took him for a big shot from Police Headquarters, told him what happened and let him into the crime scene. Thus was born

"The Inspector." It wasn't long before "Doyle from Downtown" transmogrified into "Inspector Doyle." And he did nothing to disabuse the beat cops from thinking of him that way. Why bother when he was privy to information other reporters could only dream about?

With its mix of old-timers, newcomers, the famous and its own homegrown legends, *The Daily News* is one of the most interesting places to work that I ever could have stumbled into. It has everything, even its own bar—Louie's East.

Louie's East

On 41st Street, the presses ultimately spit out the day's newspapers to be bundled and hauled away. The whole day has led up to this moment, when those trucks lumber off, delivering the paper to newsstands all over the city. The workers left standing there—reporters, editors, pressmen, engravers, you name it—after a hectic day full of deadlines and shouting, need a break and there it is, in your face, right across from the truck bays, a bar with nothing and everything going for it—Louie's East, the paper's semi-official watering hole. It ain't pretty but it is nearby and, to many, a second home.

Why it is called Louie's East as opposed to just plain old Louie's is a mystery. I've never heard of a Louie's West. No one has. Louie's has perfected the art of being a great newspaper dive, pure and simple. I'm told there was once another bar nearby called The Fourth Estate but that was before my time. Now I have Louie's and only Louie's. Physically the exterior is dark and forbidding, and giant pressmen in blue coveralls are always standing outside, giving the bar a menacing appearance that it probably doesn't deserve. Louie's is the opposite of inviting and makes no attempt to attract passersby. It doesn't have to. This bar has a dedicated customer base of newspapermen who are on the job and thirsty for drink 24 hours a day, seven days a week.

Inside, the bar is as alive as the newsroom itself, only it is far more egalitarian. The clientele here includes reporters and editors, yes, but also the musclemen of the paper, the guys who wrestle with the physicality of putting out the daily editions—the pressmen, the drivers, the composing room stiffs and everyone in between. Everyone drinks at Louie's. Editors in suits and ties sit next to ink-stained pressmen wearing funny little folded paper hats made from the pages of the newspaper. The little hats perched atop the heads of these large men look vaguely ridiculous. Actually, strike the *vaguely*—they look ridiculous but no one dares make fun of them. The hats are a badge of honor that *distinguishes* the members of that union.

Louie's is a one-stop shop for whatever you need, and mostly what people need is cheap drink. The L-shaped bar is on the corner of 41st Street and Second Avenue; it bends around the corner so one can look out the dirty windows onto Second Avenue or 41st Street. Most of the workers hang out at the bar but there is an area for food at the back where you can get a sub or a corned beef sandwich. The food is barely digestible but if need to grab a quick bite between editions, it is handy. There is even a pinball machine and a bowling game. It is all very convenient and homey once you get to be a regular which, if you work at *The Daily News*, is a given.

I spend hours at Louie's even though I don't drink much. But everyone else does so to have some company, I join them. Dick Oliver and Vinnie Lee are often perched at the bar on the Second Avenue side. Vinnie spends a lot of time in Louie's where he works from the bar. He pulls the house phone over next to him and calls people on his firefighter beat—chiefs, captain and working stiffs—all day long. It's a beautiful thing because it works for both parties. Vinnie gets to mingle, as he loves to do, and the city desk knows exactly where to find him. Vinnie is a good guy and friendly and often calls me over, tries to get me to open up. He regales me with tales of previous regimes at the paper when the infamous Harry Nichols was the editor. I'm never completely sure what Vinnie is talking about but he is so invested in his stories that I pretend to understand. I listen and try to laugh at the appropriate times. Oliver usually sits there stewing or chatting up one of his reporters. As always, I steer clear. I don't need him sounding off on me. He's a dark presence but he does have talent, about that there is no doubt. He is a born tabloid editor and, as he talks, he gets ideas which he jots down on napkins. In the morning, he pulls the napkins out of his pockets and turns those ideas into front page stories.

There is one iron-clad rule at Louie's—no tabs. The owners insist on being paid then and there, even though most of its clientele comes back night after night. Still, it keeps problems to a minimum but it's also awkward at times. Copyboy Larry Celona recalls the night one sports reporter spent his last dime drinking and turned to Celona to borrow money to get home and to buy formula for his baby boy. Celona came through.

Celona is an interesting kid and, like me, a perfect example of a guy who has one foot in each world *The Daily News* inhabits. His father runs a fish store out in Brooklyn but Celona himself is college-educated and graduated from St. John's. He was meandering through St. John's taking business courses, not really knowing what he was going to do with his life, when one day Daily News police reporter Eddie Kirkman happened by as a guest speaker. Kirkman, dapper and with more than a little panache, explained what a police reporter does and threw in a few stories about the raucous atmosphere at The News. Celona was hooked and now he's here with me, trying to figure it all out, confident it's way more fun than whatever he would've done with a business degree. We become close friends, and he tells me about the day he knew for sure that working in the tabloid trade was for him.

"I was down at the pay window and the guy in front of me had on a leather jacket and tattoos all over his arms."

He found out the guy, who looked like a longshoreman, actually was Don Gentile, a top notch reporter. The pay window was where everyone would line up to cash their paychecks but that's not all. On occasion, the City Desk would give a reporter a voucher he could cash in for expense money needed on a story. That's why Gentile was there. The Desk had given him $200 to spend at some of the illegal after-hours clubs that were operating all over the city as mini-casinos. Gentile was to use the money to gain access to the clubs and gamble the night away, all the while taking notes in his head for the story.

"I thought to myself, 'what a great job!'" Celona said.

The Copykids

The thing about the newspaper that I come to love is that it's always open. Any hour of the day, I can walk into that glorious lobby, take the elevator up to the 7th floor newsroom, and find someone that I know. There's a sense of belonging and, as the months pass, I come to know quite a few people, especially the other copykids. I am now doing pretty much what I did in those early years in the projects—sitting on a bench having conversations about life. I know how to do this.

The term copykids, which we derisively call ourselves, is of course a misnomer. We'd all be copyboys if not for the handful of women now being hired. For them the atmosphere is especially predatory. One reporter makes a point of writing a note to each female hire, inviting them out for an introductory drink. It's really a type of interview to see if he can get into their pants. Most of them take him up on the drink but ignore all the rest.

The staff of copykids is a mixed bunch from all over the city and its suburbs but we're most certainly *not* kids. Most of us have graduated college. Others—the sons and daughters of the well-to-do—are just slumming on their way to careers in finance and real estate at one of daddy's companies. Some are waiting for graduate or law school slots to open up. For still others, who have not graduated from college and never will, this is a full time steady gig where they hope to make enough dough to support a family.

The personalities are endless. There are the pseudo-intellectuals who sit around reading Thomas Pynchon novels and discussing philosophy. One especially pretentious guy with a French surname makes a great show of sitting on the bench and reading *Le Monde*, as if that would impress anyone in this place. There are the budding alcoholics who spend a little too much time in Louie's going shot for shot with men twice their age. There are the angry silent types who glare and read folded up newspapers, cursing their lowly jobs, feeling cheated that they are not already famous writers.

And then there are those we fear are mentally ill, like the copyboy who walks around the newsroom straightening out twisted phone lines and picking up teensy-weensy bits of paper wherever he sees them. (And given the number of newspapers flung all over the place, this is a fulltime job.) But even he has found a home here. He's trusted to the degree that one night he is given the task of driving Bill Umstead to his White Plains home. No one thinks twice about entrusting one of the paper's top execs to someone with obvious and severe personality problems. And so off they go except that, somewhere along the route, Umstead notices that the copyboy, let's call him Jimmy, is not wearing his glasses.

"Say Jimmy," says Umstead in his high-pitched Southern drawl, "I notice you're not wearing your glasses tonight."

"No sir."

"Do you just need them for reading?"

"Uh, no sir, I need them for driving."

With that, Umstead orders the kid to pull over, switches seats and drives Jimmy to his White Plains home where he insists the kid spend the night on the couch. Jimmy complies but later sneaks away to phone the overnight copyboy, whose nickname is Crafty, to ask a favor: will he please go into the features department and blow out the dozens of candles he'd lit earlier that evening?

The paper is a melting pot of the strange, and a place where I feel strangely at home. There are a lot of fellow copykids that I like very much and I become true friends with a few of them who make a real effort to reach out to me.

One of my closest friends is Tom Tomasulo, a copyboy whose father works in the newspaper's promotions department. Tom, who is thin with eyes that appear ready to pop out of his skull, has incredible energy, so much energy that it rubs off on everyone around him. He can barely sit still. He is always up on his feet, ready to race around whenever a reporter shouts "copy." Tom is curious and loves to talk and he's forever peppering me with questions about where I live and what kind of car I drive and who my favorite rock band is. Tom loves two bands in particular, bands that possess his kind of energy—The Rolling Stones and The Who. For Tom, the two Keiths—Keith Richards and Keith Moon—are gods and he has seemingly memorized all the bands' songs. Tom is always inviting me to hang with him and friends out on Long Island each weekend and I find myself joining him and his friends driving around the island in a never-ending search for women.

Another Italian-American who makes a special effort to get to know me—clearly attracted by our common ethnic heritage—is a copyboy with the mellifluous name of Lorenzo Carcaterra. Lorenzo is also from the Bronx and attended my high school's most hated rival Mount St. Michael. Lorenzo wants to be a *writer* so bad he can taste it. He's always talking about Gay Talese, *Esquire Magazine*, and his mother's cooking, not in that order. He aggressively tries to make connections with editors at the paper and is always pitching story ideas to them, stories that he wants to write. It's not unheard of. The copykids are free to write stories for the newspaper's feature sections if we come up with a good enough idea and Lorenzo is forever trying to come up with a good enough idea. I admire his tenacity and it pushes me to do the same just because I'm a little jealous of how much he wants it. I realize that if I ever want to get ahead I should be a lot more like him.

Another close friend at the paper is Scott Mitchell. Scott is from Manhattan and grew up only blocks from *The Daily News* in midtown. He also has an older sister who is some kind of publishing executive and for all those reasons, I think of Scott, who smokes constantly, as someone who's sophisticated. He even has his own apartment, a first-floor studio up in the East 70's in one of those buildings that depresses me for its sheer lack of imagination. His apartment is not much to look at—his loft bed is in the living room which faces the street—but it's more than I have and we spend hours there, talking about writers, and drinking. It's not really a party, more of a low-level therapy session in which each of us takes turns talking about why we can't get laid.

My other close friend at the newspaper is Deb, my old fantasy girlfriend from Fordham. She gets in touch with me after graduation and tells me she's looking for a job and I recommend her to Quinn who miraculously hires her. It's great to have Deb around but I'm always a little nervous around her, mainly because I'm still hoping that I'll somehow convince her to have sex. It never happens. We stay friends but it pains me to watch her chase other guys at the newspaper, including one who becomes a well-known sportswriter. Still, she's grateful that I helped get her the job and she remains my friend as boyfriend after boyfriend fall by the wayside.

When we're not all sitting around having bull sessions, we are ordered to do things that are just this side of maddening. Imagine spending hours feeding pencils into an electric sharpener, or being asked to create four-books and six-books, basically a piece of typing paper stapled to the same sized carbon paper. Four-book have four pieces of paper and three pieces of carbon paper and six-books have six pieces of paper and five sheets of carbon paper. We spend hours stapling hundreds of them together so they can be used by the reporters writing their stories. They feed one of these books into their typewriters and when they get to the bottom of the page, they type the word "more" to indicate another page of copy will follow, or "30" or "endit" to indicate that's it—this particular story is over. A reporter will then remove the top sheet that goes to the city desk and keep the others on his spike so he can refer to what he's already written. Hard and fast newspaper deadlines demand that stories are written and delivered one page at a time. The city desk will be editing the first page of the story before the second page is even written. Amazingly, this system works.

There are a great many newspaper terms that I learn through osmosis, just listening and being commanded to do this or that. The commands are given in such a way that assumes you know exactly what the person giving the orders is talking about. To ask a question would make one seem stupid, or at least that's how I see it and the reason I find out the hard way just what a dummy book is.

One day, Carlos says to me, "Paul, go downstairs and get the suburban dummies."

"Sure thing Carlos."

And so I'm off, having no idea of what said "dummies" are or where exactly it is downstairs that I'm supposed to find these.

I go downstairs and kind of wander around, telling one person after another, "I'm here to pick up the suburban dummies," or a variation, "Do you know where the suburban dummies are?"

Here are some responses I get:

Kid, there are a lot of dummies down here but I don't know where they're from.

Take your pick.

Dummies? Hey, this kid is looking for dummies. Joe, I guess that means you.

On and on it goes. I keep feeding various men this great opening line and boy, do they knock it out of the park. I get so frustrated I think I might cry. I consider going upstairs to ask Carlos what he meant but that would just get him pissed. So I soldier on until some kindly guy points me in the right direction, to a guy with thick glasses who hands me a small, stapled book filled with mostly empty pages. This

dummy book, I learn, is precisely what tomorrow's suburban section of the newspaper will look like. It's a stand-in
or a *dummy* for the real thing, and it shows an editor how
many ads have been sold, what pages they're on, and how
big the news hole is. By looking at this, the editor can figure
out how much room he has for how many stories the next
day. This dummy book is kind of a smart thing. Unlike me.
I am the real dummy.

Friends in The Daily News *newsroom on a quiet Saturday*

Some days are better than others. The job has more than
a few perks. For one thing, I can always bring home a free
copy of tomorrow's newspaper. And sometimes I get to drive
the radio cars on errands all over the city. The News has a
garage across the street next to Louie's and it keeps a fleet
of blue Fords, many of which have *The Daily News* logo
printed on the side. The cars are called radio cars because
they have two-way walkie-talkie radios whereby the driver

can communicate with the photo and city desks. Mainly, the radio cars are for the photographers. Unlike reporters, who can do a lot of work by phone, the photographers are mostly out in the field, hustling from one job to another.

Sometimes, the copykids are told to grab a radio car to drive to some location to pick up film or take a reporter out to the scene of a crime. It is always an adventure because the cars are kept in the same garage as the delivery trucks, usually on the top floor. Many is the time I have to drive a car down circular ramps with hairpin turns while an experienced driver is flinging his truck around those turns as though no one could ever possibly be coming the opposite way. I sometimes come face to face with a delivery truck and veer out of the way at the last moment to avoid winding up on his front bumper. I'm pretty confident he would not stop to report the accident.

But I love driving those cars because, when I do, I feel like a big shot, talking on the radio and watching people's reactions when they see that I am driving a Daily News radio car. Yeah, that's right! I work for *THE DAILY NEWS*!

One day, I am picking up film in the Bronx and I realize that the job will take me pretty close to the projects where I still live with my parents and brother and sister. I decide to show off and drive my car into our parking lot. I go upstairs and find whoever is home, my mother and my brother, and drag them out to see the car. They do seem kind of impressed and my brother even plays with the radio a bit before the photo desk begins barking orders at *"whoever the fuck is on the radio to get the fuck off."*

Okay, then. I walk them back to our apartment and exit a short time later. Unfortunately, I see that, now, our latest pack of wild dogs is circling the car, almost like they can tell it is different. There is no way I can get back in without getting attacked and yet, I feel like I better get going because I've been out a very long time on this run, and don't want to get in trouble. I ponder what to do and then go upstairs and steal some hamburger meat from the refrigerator. I go back to the parking lot, yell at the dogs and then toss it a safe distance away. The second they chase it, I run to the car and make my getaway.

Best of Times, Worst of Times

As time goes on, I cannot imagine having a more fun job. I am proud to say I work at *The Daily News*. The paper is alive. In fact, it's on fire. It has great editors who begin to make the first substantive changes at that paper since the end of World War II. Liz Smith is hired and begins to write one of the first daily gossip columns in the city. Jimmy Breslin, the quintessential New York columnist, comes on board, and then right behind him comes Pete Hamill. Both grew up in New York but they are very different men. Breslin is Breslin, a caricature of the big city newspaper columnist who seems lost in his own interior world, walking around with a notebook and pencil, grumbling and mumbling to himself about unseen enemies. He's forever smoking and growling and trying to get people to do favors for him. I can't seem to break through his cloud of cigar smoke and the most meaningful interaction I ever have with him is fetching grilled cheese and tomato sandwiches from the 4th floor cafeteria.

Pete Hamill is nearly the exact opposite. Hamill is very approachable, friendly and willing to engage anyone—even copyboys—in discussions about the news, art, and writing. It's almost like the word "gentleman" was coined for him. Hamill is a very decent guy, and that is a huge compliment in this newsroom full of runaway egos. Although he's the son of Irish immigrants, Hamill is a worldly man. He is strikingly handsome and, no surprise, he squires around a lot of women, some of them quite famous.

Hamill, like Breslin, is always writing books on the side and at one book party, held at a spacious restaurant at West 57th Street and Sixth Avenue, he invites the entire staff. The restaurant is packed, and Hamill holds court somewhere up front, talking to people and signing books. I can barely see him and am just taking it all in when the atmosphere in the room changes. What was exciting before becomes hyperkinetic. There are a lot of photographers present and they all begin taking photos of an unseen presence moving toward Hamill. Flashes from the photographer's cameras are non-stop and then I see why. Jacqueline Kennedy Onassis is walking toward Hamill. It's been rumored that the two of them are dating but I had no idea if it was true. After tonight, everyone will know it is. It is remarkable, really, and a testament to Hamill that such an intensely private person as Jackie O would wade into a roomful of journalists and photographers. She must really like him.

It's not long before another rumor shoots through the newsroom. I am on the copyboy bench one day when I hear someone gossiping about us getting a new copykid, in fact a copygirl. Some of us who are around that day are warned to *act normal* around her. I'm intrigued but don't think much more about it. I am sitting there reading a copy of the four-star final when I catch sight of her—Caroline Kennedy! She has come to join us, working as a copykid for a summer. I can barely speak. It is little more than a decade since JFK was assassinated and I, like millions of other Americans, watched her family get through the ordeal on national television. Now this daughter of our most admired modern president is sitting next to me—me, son of blue collar parents, a guy still living in a public housing project—on the copyboy bench. In what universe does this happen?

Caroline looks very young, and is a couple of years younger than I am. She's shy and doesn't say much and I'm of course tongue-tied but manage to introduce myself. We are told there are photographers poised outside the building, waiting to get a photo of the president's daughter working at this low-level job, and the paper acts before they do, taking an "official" photo of her sitting on the bench that is sent out to the Associated Press. I am not in the photo but one of my colleagues is and it would be hard to underestimate my jealousy.

That one photo does nothing to satisfy the true paparazzi who continue to stake Caroline out. So one slow news day, Oliver decides to have some fun. He asks a copygirl named Mary Beth McMahon, who is willowy thin with the same strawberry blonde hair color as Caroline, to impersonate her. Mary Beth, or MB as we call her, does not really look like Caroline but there is a slight resemblance. Oliver outfits MB with a pair of dark sunglasses, instructs her to wear her long hair down so it obscures her profile, and sends her down to Louie's on a coffee run. Someone phones in a tip to the Associate Press and, as MB leaves Louie's, she is surrounded by paparazzi. You would think experienced news photographers would be able to recognize someone like Caroline who has lived nearly her entire life in front of their cameras. But as usual, Oliver is right—they don't recognize MB as an imposter. Instead, they shout questions at her, she mumbles a few "no comments" and by the time she makes her way upstairs to the city desk, a photograph of "Copygirl Caroline Kennedy on a coffee run" is sent into the newsroom via the AP wire. It is great fun for one and all but no one enjoys the prank more than Oliver.

Fantasies run through my head. I wonder if Caroline would ever go out with the likes of me? What if she becomes my girlfriend and visits the projects? What would that be like? What if we were married and I became Jackie O's son-in-law? None of this happens of course. I do get to show Caroline a few jobs around the newsroom when she seems to be confused and I joke with her that she's going to have to move faster to make it as a copykid. She even joins us for a drink one day after work but that's about as far as I get. There is no after-work romance between us and, almost as soon as she appears, she is gone. It was surreal while it lasted.

The whole city is open to us. We're young and we're up at all hours of the night. Many times, I work the 4 p.m. to midnight shift and instead of going home, I knock back a few beers at Louie's, get in my car and go looking for fun, trouble or both. The night has all sorts of possibilities. There are always free screenings of the latest movies complete with press parties, and I learn from feature writers and photographers about press events and where celebrities hang out.

That's how I wind up at the first screening of Francis Ford Coppola's "Apocalypse Now," the most eagerly-awaited movie in the world.

Some nights, I come face to face with famous people. *Saturday Night Live* begins in 1975, the year I start working at The News, and the cast is always out and about at some bar or club. One night, I find myself at a party with Gilda Radner and, before I know what comes over me, I begin regaling her with jokes. Not good jokes, mind you, just the corniest of cornball jokes but Gilda is a great sport and laughs at nearly all of them. For 20 minutes or so, it is just me and Gilda, pushed up against the wall of a club. We've both had too much to drink and are laughing our heads off but, before I can make any more of a fool out of myself, someone grabs her arm and pulls her away. But wow! I don't care. I've hung out with one of the coolest people in New York.

Another night, a photographer lets me tag along to a press event where the actress Candice Bergen will introduce a new perfume she's promoting called CIE. I have been in love with Candice since the 1971 film *Carnal Knowledge* starring her, Art Garfunkel, Jack Nicolson and Ann-Margaret. To think that I will be physically present at an event with Candy, as I call her in my fantasies, is almost too much. I bring along a notebook and decide to play reporter at the event. We are ushered into a VIP room filled with glitter and satin curtains where, seconds later, Candy appears. I am sitting just feet away as she delivers her perfume spiel and then invites questions. The photographer I am with is snapping away next to me. "Get her to look this way," he whispers in my ear.

Somehow I get up the nerve to say, "Candice, can you tell us again how you came up with this fragrance?"

Incredibly, Candice Bergen—*the* Candice Bergen—turns to look me in the eye and smiles, the same smile she used to bewitch the Garfunkel and Nicholson characters in one of my favorite movies. It is a softball question that gives her ample opportunity to shill for her pet project one more time. I don't dare breathe as she answers, the light sparkling off her eyes just as it did in the movie. She smiles and answers my question in a few sentences before someone else chimes in and she turns her head away. I feel as though I cannot move. I do not move until the photographer pulls me away and tells me to run the film back to the photo desk in hopes of making the next day's new People Page. I am so excited I literally run the 20 blocks to the newsroom, and wait while the film is developed. When the right photo is chosen by the photo editor, I steal one away for my private collection.

In this no holds barred atmosphere, it's not surprising that sometimes things get out of hand. An especially curvaceous copygirl, who has the looks of a Mormon porn star, files a formal complaint against a photo editor, claiming that he's undressing her with his eyes every time she walks anywhere near him. He's not alone. We're all undressing her, even some of the women, but this one editor is so obvious about it that she feels compelled to file a complaint. In this atmosphere of booze, long hours, tension, and a bevy of good-looking 20-somethings, it's only natural that people are getting laid in all sorts of places at all times of the night.

But little compares with the copykid parties, which get especially frisky. One night, a copykid gets bounced from a party, held in Queens at the apartment of one of the more mature copykids who has a wife and child. It seems the host caught the raucous copykid shooting up heroin in his bathroom. But that's not the reason he gets thrown out—that happens when he puts his cigarette out on the host's carpet, raising the hackles of his young wife. At another party, copyboy John Clerkin (a fellow Hayesman who is another one of my "hires") walks into a bathroom to find two guys from the paper having a three-way with a woman in the shower. With the door as wide open as Clerkin's mouth, one of the guys in the shower—at that moment getting a blow job—looks over Clerkin and says, "We'll be finished with her in a minute."

My nights become a blur of bar, clubs and discos, and, while I almost always drink and drive, I hold back from doing any drugs, not even cocaine which is ubiquitous to the New York nightlife. A copyboy who is known for his outrageous outfits—he once wore a tophat during his shift in the city room and another time dyed his hair orange—is a health food nut who is always talking about taking shots of wheatgrass. What he talks about less are the massive bags of cocaine he hauls around that are the size of five-pound Domino sugar bags. Cocaine and wheatgrass—somehow it's not surprising in this atmosphere.

One night, the heroin-shooting copyboy gets hammered while working the lobster shift (midnight to 8 a.m.) and about an hour before the city editor is due to report in, gets hungry and begins eating a giant sandwich he'd ordered earlier in the evening. He's halfway through the sandwich when his night gets the best of him. He falls asleep with his feet on the city desk and the sandwich in his mouth. When the city editor gets there—at that point it's Sam Roberts recently promoted from his reporting duties—the copyboy is frozen in place. Sam calmly wheels the copyboy, sandwich and all, into an empty conference room and distributes the early papers himself. When the head of copyboys reports in, Sam motions to the conference room, "There's one of yours in there."

I float from bar to party and back with a coterie of various copykids, and begin to have the sort of social life I could only have dreamed of in college. I'm *still* living in the projects but, almost out of spite, I spend almost no time there. I am determined to discover something new and take Manhattan by storm or at least as much of a storm as a Catholic school boy from the Bronx can ever hope for.

I hit all the clubs and am often allowed entrance simply because I have a Daily News ID card. One night, I find a long line outside of the Mudd Club, a punk club on White Street that is a competitor to CBGB's. I flash my Daily News ID and am inside seconds later, dancing to a new group called the B-52s. Another night—actually on Halloween—I go to Xenon, a disco that is a poor man's Studio 54, and find myself pushed up against a wall where I spot Tony Curtis sharing a joint with a beautiful young blonde. Jamie Lee Curtis, star of the movie "Halloween," is nowhere in sight to watch dear old Dad.

Studio 54 proves hardest to gain entrance to. *The Daily News* ID does me no good but, one day, features writer Ernie Leogrande, an incredibly generous man—who provides an extra ticket another night so I can witness a young up-and-coming comedian named Robin Williams do standup—gives me his invite to Studio 54. I take along Dinah, a copygirl with long blonde hair who knows how to dress in an eye-catching way. The combination of her quirky coolness and my press invite gets us past the velvet rope and the giant bouncer. The excitement builds as we walk down a narrow corridor toward the giant bar and dance floor. Men naked from the waist up are everywhere and a fog machine is pumping in smoke all around us. It is a wild, exciting atmosphere, the inner sanctum where Andy Warhol, Liza Minnelli and even Mick Jagger have been known to hang out. I am wide-eyed and visit the club's infamous men's room where I find dozens of men and women crowded into the same space, snorting line after line of cocaine in full view of one and all. I stumble out to find Dinah and we dance the night away to a new song that plays over and over—"Macho Man" by the Village People.

It's inevitable that I will cross a line and it happens the night before Mother's Day, 1977. I've been out all night with Dinah down in the Village where we see an up and coming young singer named Rickie Lee Jones. Rickie is sublime, Dinah is Dinah and, after I drop her off at her upper West Side apartment, I pass another one of those street hookers who are always motioning to me. I usually smile and wave and pass them by with a laugh. I know they think I'm an easy mark because I'm a young guy driving by myself late at night. They *think* they know what I want but they have no idea, especially on this night when all I really want to do is to get home and go to sleep. I pass these women all the time; they are everywhere from Central Park South to the entrance to every tunnel and bridge in town. It's almost impossible to get home *without* passing a streetwalker. You'd think the cops would do something about this…yeah, you would think.

On this warm night, my window is open and the hooker in question starts barking and waving at me as they always do. I smile and wave back. The traffic is backed up so I'm in this one spot longer than I'd like, and she keeps talking to me.

"Come on honey, I know what you want."

"Right."

"You know I do."

I look at the traffic. It's not moving so I turn back to her. "So what do I want?"

"You tell me."

I yawn, and turn my head back to the traffic when, out of the corner of my eye, I see man's head at the driver's side window. I look at him and begin cranking the window closed.

"Sir, shut off the car and step out," he says.

Oh shit, he's got a badge hanging from his neck and a gun in his hand.

"Officer, I wasn't doing anything. I'm just trying to get home."

"Sir, get out of the car."

Fuck.

I step out of the car, and he immediately turns me around, puts handcuffs on my wrists, and frisks me.

"Look officer, I wasn't doing anything and if you'll look in my wallet, you'll see a Daily News ID card. I was working late and I'm heading home."

It's a lie, and I don't even know why I say that except it sounds better than saying I was at a concert in the Village.

The cop does exactly what I ask him, and then calls another cop over. They confer a few moments, put the ID card back in my wallet and the wallet back in my pocket. And then, without a word, they put me in the back of a squad car.

Fuck.

One of them pulls my car over, parks it and I am driven to the Midtown South stationhouse. When I get there, they put me on a bench where I have plenty of company. Seems like my hooker/undercover cop is very good at what she does. And, honestly, she does look pretty good in her short skirt and boots. It's no wonder there are at least five other guys sitting next to me. She's in the stationhouse too, lording it over us, strutting back and forth, smiling and motioning toward us while she laughs and fills out paperwork with her male buddies.

I feel my heart begin to race. I'm sweating and I know if I could touch my head, it would be ice cold. I feel like I might faint. I try to slow down my heart by taking deep breaths. The cop who examined my ID looks over at me.

"You okay?"

"Not really, I think I'm having a panic attack."

He comes over and look at me more closely. "Shit, you're sweating like a pig. You're not gonna have a fucking heart attack or anything, right?"

I sense an opening and decide this time that the truth is my best option. "Look officer, I'm not married so I have nothing to hide but I do have claustrophobia and I'm freaked out about spending any time in a jail cell. I'm having a panic attack. Isn't there anything you can do? Please."

This cop actually looks somewhat sympathetic to what I'm telling him.

"Okay, okay calm the fuck down."

He puts me on a bench by myself and goes over to his supervisor again, and then they come over to me. "Okay look," the supervisor says. "I'm gonna let you call whoever you want. Here's the deal. I can give you a desk appearance ticket if you come up with $200 as a guarantee that you'll show up in court in the morning. Come up with the 200 bucks and you can walk tonight. But you gotta come to court in the morning, understood?"

"Tomorrow's Sunday. It's Mother's Day."

"I don't care if it's fucking Christmas. You gotta show up or I'll come out to wherever the fuck you live and haul your ass back to jail, understood?"

"Yes sir."

He walks me over to a phone and takes off the cuffs. I think about who I can call who will have $200 in cash. Not a lot of people carry that kind of money. There are a few of those new cash machines sprinkled around the city but the only one I've ever seen is in the lobby of The News building and I don't have a card to get the cash out. I do have money in my room at home. I think about calling my brother but then my mother would find out. The last thing she needs is to hear I've been arrested.

My friend Scott might have the money and lives in Manhattan but then I remember that he's out of town. Tom would lend me the money but he lives on Long Island. And then I remember that there is a petty cash box at the city desk filled with about $500 in cash. I know an editor named Jean is on duty and she's pretty cool. But do I really want everyone at work to know that I've been arrested for soliciting a prostitute, even though it's a completely bullshit charge?

While I'm considering what to do, the sympathetic cop comes over to me. "Well, do you have anyone you can call to lend you the money?"

"Yeah but I don't want them to know I've been arrested for this."

"No sweat," he says. "Just tell them you were in a bar fight. I'll vouch for you if anyone asks."

"Really?"

"Yeah, make the call. You need to get out of here. You look like shit."

I don't think he really had to say that again but who am I to argue? I do need to get the fuck out of here. I call Jean on the city desk and tell her what happened.

"You were in a bar fight?" she says incredulously.

It's not exactly my reputation.

"Yeah, I had too much to drink and one thing led to another and do you think you can come down with the money? I promise I'll return it tomorrow."

There is a pause that feels about two hours long and then she says, "Okay, I'll be there in about a half hour."

For the next 30 minutes my eyes are glued to the door of the holding cell. Will she really come? And will the cops play dumb and not tell her the truth? Finally, the door opens and I can see Jean just past the cop. "LaRosa, get out here."

"Jean, thanks for coming."

I want to kiss her but settle for a quick hug. Luckily she doesn't ask too many questions and the cop does his part, lying on my behalf about some make-believe bar fight. Jean leaves and the cop hands me a desk appearance ticket.

"See you tomorrow morning. Remember what I said."

"I'll be there."

I get home around 3 a.m. Thankfully, everyone in my apartment is asleep and I can hear my brother snore as I open my top drawer and make sure that I have $200 to return to the city desk. I do, just barely. I set the alarm for eight a.m. but it hardly matters—I don't sleep at all.

The next morning I wish my mother a happy Mother's Day and tell her I have to do something at work but that I'll be home in time to go out to dinner. At least I hope I'll be back in time. I still have to go to court.

I arrive at Criminal Court to see the johns who were arrested with me the night before yawning and stretching just past the bar. I'm on the other side of the bar in the audience. The cop who arrested me gives me a smile and motions me over. "That guy over there, he's the legal aid lawyer. Go talk to him."

I go over and start to explain the situation but all he says is "What's your name?"

I tell him and he looks at the list. "Why did they let you go home?"

"I work for *The Daily News* and I guess they did me a favor."

He looks at me for the first time. "What do you do there?"

"I'm a city desk assistant."

"Okay, okay. First offense?"

"Yes sir."

"Don't lie to me."

"I'm not, and it was entrapment."

"Yeah, yeah, that's what they all say. Okay go sit down until I call your name."

I sit down and notice that the woman next to me is the undercover cop/hooker, the reason I'm here in the first place.

"Hi," she says.

"If I say 'hi' back, will you arrest me again?" I ask.

She laughs. She has changed out of her "hooker" outfit and looks quite young. If I saw her in a bar, I'd try to pick her up.

"I didn't do anything, you know that."

She shrugs. "Look, the boys were a little aggressive last night but, once they arrested you, there was no going back."

"Great."

"Hey I'm sorry."

She smiles at me and she is so attractive that I briefly consider asking her out. I shake my head. I'm out of my mind. I need sleep and need to get out of here.

"Look, I'll make sure you get out of here, okay?"

"That would be most appreciated."

She goes over and I see her whisper in the ear of some lawyer I assume is on the prosecution side of things. He looks over at me and nods.

Soon after, I hear my name called and step up to the judge. "Your honor," says the legal aid lawyer. "This is Mr. LaRosa's first offense and furthermore, he is a member of good standing of the community, and has a job working for *The Daily News*."

The judge looks over at me, looks down at some papers, and addresses the assistant district attorney. "Any objections?"

"No your honor," the ADA says. "Given that it's Mister LaRosa's first offense, the city is willing to dismiss the charge—this time only."

"Very well," says the judge. "You are free to go but the next time, it will be a different story."

"Yes sir," I say.

I try to shake my lawyer's hand but he's already onto the

next case. A court clerk tells me they'll send me a check for the $200. So I leave, and the moment I exit the courtroom doors, I feel immense relief. It's almost like I haven't been able to breathe for the past 12 hours and now suddenly have some life. I think the words "you're free to go" are the most beautiful words in the English language.

"Told you I'd take care of you."

I look over and it's the undercover cop/hooker beaming.

"Thanks."

She still looks great and the way she's standing there, it feels like she does want me to ask her out. I open my mouth to ask but then I think better of it. I just can't. Every time I looked at her, I'd be reminded of this night.

"Thanks," I mumble and quickly leave the courthouse.

I hustle up to the city desk to return the money and then, on my way home, I buy my mother some flowers with all the money I have left—five bucks.

Work

As much fun as the nightlife is, I never lose track of the reason I'm at the newspaper—I want to be promoted to reporter and make a living doing what I love most, being a writer. It's certainly a possibility. Many of the old-timers started as copyboys and, even though the newspaper is changing and trying to get more *professional*, I tell myself that I'm just what the new Daily News is looking for—I'm from the real New York *and* I have a college degree. I'm still unsure of myself around people, and feel that I'm lacking some fundamental social skills—some kind of secret way of behaving possessed by everyone but me—but I vow to push myself, even if that means behaving as someone I'm not.

It's not easy, but forcing myself into uncomfortable situations begins to work. The change happens slowly, as I move up the paper's food chain and do jobs that require me to think. I begin to make a lot more than the $127 a week I started at. For that, I can thank the Newspaper Guild, the union that represents the reporters, photographers and other editorial personnel. The Guild has strict rules so that anytime I fill in at a job out of my group, I make a lot more money. The overall pay scale goes from Group 1, the copy-boy level, to Group 10, the reporter level. Less than a year in, I am trusted with jobs that have more responsibility, like filling in as a city desk assistant, a person who operates the telephone switchboard and works closely with the city desk editors. It is a Group 8, not too much lower than what a reporter makes and way more than my father ever made at the Railway Express Company where he worked since I was born. Even with his new elevator operator job, I still make more than he does.

There are no names on the switchboard and I am expected to remember the extensions for dozens of reporters, rewrite men, copy editors, news editors, features writers, caption writers and on it goes. Mostly, I'm scared shitless that I'll make a mistake. The start of the day is easy as calls come in from readers commenting on the previous day's stories. Some are upset that we've featured a photo of a cop dressed as Santa Claus carrying a gun.

What idiot approved that?

Doncha know my kids are gonna see that?

How am I gonna explain that to them?

Other readers call in with tips about some news event they think they've seen. Still others want to recount sad stories of dealings with cops, deliverymen, kids in their neighborhood, and it's up to me to figure out which of these tips might result in an actual story for tomorrow's paper. It's an important job because I am the public's point of contact with the newspaper. I take it seriously and try to unearth stories to pass along to the city desk. I am very proud when one sometimes makes it into print.

Then there are times when nuts call in. I usually humor them for a while but, if they're especially obnoxious and refuse to hang up, I use one of three time-tested options on them:

I put them on "terminal hold" meaning they'll be holding all day.

I tell them my name is Ernie Ghento, that I'll check into their problem and they can call me back anytime. Of course, there is no Ernie Ghento, but everyone who works on the switchboard knows that and if someone calls back and ask for him, see option No. 1.

Sometimes just for fun, we'll transfer crazy people to the city desk of *The New York Times* and listen in. They make more money, let them get flustered.

But it's rare to have a quiet day. Usually, it's non-stop madness. And, as the day progresses, the pace gets faster and faster. By 2 p.m., the typewriters are clacking away and more and more calls are lighting up the switchboard. A lot of the calls are from reporters out in the field—at some crime scene or some press conference that just ended—and they are full of adrenalin. They demand to speak to "the desk," to Oli, to a rewrite man. They are brusque and full of curses.

Give me the fucking desk.

Where is Oliver?

Is Sam there?

Lemme speak to Singleton.

Hey Paulie, what's happening? How's it hanging? Give me to Cheech.

Do you have the sked in front of you? What kind of play are they giving my story?

The requests are endless. I get more and more hyped up and sometimes my hand slips and I cut off a rewrite man dumping notes. That's the worst because the rewrite man who is sitting just a few feet away starts cursing me out in full earshot of everyone in the newsroom.

Paulie, what the fuck is wrong with you?

What the fuck just happened?

Get him back—NOW!

Then, when he's finished yelling, the reporter calls back and begins *his* tirade. By day's end, I am burned out and appreciate Louie's for what it is—relief for the working man. I head downstairs to grab a beer in a place where I always find a roomful of friends eager to discuss how shitty their day was. The thought of heading home is inconceivable; I am too keyed up. One drink leads to several and before long, a group of us are doing a pub crawl all over Manhattan. For someone like me, never a big drinker, this is a big step forward or backward, depending on your perspective. I never want to go home to the project apartment I still live in with my parents, brother and sister. I know I should move out, the way adults do, but I can't bring myself to do it. I'm not entirely sure why. I was desperate to move out of their apartment to go to college but, now that I'm able to, I don't. So instead I spend an awful lot of time wandering around to bars, movies, and friends' apartments, or just driving all over New York City.

After about year of this, my body lets me know something is wrong. One day, on the way to work in an express bus, I feel as though I'm going to have a heart attack. I start sweating like crazy but, at the same time, my forehead is stone cold. I look around and feel the walls of the bus closing in on me. The people are way too close. I tell the bus driver I'm going to be sick and need to get off. My shirt is soaked wet from sweat. I wind up in an unfamiliar area and walk around aimlessly, trying to figure out what's happening to me. Eventually, I find a subway station where I let train after train go by until rush hour ends so I can sit in an empty car. Of course, I'm late for work. Back on the switchboard, I feel the pressure building again but hang on till the end of my shift when I find my way down to Louie's.

The next day's commute brings the same problem. I have to exit the bus and calm myself down for a while before whatever it is passes. I consider what to do but know there is no way I'm going to tell my bosses that the pressure is getting to me. That would guarantee that I'd never be promoted to reporter. And there's also no way I'm giving up all the extra money I'm making. Some weeks, I take home nearly $350. Besides, I know that I'm way too young to be having a heart attack. On my own time, I pull some clips from *The Daily News* library, or morgue as its called in house *(Hey Paulie, go to the morgue and get me some clips on welfare fraud)*, and begin researching what's going on. It doesn't take long to learn that I'm experiencing panic attacks. Maybe they're related to all the stress I feel from being a city desk assistant, but I can't dismiss the idea that the attacks could be caused by me pretending to be something I'm not. Am I so out of my element that I'm going nuts? Whatever is causing them, this is not good.

I refuse to tell anyone what's going on, not even my closest friends. I am certain this is a debilitating weakness that would end my career before it begins. I'm not sure what to do. I'm not a person who likes doctors but one of the articles offers an alternative solution. It mentions that meditation and yoga are sometimes successful in controlling stress and eliminating panic attacks. I re-read the article carefully. Yoga is foreign to me. I buy the book "Richard Hittleman's 28 Day Exercise Plan" but it's impossible to be quiet and meditate in my busy apartment. I begin searching for a yoga studio and find the World Yoga Center on W.72nd Street

It is definitely not convenient to *The Daily News* which is way across town on East 42nd Street but I can't find anywhere closer. I bring some shorts and workout clothes with me the following day, determined not to go out drinking after work but to head to a yoga class instead. I feel like I'm entering yet another world that's unknown to me.

The World Yoga Center is west of Broadway and up a flight of stairs. Because a class is in session when I arrive, everyone waits on the staircase. The other yoga students are young attractive women who are so beautiful and in shape that I'm sure they must be aspiring actresses and dancers. I am so self-conscious that I feel like running down the stairs but I force myself to stay. I'm having more and more trouble getting to work with each passing day. I've often had to jump off the express bus, which is not the easiest thing to do. Everyone on board has paid extra to get to work faster and here I am forcing us to stop. I am not popular on those buses.

So I resist the impulse to run, and begin to experience yoga. I've always been very active physically in the projects, playing softball, basketball and touch football nearly every day so I am in reasonably good shape. I am able to do the postures, or asanas, but nowhere near as well as the flexible women around me. I must look awfully funny because all these women are in terrific shape and wear tight body suits while I have on an old pair of gym shorts and a t-shirt. But I don't mind. The teacher is reassuring and so are the women. I become sort of a pet to them. They smile and encourage me. And the end of each class is absolute bliss, exactly what I'm looking for. It's a posture called savasana or dead man's pose. We lie on our backs while the teacher leads us through a guided meditation, telling us in a soothing voice to imagine all the stress being released from various parts of our bodies. At the end of the class, I am totally relaxed and feel much better and more alive than I ever feel hanging out in Louie's.

I'm still extremely shy around women—especially one on one—but sometimes after class, a couple of them invite me to tag along to a diner. I do and wind up getting home very late but very happy. It is in one of these classes that I meet a young woman named Kathleen who I date for awhile. What attracts me to her, besides her willingness to talk to a goofball like me, are her two different color eyes, one brown and one green. It's the type of thing I find alluring though she never believes me. She thinks it's some kind of defect. Between Kathleen and the yoga, which I keep a secret from everyone in my life, I feel myself growing more and more grounded but still not enough to move out of my parents' apartment.

Leaving Story Avenue

By the late '70s, the Monroe Houses tip fully into the danger zone. The Black Spades are in charge, the elevators and hallways are full of piss, and drugs have taken hold. Duffy, a friend about to enter the Army, makes the mistake of failing to hold a lobby door open for one of the Black Spades, and they take a blood oath to get him. He spends the few days he has left holed up in his apartment before being shipped off to Vietnam. Anything is better than this. On the long flight overseas, he looks out the window and hallucinates that the Spades are in rowboats chasing him in the plane, vowing to come get him.

The Monroe Houses feel like they're growing more dangerous with each passing day. We're living on the edge. I'm standing near my building one day when I notice some neighbors pointing skyward—hundreds of glassine envelopes filled with heroin are raining down, courtesy of some junkies who are throwing them out the windows of a 14th floor apartment being raided by cops. The second they hit the ground, they are scooped up by accomplices. It feels like

I am the last of my friends stupid enough to still live here; everyone else has wised up. I worry for the safety of my sister Karen who is 12 years old and encourage my parents to move out. My mother, who never wanted to move to Monroe in the first place, now perversely does not want to leave. She hates change, she tells us. My brother also wants to move out. His girlfriend, Kathy, one of his childhood friends who once lived in our building, has moved to a much nicer and safer project in Queens. Bob is also going to Queens College, not far from where she lives, and he tells us how nice and safe Queens is. So that's where we look.

We spend weekends driving around, trying to figure out where to move next. We're not the most sophisticated bunch, more like the Beverly Hillbillies without the "black gold" or pickup. We spot a group of buildings and say, "Hey that looks nice" and we decamp to look at a few apartments. I think about splitting off from this lackluster search and moving into my own place in Manhattan. I even check out an apartment that another copyboy is vacating. It's on the Upper East Side, near one of the off ramps of the Queensboro Bridge. The rent is low and it's considered a steal but I find it depressing. The thought of living alone in a darkened walk-up apartment in a rundown building just doesn't do it for me. I decide to stick with my family. My paycheck will help us afford a slightly better apartment.

For reasons that are not clear to any of us, we wind up choosing a three-bedroom ground floor "garden" apartment on Springfield Blvd. in Bayside, Queens. It's not really a three-bedroom apartment but we turn the small, formal dining room into my sister's room. As I have my whole life, I room with my brother. The apartment is small, especially for five people, but it's safe. The projects are far, far away. Of course, one reason this apartment is safe is that it's miles from the nearest subway line. This is a two-fare zone and commuting is a real chore. In the projects, we could always walk to the nearest subway line but here, that's not an option. The closest subway line is a 30-minute bus ride away and, while it's not a big problem for my brother or me—we each have cars at this point—it's a real hassle for my dad to get to work. But he never complains and simply goes along with our choice. For my sister, the move is great. She'll be living and attending a good public school; the immediate danger of day to day life is over.

Writing

Just about all the copyboys are filled with a desire to make it, to advance at the newspaper to a writing or photography job or something in between. I want to get my own byline, and begin to pitch story ideas to the editors. It's much easier to break into the feature side of the paper because the news side is impossible. No way is anyone going to let me or any other copyboy write about the latest gangland hit or cover a press conference at City Hall. I'm constantly on the lookout for ideas and one day, I pick up a community newspaper and read that the city's much-mocked Miss Subways contest is about to end. It's been going on for years. Some young woman from the outer boroughs—usually an aspiring actress who collects owl figurines or some such thing—becomes that month's Miss Subways and her face gets plastered all over the subway cars. When there's nothing else for straphangers to read, it's kind of reassuring to look up and see Miss Subways' smiling face looking down at you. Now the contest is ending, or at least that's what it says in this local newspaper.

I go to the newspaper's library and pull the clips on Miss Subways. That's the best way to know if anyone from The News has done a story or not. The answer is—not. So now I'm sitting on a potential features story. I pitch the idea to the Women's Editor Marie Burke. She likes it and gives me the go-ahead. I call the Transit Authority's press people and ask about the contest. Yes, I'm told, the contest is ending. A sign of the times. Feminism has swept the country and women are not into these hokey beauty contests anymore. Miss Subways served her purpose but it's all ending in a month. I get a few names of past winners, interview them along with the woman who will be the very last Miss Subways and write up the whole thing in my spare time. Then, I give the story to the editor and wait.

A couple of days later, she calls me into her office and tells me the story is very good and will run the following day. Wow! That was actually pretty easy. And I'll be paid $25. Not bad. But the big news is that I'm getting a byline, that my name is going to be in print. I decide not to tell anyone but I make sure I'm around when the first edition of the next day's paper finds its way to the city room, around 7 the next night.

Here's my lead:

> *A familiar face will be missing from your daily subway ride after tomorrow. It's that of a young woman whose name you've probably forgotten but whose hobbies you can't possibly forget.*
>
> *For how many women do you know who like to swim, ski, golf, play soccer, write children's books, dabble in ceramics, bake bread and collect owl figurines to boot? But this talented New Yorker, known as Miss Subways, has made her last run.*

It's a tradition that when the first paper—the Bulldog edition—comes up, the entire newsroom grows silent as everyone begins reading. This is why we've been going crazy all day long and these few moments are the tangible reward of that hard work. Editors look for mistakes, reporters scour page after page to see what kind of play their stories got. Today, it's all very quiet until one reporter nearby says, "Hey Paulie, is this your story about Miss Subways? Did you write this?"

All eyes nearby turn to me. "Yeah, that's mine," I say.

"What page?" someone asks.

All the copyboys turn to my story and read at the same time while I sit there, hoping for a good reaction. "Hey Paulie," the original reporter says, "this is very good. Congrats."

"Wow," says another. "I'm impressed."

And then of course, some smartass chimes in. "Did you really write this? I thought you were illiterate."

Everyone's laughing but I know they're impressed. They want to buy me a drink. We're off to Louie's to celebrate.

Now that I've had one success, I become a story-pitching fool, petitioning the editors constantly. I get taken more seriously than some of the other wannabe reporters because I've proven that I can do it. I get stories from anywhere and everywhere. One night, I hear a disc jockey on WNEW-FM talking about a novel that he's written and decide that's pretty cool, a DJ writing a book. I buttonhole John Quinn, the features editor and he gives me the green light. That becomes my second byline, the one that my buddies Andrew and Robbie notice because it runs prominently in the Sunday paper. Andrew seems bewildered by the process of how I make this happen. Like a lot of people in the projects, he grew up thinking the people in power—those on TV, radio, politicians—were beyond reach, that there's no way a kid from Monroe could possibly talk to them. I tell him that all I did was call information, get the phone number for WNEW-FM, phone one night when the DJ was on duty, pitch him the idea and he said to come on by. It was actually kind of easy. I see a new respect in Andrew's eyes. "I think you're gonna make it," he says. It's one of the kindest things he's ever said to me.

One day, the following memo is posted on one of the bulletin boards:

N O T I C E

*COPY BOYS/GIRLS AND CLERKS
INTERESTED IN APPLYING FOR
OPENINGS AS TRAINING REPORTER
ARE ASKED TO LEAVE THEIR NAME
WITH ME. WRITING ABILITY WILL
BE OF PRIME CONSIDERATION IN
THE SELECTION.*

E.F. Quinn

No one misses the implication of "*the* selection." It sounds as if one of us—and only one of us—is going to be promoted. The gossip and conspiracy theories among the copykids, each one more jealous or determined to make it, never cease. Some suspect the test is only a ruse for promoting this or that copykid while simultaneously, and falsely, making it seem like all of us have a chance. Rumors spread that the top three will absolutely be given tryouts as reporters. Others speculate it will be the top five. On and on it goes. I can write and have already proven it but that does not mean I'm a shoo-in. I don't take the test lightly because I know I have some very talented colleagues—Lorenzo, Murray Weiss, Vince Cosgrove, Thom Forbes, John Melia, to name a few. I study the newspaper and the way the stories—hard news and features—are written like I'm cramming for a final exam.

The day of the test arrives and they sprinkle us throughout the newsroom after deadline when it's quiet and a lot of typewriters and desks are available. What they ask of us is nothing special—it's your classic newspaper writing test. They give us a bunch of facts and ask us to write two news stories. One is a straight hard news story about a drug distribution ring in Harlem. It's based on a real story that made a very late edition of the paper so whoever created this test made the safe assumption that not many of us would have read it. In this particular drug ring, dealers used kids who would only be charged as juveniles if caught. The cops ruined those plans by breaking into the dealers' drug den "Batman & Robin" style, or so we are told.

The second story is intended as a humor piece so we can show off our writing chops. It's about Mayor Ed Koch and his supposedly jinxed city-owned car. The News runs a lot of these off-news feature stories and you'd better know how to write them if you want to be a reporter here. "Just the facts, ma'am" won't do at *The Daily News* which prides itself on catchy headlines and clever writing.

We all dig in. There is, of course, an artificial deadline they impose because *this is a daily, son.*

I study the facts and scribble a couple of paragraphs on a piece of copy paper. While I'm still trying to craft the proper lead, I hear the first typewriter begin to clack. Nervously, I slide a four-book into my manual typewriter, look down at the lead I've hand-written and begin to bang out the news story. It's exciting and I feel the rush of competition. Soon, a bunch of typewriters are clacking away and the newsroom sounds as it would if this were a real deadline. I finish my news story, read it over and am satisfied with it. In goes another piece of copy paper and I begin the human interest story. Afterwards, we all head down to Louie's to mull over the test long into the night.

Months go by before we hear anything but then one day, a few of us find notes like this in our mailboxes:

Dear Paul:

If you are interested in a possible opening in the training classification, please put together your credentials for interviews with Dick Blood, Larry Craft and me.

Let me know when you are ready, and I'll arrange the other meetings for you.

Sincerely,

E.F. Quinn

The Crazy '70s

The last years of the 1970s—my first five years at The News—prove a boom time for news stories. The city nearly goes bankrupt in 1975 but Governor Hugh Carey and others pull it from the brink. Still, the city is a mess and feels out of control. Graffiti is everywhere, the subways have constant breakdowns, and a serial killer who calls himself the Son of Sam is stalking young lovers. Safe to say, nothing is going New York's way except for the New York Yankees who pick these years to roar back into being the pennant-winners they once were.

But as much as these are bad years for the city, they are salad days for a tabloid newspaper like *The Daily News*. It feels like I am at the center of the universe, especially when The Son of Sam killer begins sending crazy hand-written letters to Daily News columnist Jimmy Breslin. One of my jobs as a city desk assistant is to open reader mail and now the formerly tedious job takes on new urgency. Every weird looking letter is opened immediately in the hopes that our very own crazed serial killer has written to Breslin again.

Couples across the city are on high alert for this killer who stalks lovers in their cars and unloads his .44 caliber gun into them without saying a word. Whenever I go out, I watch for this lunatic and, after a night of barhopping in Bayside, Queens, I come in to work the next morning to find out that the Son of Sam has struck again—in Bayside at the Eliphas Disco only blocks from where I'd parked my car. This is getting much too close. That shooting of Judy Placido and Sal Lupo, two kids sitting and talking in their car, is the seventh time the Son of Sam has struck and the entire city is in a panic.

A month later, the Son of Sam strikes for the first time in Brooklyn, killing Stacy Moscowitz and partially blinding her date Bobby Violante. Breslin is nearly foaming at the mouth to catch the guy, blustering around the newsroom and writing one open letter after another urging the guy to surrender, preferably to Breslin here at *The Daily News*. Half of me wants him to walk through the door and the other half is scared shitless that he just might, along with his .44 caliber gun. But the end for the Son of Sam is not nearly as exciting as his reign of terror.

He gets captured in a way every New Yorker can relate to—by a parking ticket. He parked a bit too close to a hydrant at the scene of one of his shootings and the resulting ticket led cops right to the front door of a post office worker, a loser from the Bronx named David Berkowitz. (I later find out he's friendly with some of the guys in the projects and frequented Shorehaven, the neighborhood swim club my parents never allowed me to join.) When cops question a neighbor about who the hell "Sam" is, he tells them—it's a neighbor's dog. Berkowitz was convinced the dog could talk and was giving him orders, hence the nickname he gave himself "Son of Sam."

While all this is going on, The News city room incongruously is taken over by a Hollywood production team who are turning the *Superman* comic books into a major motion picture starring Marlon Brando as Superman's father, Margot Kidder as Lois Lane and a newcomer, Christopher Reeve as Superman/Clark Kent. For me, it's a melding of fantasy and reality. One night I report to work to find actress Margot Kidder—a.k.a. Lois Lane—posing for publicity photos while sitting at my desk. I am dazzled and cannot focus on anything except Margot's stellar legs kicking out from the spot where I usually write obits. I am speechless as a photographer takes photo after photo. Margot is in a great mood and gives me a great big smile. "I love this place," she says to me.

I follow that up with something witty like, "Yeah, me too."

The movie production takes over the office, parts of the building, and the street outside. They are still shooting outside on a hot night in July 1977 when the city experiences its second massive blackout in a decade. This one, however, is nothing like the one from the 1960s which, in retrospect, seems absurdly good-natured. That one inspired the film "Where Were You When the Lights Went Out?" This time, the reaction to the blackout is vicious. The neighborhood of Bushwick, Brooklyn, explodes, and thousands storm into stores that no longer have functioning alarm systems. The shop owners find themselves confronted by mobs with no protection from the NYPD who are spread too thin trying to control the chaos breaking out all across the city. Some Bushwick residents, sensing opportunity, steal whatever they can carry. Photographers and television crews get disturbing and damning pictures of men, women and children hauling away furniture, television sets, and anything not nailed down.

Back at *The Daily News*, we are not immune to the lack of electricity. There are no lights in the newsroom, no way to put out the evening edition of the biggest story in town. The manual typewriters are the only part of the newspaper truly functioning. All of us in the newsroom are helpless, sitting on the biggest story of the year and not knowing how to report it.

And that's when my crazy childhood fantasy about *The Daily News* building being the true home to Clark Kent comes to life. On this night, when The News is nearly down and out, it is Superman to the rescue. The movie's production team lends its lights and generators to the newsroom so we'll have the enough basic power to at least write and edit stories. We work by klieg light as one reporter after another makes his way in to write a first-hand story of what he's witnessed. A deal is made to print the newspaper at a rival's presses outside New York and the next day, the News is able to come out with a special blackout edition. Quite literally, Superman saves the day.

At this point, I am still in the training program offered up by E.F. Quinn, and every once in a while, I am allowed to fill in as a reporter at nights or in one of the borough offices. I get good reviews for my writing but nothing, I am told time and again, is guaranteed. I watch jealously as my brother copyboys—Vinnie Cosgrove and Murray Weiss— are promoted ahead of me. I hope that I'm not being over- looked. I know I have a mild-mannered personality but, hey, it worked for Clark Kent, right?

And then in the summer of 1978, it happens. Quinn gives me the news that I am being promoted to reporter in the Brooklyn section. The fact that he ruins the moment by making me feel worthless at the same time—by telling me "I don't think it will last long"—only serves as motivation. I want to take one of my bylines and smear the newsprint all over his face. The words still sting and I am determined to show him and everyone who doubted me what I can do.

Brooklyn Daze

I am assigned to the Brooklyn office of the News which is kind of funny because I've only been in Brooklyn three times in my entire life. Even though I'm a New York native, I know less about this borough than a newcomer to the city would. I might as well be moving to another city by being assigned there. But I'm in luck because the editor of the Brooklyn section is a guy named Bill Federici. Federici is a larger-than-life personality, a movie-star handsome guy who's been at The News forever. He's a Brooklyn native and, even better for me, he's Italian-American. The dirty little secret of New York, the purported "melting pot," is that it's really no such thing. Every ethnic group—be they Jews, Italians, Chinese or Puerto Ricans—flocks to their own and looks out for their own, and Federici looks out for me.

And I need looking out for. Here's the thing: I've studied writing for years, and have been in the center of the newsroom for three years but I never went to journalism school. What I know about reporting is what I picked up in college (where I mainly reviewed movies) and from watching those around me. But in a very real sense, I have no idea what I'm doing when it comes to reporting hard news. I've got a lot to learn.

This becomes all too apparent when I'm sent out on my first news story, some type of chemical spill not far from the office. It's far enough that I have to drive there, and I waste ten minutes looking for a legal parking spot, clearly a rookie mistake. By the time I run up to the scene, I'm sweating. I did remember to bring a reporter's notebook and pen, and I go up to the first cop I see and ask him what happened. The disgusted look he gives me makes it very clear very quickly that he wants nothing to do with me. First lesson: only those cops authorized to speak to the press will speak to the press—sometimes. Cops don't trust reporters they don't know. Without saying a word, this cop tilts his head toward a scrum of other reporters who I've somehow missed despite the fact that they're holding large cameras and microphones.

I stand at the edge of the crowd, whip out my notebook and listen in. The firefighter who is speaking—I have no idea what his name is or how to spell it—details what happened with the spill, how they are cleaning it up and how it's not really a threat to anyone. I take it all down and think it's crystal clear. But then the reporters—especially the radio and television reporters—begin to ask questions. The questions strike me as ridiculous. Didn't the firefighter explain all of this? Why are they asking these inane questions? I don't understand at first but someone soon clues me in—the radio and TV guys need sound and it's even better when their voice is on the other end of the question. That way, it seems like the firefighter is talking only to them and they can appear extra smart or tuned in or whatever for the 6 o'clock news or the most recent radio report.

I walk around the scene and interview a few people in the crowd who say they're afraid or not afraid. I take a few more notes on what everything looks like and then I spot one of the paper's photographers, a guy named Chuck.

"Pretty good story, huh?" I say.

He doesn't even look at me while he takes a few more pictures. "Nah, this is a rope. Waste of time."

A rope is a photo that will appear in tomorrow's paper with a fat caption. There will be no story and hence, no byline.

"Really? You think that's all it's worth?"

"Yeah, these things are a dime a dozen. What is this, like your first day on the job?"

I don't say the obvious—yes it is!!

"You need a ride back to the office?" he asks.

I tell him I've got my own ride and head back. Feeling a little confused, I enter the Brooklyn office and walk over to Federici.

"Okay Bill, I got a bunch of quotes. Doesn't look too serious but I'll follow up with some calls. How many takes do you want?"

"Forget it," Federici says, "Chuck told me it's a rope. Type up a few notes and give 'em to me. We'll put it in with his film."

And it would have made a nice rope in the next day's paper if only Chuck had remembered to put film in his camera. "Shit," he says back at the office, "I forgot."

Everyone except me starts laughing. *Fuckin' Chuck, he does shit like this all the time.*

My first day was more than a little deflating but I don't have time to dwell on it. The next day I am sent out to some kind of protest meeting at the House of Our Lord Church, the Reverend Herbert Daughtry's church on Atlantic Avenue. The meeting is in the basement and I am pretty much the only white person in the room. The Rev. Daughtry is known as a bold leader in the black community who is only too happy to take on the white establishment. I dutifully take some notes of the long-winded speeches but grow especially interested when a fiery speaker named Amiri Baraka takes the microphone. I have no idea who he is but later learn he is a poet whose former name was LeRoi Jones.

Baraka gives a compelling talk about a recent beating he suffered at the hands of the NYPD. I am astonished the police officers would do what Baraka says they did to him. After he steps down, I buttonhole him and ask him more questions about the beating. He lets loose with a story that gets more and more incredible, at least to a naïf like me. By the time he finishes, I am outraged a black man would be treated like this.

I race back to the office and tell Federici that the protest was nothing—the real story was told by this black poet who was beaten by cops. Federici looks a little bemused but says, "You need to get the police response if you're gonna write a story like that."

"Yeah, sure, no problem," I say.

I call the cops' press office, better known as DCPI (Deputy Commissioner for Public Information) and relay what I want—some kind of official response to Baraka's story of being beaten and humiliated by New York's Finest. The cop on the other end listens quietly and at the end of my rambling, says, "You finished?"

"Yes."

"Okay, we'll get back to you."

I write up my story and man, it's good, filled with the type of outrage I am feeling about this black guy who was beaten to a pulp. Federici comes and looks over my shoulder. "How ya doin'?"

"Good, getting close to being finished but I'm waiting for the cops to get back to me."

"They know you're on deadline, right?"

"Right."

"This story can't run without their response you know that right?"

"Yeah, of course but they said they'd call me back."

Federici puts his hand on my shoulder. "Paul, they're not gonna call you back."

"But he said he would. I have his name."

"Well, let's see what happens okay?"

"Okay."

It's now 3 o'clock and our deadline is 5 p.m. I call back a couple of times but the cop I spoke to is never available. I pace back and forth, look out the windows, re-read my story for the hundredth time. It's damn good. All it needs is the police response.

At 6 p.m., I'm still waiting and most of the reporters have left for the day. Federici and I are the only ones left. "Paul, bring me your copy," he says.

He reads it and sighs. "You've got no proof any of this happened, you know that, right? He could be making this whole thing up."

"Yeah he could but why would he?"

"Because he hates the cops?"

"No way was he making this up. It was too real."

"Well, it may be real but this paper will never run it without some sort of official response and Paul…"

"Yes."

"It ain't gonna happen."

With a flourish, he plunges my story onto the metal spike sitting on his desk. Every editor has one and every reporter fears it. If your story winds up on that spike, it's dead. Now, my story is official *spiked*, meaning it's not going to run in tomorrow's paper or any day's paper.

"You'll learn," he says.

And I do. Slowly. I begin to realize, and so does Federici, that my real talent lies in writing feature stories, little neighborhood profiles that are the bread and butter of a borough section. I work on stories about ham radio operators helping direct truckers around the city's traffic jams,

> *"Listen up, everyone. We've got a Kojak with a Kodak hanging out near the top of the world so take it easy up there."*
>
> *Translated, that means an eagle-eyed trucker has spotted a police car with radar stationed at the high point of the Brooklyn-Queens Expressway near the Hamilton Avenue exit.*

Group homes for the mentally retarded moving into up and coming neighborhoods like Park Slope (Headline: Retarded Are Good Neighbors):

> *It's a long way from Willowbrook to Park Slope and for some the distance is never bridged.*

And a story about an Italian-American puppeteer who happens to live in Brooklyn:

> *When Miguel Manteo moves his hands, people notice.*
>
> *That's because his hands are usually at the end of one of his intricately-designed marionettes—creations that seem so real that people have been known to treat them as...other people.*

I have a way of turning a phrase that the editors back in Manhattan appreciate. And I can write fast. On any day, I might have three, sometimes four, bylines in a single edition of the Brooklyn section.

I am gaining some traction for my writing when it all comes crashing down. Barely a month after I start in Brooklyn, the newspaper unions, led by the pressmen, call a strike. *The Daily News* shuts down, as do *The New York Post* and *The New York Times*. No one is exempt from the wrath of the unions who feel the looming shadow of the computer age. All of the newspapers are about to make the switch from manual typewriters and hot lead to computers and cold type, just as Quinn had predicted. It's been happening all over the country and finally it's reached New York. Jobs will surely be lost and the notorious newspaper unions are not happy.

I am a member of the Newspaper Guild and, though I know precious little about the strike, I am compelled to walk out with everyone else.

There's no doubt that I am much luckier than most. I still live with my parents, have a used car and virtually no expenses, no family to feed, no mortgage to pay. When the strike appears as though it may go on a long time I round up a couple of fellow copyboys—John Clerkin and Scott Mitchell—hatch a plan to drive to Los Angeles. There is a woman living there whom I know from college and I'm eager to reconnect. John and Scott agree and we contact a car transport company that hires drivers to move cars from one end of the country to the other. Incredibly, the car we are given to deliver to Encino is a sleek Mercedes 350 SL. We have five days to get it across the country. We do it in three, never stopping overnight, taking turns driving. Someone is always sleeping in the back seat. We keep the car in L.A. for the two extra days we have before renting cheaper wheels. It is great fun. I look up my old college girlfriend, and we all spend a lot of time on the beaches of Santa Monica, pretty much ignoring everything happening back in New York.

The strike goes on for 88 days and, when it is finally settled, I am once again assigned to the Brooklyn office, but not for long. The strike has taken its toll on the newspaper's staff. Management is determined to make the staff younger and cheaper, and generous buyouts are offered to dozens of senior employees, many of whom leave. I am transferred to the Manhattan office to work nights.

Nightside

Working nights at *The Daily News* is like sitting at a bar where every once in a while someone asks you to write a news story.

After 7 p.m. each night, the city room empties and only a skeleton crew of reporters, editors, copy editors and photographers remain. A hush, or what passes for a hush in a busy newspaper office, descends on the room. A bundle of papers—the one-star edition—is brought up hot off the presses, distributed and perused by one and all. The clacking of the typewriters slows to a trickle. Finally, there are enough chairs for everyone and you can look across the vast newsroom to see only a few heads here and there. The daysiders are gone. There's a romance and mystique about nights that some prefer. There are more practical reasons as well. One veteran reporter tells me he works nights because "there are fewer assholes to deal with." There is also night differential pay but he doesn't mention that.

The nightside shift attracts lifers who have a bit of the loner in them, who don't want to be around others for one reason or another. Dayside is where the action is. The best reporters and editors work days. Nightside is a mindset, not too different than being a firefighter—long periods of nothing and then, *boom*, a calamity! A cop is shot. A young woman is pushed off a subway platform. A polar bear eats a kid. Nights have their own peculiar karma.

It's often so quiet and boring that the best way to pass the time is to think of a prank. One night, Teddy, one of the older reporters whose wife has recently passed away, becomes the perfect patsy when he falls asleep at the photo desk after going out for his nighttime blow job, a habit he picked up since his wife's death. Of course, everyone in the newsroom is aware of his new hobby. Reporter Harry Mathos spots Teddy snoring away, his head inches from the pneumatic tube that carries photographs from the darkroom to the photo desk. Harry excuses himself and sneaks into the dark room where he begins speaking into the tube in as feminine a voice as he can manage: "Teddy, this is your wife. Teddy, wake up."

Everyone watches as Teddy slowly awakens. "Teddy, this is your wife. I want you to stop spending all my money on blowjobs."

Teddy turns ashen and runs out of the newsroom as everyone collapses in laughter.

Some of the pranks, however, border on the cruel. On Saturday night, when *The New York Times* comes out, one reporter named Tommy focuses all his attention on the wedding announcements. He seeks out the most WASPY of the many WASPY names, and calls the bride's mother who inevitably is a matron living on the Upper East Side.

"Hello," says Tommy, "Can I please speak to Muffy."

"I'm sorry, she's not here. May I ask who's calling?"

"Sure, it's Tommy. Do you know when she'll be back?"

"Well, she just got married and she's off…"

"What?" shouts Tommy into the phone in his most indignant voice. "That slut! How could she get married? We've been screwing for the past two years."

The mother of the bride is aghast but Tommy never lets up until she finally hangs up on him.

Running the desk at night are a handful of colorful editors who are divided between those eager to make their bones, and others jaded beyond belief. Editor Dick Blood falls into the first category, desperate to put his mark on the paper crafted by the dayside editors. He likes nothing better than to change the front page headline to something that happened on his shift. He drives his reporters hard and demands they get every tiny detail and get it correctly. One time, he sends reporter Don Gentile to a school that has been trashed, warning Gentile that his reporting better make the reader see, feel, smell and taste everything that happened there. Gentile talks himself inside, takes a lot of notes and, among other things, notices there is a pile of shit left behind. He calls Blood to tell him what he's found and casually mentions the pile of shit. "Human or dog shit?" Blood asks.

But when Blood is not on the desk, one of his fill-ins is an editor who is Blood's polar opposite—a guy named Hank who would rather not change anything in the paper. Legend has it that, when Hank was a young reporter, he was sent to Dallas to cover the aftermath of JFK's assassination. Once there, Hank decided to go out to lunch rather than attend Lee Harvey Oswald's perp walk, and didn't find out until much later that the presidential assassin had himself been gunned down. He wasn't too upset and, incredibly, did not lose his job. Instead, Hank was promoted to where he is now—a substitute editor on nightside. The word "jaded" doesn't begin to explain his attitude. No matter what story is suggested or what crime happens on his watch, his answer is always the same, "Nah, a piece of shit."

The big problem with nights is that you can wind up liking them a bit too much. You can embrace the lifestyle of being apart from the hurly-burly of the day and before you know it, you've got a pasty complexion, never work out and consider a pickle a vegetable. You become a fat, hard-nosed alcoholic. The thing is, it's hard *not* to drink on nights because it feels *unnatural* to head home at the end of your shift, which also happens to be midnight. Hey, the night is young. You feel the need to unwind and it's the perfect time for a cocktail or two or three.

One night shift I look around and realize that the other four reporters, including the assistant city desk editor, are all downstairs at Louie's. It's me and the city desk editor manning what is the largest circulating newspaper in America. On quiet nights, my co-workers spend a lunch hour or two down at Louie's before returning to their desks with a Styrofoam cup filled with scotch or vodka and a glazed look in their eye. I joke that I'm working on the all-alcoholic shift. One night, as I return from actually eating a meal during my lunch hour, I see a co-worker, another reporter on the same shift, walk face-first into a city bus shelter as if it wasn't there. He is that drunk. He bounces off, falls down, gets back up and continues on his way. I'm so stunned that I watch him walk on down the street. His nickname becomes "Just One More" because those are words that escape his mouth down at Louie's about 10 times a night.

Aside from drinking, nights are all about crime and I cover my share. Knife fights, gun battles, husband and wives, stranger on stranger attacks. You name it and I cover it. We go headlong into crime scenes where I sometimes see dead bodies lying around. One particular night, I watch as the guys from the morgue cannot seem to get a gunned-down mobster into his body bag. His bloody body slips out a couple of times as the reporters moan and groan along with the family who are watching horrified.

Yours truly in The Daily News *city room, sometime in the late 70s*

The News always keeps a man stationed inside Police Headquarters, the ugly brown brick building just north of the Brooklyn Bridge, nicknamed *the Puzzle Palace* by cops who can't understand the inner workings of the commissioner and his higher-ups. Most nights, our man at Headquarters is the infamous Pat Doyle, a.k.a. "The Inspector."

By the time I begin working nights, Pat has been at Headquarters a very long time and he's become quite the character. It's rumored that, as the building was being built in the early 1970s, Pat would visit every night to monitor its progress. He also helped himself to some of the brown bricks used on the building's exterior, placing one or two in each pocket of his raincoat every time. He then used the bricks to build a new patio wall at his suburban home, or so the story goes.

There is a ton of folklore surrounding Pat. Reportedly, he no longer leaves Police Headquarters for fear of missing an important phone call. He cooks on a hot plate and throws the grease out the window. He smokes cigars and puts the butts in a drawer. He does not even leave to go to the bathroom, preferring instead to pee into one of the wastepaper baskets. When the building's janitors complain and point the finger at Pat, he tells them not to worry, that he will get to the bottom of who is the offending party. About a week later, he sidles up the janitor with his report and whispers conspiratorially, "I found out who's making the mess—it's the guy from *The Times*."

The editors on the city desk tolerate Doyle but do not believe much of what he reports. The reporters, me included, are told we have to check everything Doyle tells us. Not surprisingly, this double-checking makes him paranoid. One night, he demands to know why I called DCPI when he had given me the details of a crime. I am so surprised at being confronted, I tell him the truth—the city editor made me do it. Perhaps it's not surprising that Doyle becomes more and more suspicious. I often answer my phone to hear his voice on the other end: "Is [Editor Dick] Blood on the desk? Don't turn around. He'll know it's me. Say yes or no."

That was inside the paper. Outside the paper, Doyle's reputation as a hard worker (which he is no doubt) and his tenacity for stories and bylines makes him a well-respected man. One night, copyboy Larry Celona is told to head up to the bar P.J. Clarke's to deliver the Night Owl edition to Doyle who is holding court there. "I go in and Doyle is sitting with Walter Cronkite, the most trusted man in America with the most mistrusted," Celona says.

Different rules apply at nights when the grownups are away. One night, I'm passing by a darkened office and hear some voices coming from inside. I see five grown men—including a copy desk chief who weighs close to 300 pounds—standing on top of a heating unit with their faces pressed against the window.

I turn on the light and whisper, "What's going on?"

They turn around in unison and hiss: "Shut that fucking light."

I do and they fill me in. It seems that a shapely young woman in an apartment across the way has come home from a shopping trip, and she's trying on one new outfit after another in her well-lit apartment. She is not wearing any underwear, only trying on one article of clothing after another. As she pulls on each new skirt or slinks into a dress, she parades around in front of the mirror before stripping everything off to begin again.

Holy shit.

Thank you God.

This has to be the best night of my life.

I look over at the copy chief and he's sweating profusely;

I'm afraid he may have a heart attack or push so hard against the glass that he'll go through the window. The show goes on like that for a half hour until her new wardrobe is exhausted, and we all go back to work, except for the copy chief who heads for the bathroom. Hmmm...

A lot of guys don't like this shift because they have families or girlfriends but I have neither, because, yes, I am still living at home. And that's becoming more and more embarrassing. I'm a reporter now for God's sake. I spend a lot of time at Scott's place on the Upper East Side discussing: a) whether I should get my own place, and b) how I can find a girlfriend. I meet a lot of women and go out on dates but nothing ever is long-lasting. I begin to think there's something wrong with me. Maybe I'm not capable of a long-term relationship. I feel different than the people I work with, nearly all of whom grew up middle-class. I almost never meet people from the projects unless I'm doing a crime story.

My life now revolves around my work friends. I have almost nothing to do with the guys I grew up with. I'm still in touch with Andrew and Robbie, but I don't think we have much in common anymore. They want to spend all their time in the boroughs or the surrounding suburbs getting as drunk as possible while for me, Manhattan is the only place to be. When I'm honest with myself, I realize that I've consciously turned my back on my past in order to live in the present. I feel like my friends from the Monroe Projects know too much about the old me—the meek, quiet kid who more often than not would get pushed around in school and in the projects for being too studious, too mild-mannered. That's no longer the way I see myself and I don't want to be around those who do. I want to shed that identity in favor of the new me—the hard-bitten, street-smart, foul-mouthed reporter who doesn't take any shit. Deep down, I know that's not true because I get constant reminders. One night, the brother of a priest who's been murdered calls me up about a story I wrote for that day's paper. My story recounts for the umpteenth time the circumstances of how and why the priest was murdered. He picked up a transvestite prostitute and was getting a blowjob when things went awry. The priest's brother implores me to stop repeating the basic story every time there's any kind of update on the case. "My mother's reading this stuff and it's killing her," he tells me.

I am sympathetic, and seek the counsel of a more seasoned reporter who listens for half a second and says, "Fuck him. He's a priest for Christ sakes. He shouldn't have been out getting a blowjob anyway."

Right. It's just that there are times when I prefer to be more human.

I push on, doing what the editors ask of me, even when it gets extremely uncomfortable. One afternoon, the assistant editor comes over and tells me about a construction accident in midtown. It's been a windy day and a wooden beam has blown off a high floor and hit an aspiring actor square in the head. "He's dead. Go on up to his apartment and see what you can find out about him."

This is a typical assignment for a reporter and, if you don't have the stomach for it, then you should find another job. I've done this same thing dozens of times now. I've been to horribly poor areas of the city where I knock on the doors of friends and family to ask about the poor victim. This should be no different. I grab a notebook, some cards, and head out the door. Because the actor lived on Ninth Avenue in Chelsea, this assignment is easier than many I go on. I've been out to the far reaches of Brooklyn and Queens many times and I'm thankful that all I have to do for this one is grab a cab and be there in minutes. I am. I look over the buzzers downstairs for the guy's name. He is all of 30 years old when he had the horrible luck to walk by that building. He wasn't even walking under the building—he was across the street but the beam still found him.

As usual in New York, there are no names on the buzzers but I do have his apartment number. There is no answer so I begin ringing all the buzzers. As usual, someone impatient or plain sick of the whole buzzer system presses the enter button and in I go. I begin the climb to his fourth-floor walkup. The aroma of cooking is all around me because it's dinner time. Whoever buzzed me in does not come out of his apartment to see who he let in the building. At the kid's door, I ring and wait. Then I knock. Nothing. No big surprise, he probably lived alone. The door behind me and across the hall opens partway. A young guy peeks out but keeps the security chain on.

"Can I help you?"

"Hi, my name is Paul LaRosa and I'm a reporter for *The Daily News*. Do you know an actor named John who lived here?"

"Yeah," he says. "I knew him and I know what happened."

"Well, can you tell me a little bit about him?"

The neighbor opens the door and steps into the hallway. "What do you want to know?"

"What kind of guy was he? Where did he work? I hear he

was an actor. Do you know anything he's been in?"

The neighbor tells me he was a friend and he and John discussed their careers. "Do you need a photo of him?"

Bingo! I was building up to that but here the friend had jumped ahead. I know how the editors think. Nothing like a good-looking victim—and I'm sure an aspiring actor will be good-looking—to personalize the tragedy. It also means my story will get much better play. What a lucky fuck I am, I think.

Then the neighbor pulls out some keys and says, "I'm sure John has some head shots in his apartment."

He steps across the hall, opens John's apartment and here we are—inside a dead man's apartment only hours after he's been killed. This feels very wrong. I look around. The place has the lived-in look of a million small New York apartments. Everything is crowded together. The bed is unmade. There is a pile of dirty clothes, some takeout food containers. I look around but I don't like being here. It feels like a violation. This doesn't normally happen. I usually do not get so close to the victim, especially within hours of his death.

The neighbor pokes around John's belongings until he finds what he's looking for—an actor's smiling head shot. John is a good-looking guy and this will go nicely in tomorrow's paper. I reach out and take the photo. "Thank you."

"Is there anything else you need to know?"

"Yes, you said John was a waiter. Do you know where he worked?"

He does and tells me about a bar-restaurant I've always meant to visit. Looks like I'll get my chance this night. I thank him and leave. Outside I run into a News photographer and hand him the photo. "Hey good job," he says.

"Looks like a nice kid."

"Yeah."

I call the desk and the editor asks me to dump my notes to a rewrite man. He doesn't want me to go in and write the story myself because he'd rather I head downtown to visit the bar where John worked so I can get even more color from his co-workers. I tell him about the attractive head shot. "Hey, nice job Paul."

I go down to the bar and steel myself. I have a bad feeling about having been in the apartment of a man who just died and I don't think this is going to be any better. I walk up to the bartender. "I'm a reporter with *The Daily News* and I'm here doing a story about John the actor who worked here."

"What do you mean, 'worked'? John works here. What about him?"

Uh-oh. They don't know. "Well, uh, there was an accident this afternoon..."

"What kind of accident? Is John all right?"

There's really no right way to say this so I just plunge ahead.

"Well, no he's not. John's dead."

"What!!??"

The bartender starts calling over his co-workers who are all looking at me. "This guy says John's dead."

A waitress's face crumples. Tears are close. "What happened?"

Oh, man, I didn't sign up for this. This is horrible but there's nothing I can do. I have no choice but to push on.

"There was an accident this afternoon. A wooden beam fell off a construction site up on 57th Street and it hit John in the head. I'm sorry."

The waitress begins sobbing loudly, and a couple of guys hug her close. "Oh my God," says the bartender. "Are you sure?"

"Yes, I was up at his apartment and his neighbor knew all about it. It's true."

"What do you want from us?"

"I'm trying to find out what John was like?"

"John was a great guy man. I need a drink. You want one?"

"Sure," I say.

The bartender pulls out a bottle and starts pouring for everyone. All the workers and the people at the bar are staring at me as I take notes. I know what they think of me. I think the same thing.

Thankfully, every night is different. Another time I am given an assignment to follow-up on the mugging of well-known New York City philanthropist George Delacorte. Even New Yorkers who don't recognize the name surely recognize his good works. Delacorte has donated several famous public art works to the city, most of them in Central Park. There's the statue of Alice in Wonderland near the boat pond, the Delacorte Clock at the entrance to the Children's Zoo, and the Delacorte Theater where thousands enjoy free "Shakespeare in the Park." On this day, Delacorte and his wife, both senior citizens, are mugged while walking through his beloved park. His wife is stabbed in the hand, and has her mink stolen. The story is filled with the sort of delicious irony that sells papers: *Millionaire Mugged in his Favorite Park.*

My job on this night is to secure an interview with Mr.

Delacorte only hours after the mugging which took place that afternoon. I'm not optimistic. If there's anything I've learned about covering crime, it's that the higher you go up the socio-economic ladder, the less willing crime victims are to talk. And it's not only that. The idea that I can get anywhere near the Fifth Avenue apartment of a millionaire like Delacorte is ludicrous. Undoubtedly, he lives in a doorman building where I'll get nowhere. If I'm lucky, he'll live in a townhouse where speaking to him, though still unlikely, might be a possibility.

But uptown I go and at the corner of 79th Street and Fifth Avenue, I see what I'm up against. Delacorte lives in a huge building with not one but two doormen. I decide to go for it, walk up to the doorman say "Paul LaRosa to see George Delacorte."

One of them phones upstairs and I count the seconds before I get turned away but then the doorman says, "Go right up Mr. LaRosa."

Okay. "Which floor? I haven't been here in a while?"

He tells me and up I go, sure that the moment I get to his apartment, *that's* when I'll be tossed out. The elevator opens and a maid appears. She tries to communicate in English but with a heavy French accent. Now I understand that she probably answered the phone and said, "Oui, oui." Great security this building has.

She escorts me into the living room where a miniature version of the great Delacorte clock has a place of honor on a sideboard. The walls are adorned with artwork and I believe I see a Matisse or is it a Degas? I have no doubt it is an original.

And then I hear a shuffling of feet. George Delacorte,

now a little old man, comes into the room and smiles. "Mister Delacorte, my name is Paul LaRosa and I'm a reporter for *The Daily News*. I'm here to ask you a few questions about the incident in the park this afternoon."

He looks at me through thick glasses and I think, okay *now* is the moment I'll get tossed out.

But instead, he smiles and ushers me toward a chair. "Well," he says, "Aren't you an enterprising young man? Please sit down."

And then he proceeds to give me an exclusive interview that leads the paper the next day.

The old-timers *say anything can happen at night*, and that proves to be true but it's not always a good thing. One night, instead of stopping off at Louie's, I walk down to my car in back of the building along with another reporter, also named Paul. My car is parked at 40th Street and Second Avenue while Paul's is down the block, closer to First, so we part company at the top of the block.

I spend a few moments in the car, picking out which Bruce Springsteen eight-track I want to listen to on the drive home and then pull out with the windows open and the eight-track blaring. As I head to first, I spot Paul but something's wrong. He's surrounded by four guys, and I know instinctively that I am witnessing a mugging. I'm not sure what to do but, full of bravado, I speed up to the scene and slam on the brakes before I hit the thug who's standing next to Paul in the street.

I figured they'd all run away but I figured wrong. The leader does not appear the least bit concerned. He looks at me and starts walking toward me. When he's about five feet away, I see the gun, and freeze. He's moving toward me with menace in his eyes and a gun in his hand but I am stuck. Everything is moving in slow motion and he's nearly at the window when I snap out of it. Without a thought for any cars that might be behind me, I throw the car into reverse and push the gas pedal to the floor. The car and I go flying backwards and recede from the thug and the gun. A good thing. I see his mouth form a little "o" but he doesn't raise the gun to fire. Instead, he and his buddies hustle into a car and take off. I drive up to Paul.

"Get in, we'll follow and get their plate number," I say.

And we do follow but they're too far ahead of us and, really, do I want to catch up to a car filled with thugs who have at least one gun? We call off the chase and I drop Paul at his car and wait until he's pulling out. I follow him for a while and it's only then that I realize Springsteen has stopped singing. I futz around with my eight-track but it's no use—it's broken. I decide then and there to invest in a cassette player.

The Olympics

Everyone is excited during the winter of 1980 because the Olympics are being held upstate in New York at Lake Placid. The paper plans a lot of sports coverage and sends practically the entire sports department and several photographers up to cover it. Big splashy headlines and stories herald the coming games.

But as the events begin, there is unexpected trouble with the buses that are supposed to transport tourists from one event to another. People are waiting for hours and missing events and they're plenty mad. That's when the news desk decides that it might be nice to have a cityside reporter up in Lake Placid to cover the bus debacle and whatever other non-related sports stories happen to pop up. And for whatever reason, someone decides that I'm it. One day, an editor says simply, "Hey you wanna go to the Olympics?"

At first, I'm sure he's kidding. Everyone in the newsroom loves to bust balls, more or less incessantly. "Yeah, okay," I say, "What's the punch line?"

"No punch line. We need someone up there and if you

want the job, you got it. Go see Debbie in sports and she'll tell you how to pick up some gear."

In an hour, I'm standing in the Scandinavia Ski Shop on 57th Street trying on a red ski jacket and being outfitted with hefty snow boots. Seems it's cold up in Lake Placid and everyone covering the event for The News is given a clothing allowance. I can barely believe my luck. I am told to report to the White Plains airport to catch a plane upstate. I don't ask any more about it until I get up there and realize I am flying to the Olympics in a two-seat mail plane! I am a bit daunted but what the hell? It's the Olympics, right? I hop into the only available seat—the one the pilot is not in. Before we take off, the pilot says, "I've gotta check something."

He jumps out, reaches into the wing and pulls out a dip stick. Then he goes into a nearby hanger when he carries out a couple of quarts of oil, and pours them in. *So maybe this is why they asked me, I'm thinking. No one was crazy enough to fly in this thing.* But I sit still and wait for him to come back. In minutes, we're airborne over Westchester where I notice that the pilot—who looks to be in his 50s—is sweating profusely. I think, if this guy has a heart attack, I'm going down.

So I feign more interest than I normally have about planes and begin asking him about the instruments. He tells me what everything is until I run out of questions. I'm not sure I can fly this thing but at least now I have a fighting chance. Besides, the conversation seems to have taken his mind off his pending heart attack and he's stopped sweating. It looks like it will be a fairly smooth ride.

Tony the photographer picks me up at the airport and

off we go, past the Olympic Village to the house where I'm rooming with Tony, columnist Mike Lupica and the outdoors reporter Jerry Kenny.

The next two weeks are a whirlwind of covering the news side of the Olympics. I file several stories about the bus problem but it soon gets straightened out and I have plenty of time on my hands. The sports guys are covering the actual events; my job is to file color pieces. Because I have some sort of special access pass, I can get into most Olympic events without any trouble. For the most popular ones, I need to score a ticket from Sports Editor Buddy Martin but he's pretty accommodating. In return, I help him shuttle reporters and photographers from one event to another.

I realize very quickly that attending outdoor events like the luge and bobsled are a major waste of time. They are nothing like what you see on television when the runs are compressed into something resembling a competition. In the frigid temperatures, you wait through snow squalls for hours while every country in the world—hello, Albania—goes through the motions competing for a medal they know will never come. Even with all my new gear, I freeze my butt off waiting for that millisecond when either a luge or a bobsled (who can tell when they're going so fast?) whooshes by me as I try to maintain my footing on the slanted, snow covered ground. I wouldn't recognize my own brother in this competition. After one day on the bobsled run, I flee Mother Nature for the indoor events and find that watching a lot of limber young women performing in scanty ice skating outfits is more my speed. What's not to like? They're young, pretty, and the temperature is somewhere in the 70s. I even get invited to an ice skating party one night. I point out a woman to one of the newspaper's female sports writers: "Man, she really has that Dorothy Hamill haircut down. She looks exactly like Hamill."

The sports writer looks at me curiously: "That is Dorothy Hamill, you idiot."

Oh.

Because part of my job up here is to find news stories, I spend a lot of time at the medal ceremonies that take place on frozen Lake Placid. City boy that I am, I become convinced that the giant stage is destined to fall through the ice. It can't be that thick, can it? I mean, there are trucks sitting on that ice and thousands of spectators. I move to the periphery, notebook and pen in hand, waiting for moment when the ice will crack and I can begin taking notes about the disaster unfolding before me. It never happens.

At the 1980 Olympics in Lake Placid, New York

What does happen is the United States hockey team. Led by the dapper Herb Brooks and a goalie with an unbearable (to a Yankee fan) Boston accent, the team advances through the early rounds until they come face to face with the team from the USSR. It's the culmination of the cold war—the United States vs. Russia for world domination, hockey style. It's not the finals but it's damn close and the winner of this game most likely will win the gold. The United States team was never supposed to get this far, and everyone—people who never watched a hockey game in their lives—are excited. I begin filing some non-sports stories in the days leading up to the event but realize that my special access pass will *not* get me into the arena the night of the game. I ask sport editor Buddy Martin for a ticket and he comes through at the last moment, knocking on my dorm room door about an hour before the puck will drop.

I take the ticket and decide to lie down on the couch for a few minutes to catch a quick nap. Whether Team USA wins or loses, it's going to be a long night of running down quotes and writing a deadline story. I should really get a little rest.

I am awakened by screaming coming from outside. I run out to discover pandemonium.

"What's going on?" I yell to no one in particular.

A joyous and obviously drunk fan screams in my face: "U-S-A, U-S-A."

"What's going on? What's going on? Man, we fuckin' won. Where have you been?"

Nooooooooooooo! I can't believe it. I've missed the defining event of the Olympics while sleeping on my couch with the ticket in my hand. I look at my watch. Hours have slipped by. I do the only thing I can—grab my notebook and run out to get some quotes on the big event, all the time smiling and gritting my teeth as people regale me with stories of where they were and what they were feeling during the spectacle. I head over to the sports center and dump my notes to Mike Lupica who is writing the front page story. "What a great game," he says over and over.

Who am I to disagree?

Lobster

One day I hear the words every reporter fears: "We're putting you on lobster."

Lobster is the most dreaded shift of all. It means you're working midnight to 8 a.m. Your world is turned upside down. When you're going to bed, everyone else is waking up. When everyone else is heading out for the night, your shift is starting and you'll be there all fucking night. I hate the thought of it but there's nothing I can do, still being one of the new guys. I'm not the lowest man on the totem pole but I'm damn close. And so it begins.

The first night I report for duty at 11:45 p.m. so does Tom Raftery, a reporter I've worked with in Brooklyn. It is the first night for both of us. Raftery is a genial family man from Staten Island who is, I seem to remember, very big into the Boy Scouts. Turns out, he is kind of a Boy Scout himself; he has a lot of moral underpinnings and is fairly religious. We're not exactly a like-minded pair.

I'm very aware that I'm becoming more and more sarcastic and cynical every day. I have a general distrust of people from living in New York my whole life, and being a reporter only serves to make my outer shell even harder now that I have a front row seat on the horrors man is capable of inflicting on his fellow man. Sure there are some bright spots, stories of the "Hey, the cabbie returned my wallet" variety, but isn't that what cabbies are supposed to do? The answer is yes but it doesn't stop us from doing stories like that, ones that focus on the smallest gesture of kindness one New Yorker bestows on another. What is routine in cities across the United States is front page news to us, and that's just sad.

After a few weeks, I begin to look upon the lobster shift as a jail sentence. I just want to stoically put in my time until the parole board deems I can leave. The biggest challenge is the effort it takes to stay awake. Every night, no matter how much I fight it, my eyelids get heavy and I am pretty much forced to close my eyes, put my feet up and nod off. It comes with the territory, I'm told by veterans—everyone sleeps on lobster. The only question is how much shut-eye you get in. You don't want the early shift to find you fast asleep although it happens. I limit myself to three or four hours max, partly because sleeping on a chair is so damn uncomfortable.

Most of the time I think lobster sucks, but there are days when I become aware that, from midnight to 8 a.m., I'm running *The New York Daily News*. Me. Incredible. As those first weeks roll by, I realize that I'm never getting enough sleep no matter how many hours I sneak in during my shift. I get home at around 9 a.m., eat breakfast, and then go to sleep by 10. I'm usually up by 3 p.m., sometimes earlier when my younger brother, now in college and study-ing music, decides to practice his piercing piccolo trumpet. And still I don't move out, figuring why pay rent when I'm working lobster and have the life of a nun? It's very hard to do anything even on my days off because I'm always tired.

Raftery and I only work together three nights a week. The other two he's off and I man the phones alone. I like it better that way because Raftery has a way of driving me a bit nuts. Between 3 and 4 a.m. both of us settle back in our chairs, put our feet on the city desk and doze off. But God forbid that phone rings. Raftery jumps for it like his life is on the line. He does not want to take a chance that I will answer first and get a story tip or learn of a murder before he does. It's insane. There are two of us here, and the phone rings about 5 times a night. There's plenty of nothing to go around.

But no, he has to hog every call that comes in. He makes sure the phone is closer to him when he takes his nap so there's no way I can answer before he does. At first I chal-lenge him for the right to answer the phone and, like school-boys, we fight for each call. Soon enough, I realize that we're both being jerks and I bow out of the competition. He wants to answer every call? Fine! All it means is more work for him. The stories that come in overnight are, 90 percent of the time, nothing but minor murders that will become briefs in the next day's paper. We're supposed to call police head-quarters and talk to the duty officer who, like us, is manning the lobster shift. Like us, he's trying to get some shut-eye. The overnight cop swears he will call us if anything remotely newsworthy passes by his desk. He begs us not to call him because he, too, needs his rest. It sounds reasonable to me but not to Raftery. He calls the police desk every hour on the hour. Each night, the ritual is always the same. He sits up straighter than usual, peers at his watch, and begins dialing. Raftery is very chipper (except when he's fighting me for the phone), has a hint of an Irish brogue and pretends to be the cop's best friend, the cop who would rather eat glass than hear Raftery's voice every hour on the hour.

"Hello, Sergeant. It's your favorite lobster reporter. How are you this fine evening? Anything to report? Okay, well thanks anyway. Keep me posted."

Whenever I talk to the overnight cop—on the nights Raftery is off or happens to be in the bathroom when the phone rings—he asks me, "What's with your buddy? Can you tell him not to call me ten fucking times a night? I'm trying to get some sleep down here."

I tell him I'll do what I can—and I do ask Raftery not to call so much—but he doesn't listen. Instead, he writes up every mundane story that comes across his desk, trying his mightiest to find an angle or twist that will force the dayside editors to include his overnight stories in the next day's paper. Over time, Raftery's memos become the stuff of legend.

There are attempts at irony:

Four bullets fired through an apartment door at a city housing project may have been a family affair. No one was hit, but feelings appear to be hurt, police said.

There is word play:

Some go to church to pray, some go to prey. Words failed, but a knife didn't.

There are stories that combine crime and weather:

A man caught his death of bullets in the chill Washington Heights night air.

Mixed metaphors:

Three bullets were enough to nail the coffin shut on Matthew White, 30, just before midnight on a Harlem street corner.

And there are lead paragraphs that seem to spring directly from Raymond Chandler's typewriter:

An order of protection didn't cut it. A knife did.

There are even Raftery classics that only he could have written:

That old saw, out of sight out of mind, apparently fell on deaf ears as a blind suspect was charged early today for rape. Wearing dark glasses and handcuffs, he was led to central booking with a cop holding his cane, police said.

I do have to hand it to old Raftery; he is making the best of a bad situation but I still I have much more fun on the nights he is off. Then, I wait until the last person goes home and I am alone in the newsroom. That's when I begin to walk around and do a little spying. I am a burglar at heart and I find it thrilling to look through the papers of my fellow reporters, check their mail and sometimes take the food they've stored in the refrigerator. It's not like I'm boosting computers. It's all pretty harmless and it helps me pass the time. My real find comes in the office of Claudia Cohen, a gossip columnist. The woman gets every book imaginable for free and many that I'd like to read. So I help myself. At first, I read what portion I can while at work and then return the book to her pile but soon I am taking the books home like she's running a lending library. I usually bring them back but over time I get sloppy and keep them. That's when she leaves me a note one night. Well, she doesn't actually leave it for me but I know who it's meant for.

"I hope you're enjoying the books you're STEAL-ING from me. You might be interested to know that I donate these books to public school libraries so you're actually stealing from children."

I look at the note and start laughing. Who is she kidding? I know she's selling her review copy books to The Strand bookstore to make a few extra bucks. That night, I take a couple of extra just to teach her a lesson.

Like I said, 90 percent of the time nothing that happens during the lobster shift amounts to anything more than a brief in the next day's paper. The other 10 percent of the time are the stories we live for. One night in December, 1980, at around 11 p.m., I'm getting dressed to drive from Queens to the News office on East 42nd Street when my phone rings. It's the desk—"John Lennon's been shot. Get your ass over to the Dakota."

"What? Are you sure?"

"Yes, he's at Roosevelt Hospital and there are rumors that he's dead. We need you at the Dakota. That's where he was shot by a crazed fan."

I rush out and hop into my blue Dodge Dart, driving as fast as possible to get to Lennon's residence—the famed Dakota Apartment building on West 79th Street and Central Park West. Everyone knows he lives there and everyone knows he's very approachable. There are always photographs in the paper of him and Yoko walking in Central Park. He has just come out of his self-imposed "house husband" phase, and has released an album called "Double Fantasy." It was not one of my favorites, and I was always a "Paul" man, but still. This is beyond outrageous. Who assassinates a musician?

Driving there, I begin to wonder if maybe Lennon was too approachable. I think of the News photographer who casually told me a few weeks before that he had jammed with Lennon on guitar in his apartment and smoked pot with him and Yoko. The ongoing reports on the car radio are sketchy except to confirm that Lennon is indeed dead. It is a stunning blow. Fans everywhere had still hoped, despite their bitter breakup, that the Beatles might some day reunite. Now that's impossible.

I turn on WNEW-FM, the city's premiere rock station, to learn what they know. The DJ is of course devastated by Lennon's murder and does the best thing he can—he plays music. As I'm crossing Central Park from east to west, getting very close to the Dakota, the song "Jungleland" by Bruce Springsteen comes on the radio. It seems too appropriate and I moan along with Bruce on the song.

And then, I am there—at the Dakota. The building has always been a bit eerie with its dark brown exterior festooned with gargoyle heads. It is, after all, where Roman Polanski shot the film "Rosemary's Baby." And now, it is the site of the worst tragedy my mind could conjure up—the death of one of The Beatles. By now, it's a bit past 11:30 p.m. because I've broken every speed limit and used every short cut I know to get there quickly. A few dozen people are gathered around the front entrance to the Dakota, and a few policemen are trying to keep the growing crowd away from the entrance. I pull out my notebook and begin to interview the fans. Some are from New York, some from out of town who happened to be in the city on this horrible night. All have rushed here because they've heard the news. Someone produces a guitar and begins strumming and singing "All We Need is Love." When that ends, someone else begins singing "Give Peace a Chance."

But mixed in with the calls for peace and love, there is also outrage and bitter denunciation of the supposed *fan* who killed this brilliant man, musician and icon. Soon, word spreads that the fan—Mark David Chapman (of course, like all assassins he is given three names almost immediately)— had approached Lennon earlier that day and Lennon had signed his album. Crazy.

Back in the city room, people are called in or come in to help the small nightside and lobster staff deal with this headline-busting story. A grumpy photographer happens to be manning the photo desk and filling in as the photo editor. It's his worst nightmare. Instead of getting to sleep through his shift, a major story breaks. He's not happy, and he takes out his pique on an amateur photographer named Paul Goresh who calls in and says he was at the Dakota earlier that day and believes he photographed Lennon signing a copy of "Double Fantasy" for Mark David Chapman.

"You think or you know?" shouts the photo editor into the phone.

Reporter Bob Lane who is sitting nearby hears the exchange.

The photographer is known for his gruff manner and, given the events of the night, is more uptight than usual. The switchboard is lighting up with calls from all over the world from fans and other media outlets wanting to know what's happened. "Well," the photographer screams into the phone. "When you find out if you've got that picture, bring it here. The address is in the paper."

Lane stares at him. "What was that?"

"Some guy who says he might have a photograph of Lennon signing an autograph for his killer."

"And you hung up on him?"

"I told him to figure out what he has and bring it in."

Lane is beside himself. "Did you get his number?"

"No."

"Shit, if that guy calls back, I wanna talk with him."

Within minutes, the phone on the photo desk rings again. The gruff photo editor takes the call. "What, you again?"

This time, Lane grabs the phone away from him. "This is Bob Lane. I'm a reporter here. Can I help you?"

Lane listens, becomes convinced that the caller might have the goods, and tells him to sit tight. He drives out to Goresh's house in New Jersey and brings him and the roll of film back to be processed in the News' darkroom. The caller does indeed have the picture of the year. It shows Lennon signing Chapman's album with Chapman in the photo hours before this madman returns to the scene to shoot Lennon dead.

Back at the Dakota, I'm joined by reporter Bob Herbert who lives up the block from Lennon. After spending an hour or so taking notes, we head up to Herbert's apartment to call the city desk and dump our notes. I tell Herbert I'm heading back downstairs to stay until the morning. Slowly, the block fills up with more and more fans until the police have to close it off because no traffic can get through. The singing goes on all night and I get plenty of material for another story. I can write my story for a special afternoon edition that will appear on the newsstands in only a few hours.

I tell the editors I want no help from rewrite. I am determined to write this story from my heart and soul, to connect with all of Lennon's fans and make them realize that a Beatles fan—not just another hack reporter—wrote this story. I don't know if I succeeded but within hours, my article on Lennon's death is on page 3 of that afternoon's paper.

Susan

In July 1981, there is one less person living in our Bay-side apartment after my younger brother Bob marries his longtime girlfriend Kathy who he's known since they were both around six years old. They grew up together in the projects and seemed destined to marry since nearly forever. So Bob moves out and soon after, I convince my parents that *they* ought to follow. It's a bold move. Since I'm still resistant to finding an apartment on my own, I suggest to my parents that they should get their own place. It's a neat trick and, even more amazingly, it works. The truth is, it makes sense for all of us. We're still living in the Bayside rental we moved to after leaving the projects but right across the street there is another development that is in much better condition. It is a cooperative for military veterans and, since my father served in the Army during World War II, he qualifies. The cooperative will provide stability for my folks as they get older and me, well, I am finally on my own.

It's probably no coincidence that I begin to have much more luck with women. After all, I now have an apartment to go to and no longer have to hem and haw about living with my parents. That phase of my life is over.

Everything seems to be clicking all at once. At work, I am transferred to dayside, working in the Manhattan section. The Manhattan section had been the centerpiece of the experimental afternoon edition of *The Daily News*, and it was filled with high-salaried, well-known writers, but no more. The editor was the dashing and daring Clay Felker, the man who invented *New York Magazine*. But all those big names didn't help bring in extra readers and, with the newspaper hemorrhaging millions of dollars, the decision is made to pull the plug on the ill-advised afternoon edition, and the entire staff of the Manhattan section is shown the door—immediately. But the section itself remains. So now there are pages and pages to fill and virtually no one to do it. I am transferred in with a couple of other reporters. The Manhattan section is the opposite of everything I've learned in newspapers about writing tight. With all this space to fill, I am instructed to "write long." The news hole is enormous and if I want lay out anecdotes and quote entire speeches, so much the better.

The new editor of the section is Marty Gottlieb, a News veteran only a few years older but with vastly more experience. Marty, like Sam Roberts, is one of the new breed of journalists Editor Mike O'Neill has hired to replace the old-school guys who have been holding down the fort since World War II. Gottlieb is well-regarded for his long running series on rebuilding the Brooklyn neighborhood of Bushwick after the blackout. Gottlieb wrote so many stories about one particular block and its struggles to reinvent itself, that he shamed politicians and developers into providing money. He probably should have won the Pulitzer but instead he settled for a slew of awards and the admiration of the newsroom. Now Gottlieb is my editor and he's a creative dynamo, always coming up with some interesting story or angle for me to pursue. It's great being his soldier but it's often hard to match his energy. He's always challenging me to do more. His ideas are ambitious and smart, and suddenly the Manhattan section is covering topics that were formerly the purview of *The New York Times*. Under Gottlieb's tutelage, I begin to write about housing, preservation, gentrification and many features about unique New York characters. It is a head-spinning experience and great fun for a young reporter. Some days, I am responsible for two long feature stories that fill the section.

But even dynamos need to take a vacation now and again and it is during one of Gottlieb's vacations that George James, a veteran newshound who's toiled mostly in the borough sections his entire career, takes over. James lives in New Jersey and is nothing like Gottlieb but he's a good guy who wants to do the best he can while Gottlieb is away.

One day, he rushes over to me holding a piece of paper. "You've got to call this woman right away," he says. "She's got the greatest idea for a story. I want you to call her right away."

The name on the paper is Susan Glauberman, a flack for New York University. I dial, having no idea what the story is about. Susan, who is friendly on the phone, tells me the story she's pitched is about an archival radio series about ironworkers and the building of New York's skyscrapers that recently landed in the NYU library. *Huh?* I don't know what to say. I look across the room to see if maybe George

James is playing some kind of prank. But his head is down and he's not even looking my way. *This* is one of the best story ideas he's ever heard? *A radio series?* How the fuck do I turn this into a story Daily News readers will care about? *What the fuck?*

I've been at The News long enough to know that this story is a non-starter. If James had told Dick Oliver about this story, chances are he would have transferred James to lobster. Either that or he'd give him one of his death stares until James slunk off on his own. I don't have those options. I hang up with Susan, and walk over to James.

"You're kidding about this story, right?"

"What? No, I think it's great. You know, my father was an ironworker"

James keeps talking but I'm no longer listening. *Now* I get it. James isn't really interested in this story—he's interested in his father!! Of course. Well, at least it's not a joke. It's a contract—I have to do this story.

"I don't think this will have any resonance with the typical News reader," I say.

"Are you kidding, Paul? Look, it's all in the way you write it."

And he's off again, basically convincing himself that this story is great. Whatever. I call Susan back and reluctantly tell her I'll come by tomorrow to listen to this fucking radio series and write a feature about it. She's ecstatic of course, for good reason. I'm sure she's already called 50 reporters without even a nibble. This is what flacks live for—paydirt on the 1,000th call. It proves they're not insane. Not totally.

The next day I head down to NYU. The only interest I have in the entire story is meeting Susan. She's been fun to talk to and I'm curious to see what she looks like. For whatever reason, I think there is something special about her, something I can't describe. I stand at the reception desk and wait for her to turn the corner. She comes around that corner beaming from ear to ear, happy to see me. She's young and cute, slender. She wears her hair in the style of the day, a wavy permanent. She's dressed in a knee-length skirt and a silk burgundy blouse. Very professional and, yet, there is something undeniably sexy about her.

We engage in small talk as she takes me over to NYU's Bobst Library where I sit with headphones and listen to an entire radio series. It's a wonder I don't fall asleep but I do manage to take some notes because I know George James will want to play this up on the front of the Manhattan section. Somehow, I have to figure out how to make it interesting to the average Daily News reader. Susan sits nearby, watching me and reading the newspaper—*The Times* of course. After a couple of hours, it is past 2 o'clock and I announce I'm finished. Susan walks me downstairs and we are about to go our separate ways at a corner near her office when she asks if I'd like to go to lunch.

Why not?

We go into this place called Garvins right near NYU. Because it is after lunch, it is empty except for one other table of three people. I'm astonished to see that one of the people at that table is Father Rafferty, a priest I know from Blessed Sacrament. He was never as popular as Father Dolan and Father Gorman but I remember him as a good guy. Still, I have no desire to engage in awkward small talk so I ignore him. Because I am older and out of context, he doesn't seem to recognize me, and that's just fine.

The waiter comes over. We place our order and Susan orders scotch. Hmmm. I order a vodka tonic even though I've never before had a drink while lunching with a flack. But this one is kind of pretty. We talk and talk and Susan is great fun, laughs at all my dumb jokes and before I know it, I lean over and kiss her. She kisses me back and soon the lunch evolves. I forget all about going back to the office. This is too much fun and the coincidence of having this tête-à-tête *in front of a priest whom I know* is too delicious. I cannot stop. I am smashed and so is Susan, who excuses herself to go to the rest room and walks into the kitchen. We laugh and laugh all the way back to her office where she closes the door. When we exit, the cleaning woman is in the hallway asking if we're done. We both blush and hurry out.

Four months later, I propose.

I hardly know what I'm doing and I don't think Susan does either when she accepts. We're both very different. To begin, Susan is Jewish and I'm not, and that's a fact that doesn't go over so well with her parents who are, nonetheless, very polite Midwesterners from Akron, Ohio, the city where Susan was raised. To them, Akron is home. To me, it has always been kind of a joke. You know, like Akron, the rubber capital of the world? The word Akron is innately funny to me but neither Susan nor her parents get it.

But our different religious backgrounds don't faze me. What really throws me is visiting her hometown for an engagement party where I am to meet her whole family. Her parents are fine, as are most of her relatives, but the way they live!! Turns out they reside in the Akron suburb of Fairlawn and it's something out of "Leave it to Beaver."

I've never lived in a house in my life and I cannot conceive of existing in this totally residential world where the neat little houses are lined up one after another. Most people in American feel comfortable in places like this but, me, I feel trapped. I am nothing if not a native New Yorker used to stepping outside and seeing hundreds, sometimes thousands of people. Here, I step out and see more houses and not a person in sight. It is so quiet you can hear a cicada chirp and believe me I do—they keep me up all night.

But it's not only the lack of people—there are no stores anywhere! This is really residential and to get anywhere you need a car. I never before realized how comfortable I felt knowing that there was a bodega on every corner. In New York, I can walk to get a container of milk or a bag of chips or even stop by any number of pizza stores to get a whole "pie," as my father calls pizza. Akron strikes me as terribly deprived. All that exists in this neighborhood are homes, cars and a nearby mall. I've never felt so isolated in my life. We don't even have our own car. It makes me antsy and I'm sure I present a pretty pathetic picture to her parents.

The engagement party goes not so well. Just before the party gets started, one of Susan's relatives comes up to me and matter-of-factly says, "I hope you know what you're doing—she's a ball-breaking bitch."

I am so shocked I say nothing. I think he must be kidding but he looks at me without a hint of a smile. Before I can bolt out the door, Susan's extended family comes through it, including her Uncle Murray, who buttonholes me in front of everyone.

So Paul do you golf?

No.

Play tennis?
No.
Ski?
No.
What do you do for fun?

I briefly consider telling him that I sit in bars and drink, or sometimes walk the streets of Manhattan to people-watch and visit book and record stores. It always seemed enough for me but now it suddenly dawns on me (and every other member of Susan's family listening intently to this conversation)—that what d'ya know? I don't have any hobbies! I mean, there are the times I change the oil in my car just for fun but I don't think that would score me any points with this country-club crowd. I realize that I must seem awfully un-American in their eyes. Forget not being Jewish. Susan is perhaps marrying an alien! The rest of Susan's family stares at me like they've come upon a strange new species. In a pathetic attempt to win them over and gain back a measure of respect, I tell them that I'm a pretty good softball player. They smile politely and offer me cheese. I decide not to follow that up by telling them I used to hunt rabbit and pheasant with a bow and arrow and, for a few good years, was a hell of a shoplifter.

Despite this disastrous party, Susan and I decide to go ahead with our union and eleven months after we met over a story about a radio series, we marry in a loft apartment and, after a honeymoon in the Caribbean, we move to the Cobble Hill section of Brooklyn. It's a long way from the Bronx and that's fine with me, and I think Susan feels the same way about Akron.

Trying Harder

One day, not long after I am married, Gottlieb, perhaps my favorite editor of all time, asks me to walk with him to J & A, *The Daily News'* official deli of choice. Once we get outside, it's clear he has more on his mind than what type of sandwich to order. I am in for a lecture. He tells me he thinks I'm a good reporter but could be much better. He tells me that sometimes it seems like I cut corners or don't put as much effort into an assignment as I could. "Paul," he says, "you've got to want it more. You've got to work harder. You need to make that extra phone call, talk to another person. You have a lot of potential but you need to really concentrate and not take the easy way out."

The words sting and I'm a more than a little astonished. Here I thought I was doing great work for Gottlieb but, evidently, it was not good enough. My first reaction is to get defensive and the next is to feel hurt. The walk back from the deli is a long one. I don't say much. Gottlieb keeps chattering away. He keeps telling me straight out that he likes me and thinks I'm talented but...

Back in the newsroom, I eat my sandwich alone and think about what he said. For better or worse, I've been raised to be a reporter in a newsroom where the union mentality is dominant. The overall vibe is to work hard but not too hard. The job is supposed to be fun, not a life's mission and you've got to leave time to go down to Louie's and drink for a few hours.

I decide that maybe I'm misinterpreting that vibe. Sure there are the "union" reporters who only do the bare minimum to get by but I am also surrounded by intense hard workers. Guys like Vinnie Lee and even Pat Doyle are workhorses who care about nothing more than seeing their bylines in the newspaper. I realize that maybe, just maybe, I've been blinded by their love of a good time and have missed how hard they really work. Gottlieb is right; I need an attitude adjustment. I don't tell Susan or anyone else about the conversation with Gottlieb. I'm too embarrassed. Instead, I resolve to work harder, longer and put more thought into my assignments.

I always prided myself on my writing but now I double down, and add little flourishes whenever I can. I study *The New Yorker* and *The New York Times'* Metro section to see how they do what they do. I come to the conclusion that what I'm most interested in are those quirky features about quirky New Yorkers. I do not believe I have the tenacity or drive to be a great investigative reporter. So I concentrate on what I believe I do best. One day, after a window washer falls 50 stories to his death, I suggest to Gottlieb a story on the guy who washes the windows at the Empire State Building, and Gottlieb enthusiastically agrees.

Turns out the Empire State Building's chief window washer is a guy named Tom Smith who, despite his boring name, gives pretty good quotes. He tells me he's always considered himself an outdoorsman and feels he has fulfilled his life quest by hanging off the side of a tall building smack in the middle of eight million people. And he's fearless. He doesn't use a scaffold but attaches his leather belt to bolts affixed to the building's windows. Once secure, he leans back and begins washing. He says he never worries, not even when one of the bolts breaks. "Even if a bolt comes out, you'll still be secured to the building by the other one and you should be able to get back in the building—if you don't have a heart attack first!"

This is great material. I ask him how he handles cold weather and he says, "It always makes me laugh because people ask me what I do in the winter. They don't realize that there are two sides to a window and, in the winter, we do the insides."

I love this guy and I know I'm going to get a good story out of him. I'm lucky that Gottlieb's deputy for the Manhattan section is a guy named Mike Neill who is terrific at layout and headlines. Most of the time, my stories are featured on the front of the Manhattan section with a large photograph, a provocative headline, and a prominent byline. For the window washer story, Mike keeps it simple: *"It's a long way down"* because the photo of Tom, shot from above, says it all.

The story begins with a quote from Tom Smith:

> *"Window cleaners resent everyone calling us nuts. We want people to know we're not supermen. We're regular guys just doing a job."*
>
> *"They might be 'regular guys just doing a job,' but the city's 1,500 unionized window cleaners do some-*

thing that almost none of us has to do every day—confront death."

Gottlieb has assigned me to cover Manhattan below 14th Street and I scour every little ad or community board meeting to find stories with that little zing. In the Village Voice, I spot an ad for a Tupperware party to be held at the Pyramid Cocktail Lounge, a club on Avenue A, between Sixth and Seventh Streets in the heart of Alphabet City. It's also the heart of thriving downtown art scene. The Pyramid was a stripped-down former blue-collar bar that has changed with the neighborhood. Instead of union men knocking back shots and a beer, the club has been embraced by a coterie of actors and performers—gay, transvestite and straight—who put on vaudeville and burlesque shows, and just about anything else that will get a laugh.

The Tupperware party falls into the "anything else" category, weird but just weird enough to be hip. I arrange to attend with a photographer, and we're not disappointed. Our upbeat host is Malcolm Kelso and he's invited Vera Castellone, a Tupperware party-giver from West Hempstead, Long Island, to show off her wares. The bar is jammed with friends and regulars who hoot and holler with gusto at the very latest Tupperware gizmos that Vera has to offer.

"Tupperware," Kelso informs the crowd "is exclusive. You can't buy it anywhere—not even Bendel's!"

Vera, whose hair and glasses scream *Middle America*, is determined to impress and she does, doling out suburban hors d'oeuvres like Reddi-Whip on Ritz crackers, Marshmallow Fluff and Velveeta. The crowd literally eats it up. Vera, who even makes a bit of money at the event, beams with pride. "I've never done this kind of thing at a club," she says, "except for one or two held at yacht clubs."

The story runs on the front of the Manhattan section with a photograph of Castellone and Kelso, the odd couple, and my lead is: *It was the day suburbia came to the lower East Side.*

In-house, my articles begin to get noticed. I have the good luck of writing for the Manhattan section which is included in the newspaper distributed throughout the newsroom. The sections for the other boroughs are more or less invisible to those in power. Editor Syd Penner, who writes an internal newsletter called The Printer's Devil, cites my articles as examples of what the paper should be doing more of. Gottlieb congratulates me, but warns me not to sit on my laurels and asks me what I have for that day's paper. That's the thing about daily journalism—it's relentless.

I follow up with a series of pieces on unique New Yorkers and those in trouble for one reason or another. These are "small" stories that are not news and would not be able to fight their way into the news pages but they make great features and I believe they're the kinds of articles News readers love to read. Take the article that Neill headlines: *The People vs. Mary King.* It is about a cleaning woman who gets a city violation for taking garbage off a city street. Mary got in trouble when she spotted a couple of cardboard boxes left on a city street. She took some paper out of one and put it in the other and started on her way with the now-empty box under her arm. That's when a Sanitation Department worker stopped her. "What do you think you're doing?" he asked.

Mary told him she needed an empty box and he told her that what he had just witnessed– what he termed "unauthorized removal of garbage"—was against the law. The result was a ticket that could cost Mary up to $250.

Of course, The News comes to her rescue. Once my article is published, the city drops the whole thing. I feel the power of the press—I can change lives, help people, keep the city off their backs. It is exhilarating.

I've tapped into a desire to help people that I was not aware I had. Soon after, I am assigned a piece about a gay senior citizens' group called SAGE (Seniors Action in a Gay Environment) whose members humor me and assure me that the article I am taking notes for will never be published. "We've had other reporters try to do what you're doing," one of them tells me. "I have no doubt you'll write it, but you watch—your piece will be killed and you'll get some bullshit answer when you ask why."

"No, no," I say. "It's really going to be published. I have no doubt."

Gottlieb, after all, has assigned it. The group members are polite but don't believe it, not until the next day when a story runs prominently on the front page of the Manhattan section headlined:

> *"Within a minority, another minority: Being old and gray is tough; being old and gay can be hell."*

A couple of the members call me, clearly astonished at seeing their quotes in print. "We couldn't even get that article in *The Times*," he says.

I begin finding stories everywhere. I write about identical twins who, because of an accident of birth, wind up with very different lives. One graduates from Brown and becomes a successful writer; the other attains the status of bicycle messenger. I write about the Cat Woman of Chelsea who feeds cats peacefully for 24 years until her rental apartment becomes a cooperative and her once-tolerant neighbors demand she move out. I write about one of the city's first dedicated dog runs; it's down near SoHo, causing Mike Neill to dub it DoHo. I write about my own love of papaya juice, especially at the hot dog stand—Gray's Papaya on E. 86th Street—that I have been patronizing with my parents since I could walk. I write about Ms. New York State Senior, America Henrietta Bundy, 67, who wins the talent competition at a Catskill resort by doing a little soft shoe. I write about the renegade barber of Union Square who holds up the construction of a 45-story building by refusing to move from his little shop where he is paying all of $200 a month rent. I write about a reunion of kids who grew up in the Hebrew Orphan Asylum, kids with fond memories of being orphans. I write about 83-year-old Ruth Wittenberg, a.k.a. Mrs. Greenwich Village, who was once friends with journalist and communist John Reed when the Village, and they, were young. I write about building superintendant Nick Mazzuco who is dubbed "an atomic vet" because he was exposed over and over to the fallout of nuclear tests when he was a kid in the Army during World War II.

And it isn't only unknown New Yorkers that I profile. One day, I get a call from Howard Rubenstein, who runs a big public relations firm that represents the Dime Savings Bank. They are holding some hokey stickball competition for kids near Lincoln Center and want to know if I have any interest in covering it. *Uh, no.*

But it turns out Howard is playing with me. He tells me that Joe DiMaggio will be attending said stickball competition to repay a debt to one of his benefactors, Dime Savings Bank.

"I was going to ask if you'd be interested in going up to Joe D's room and hanging out with him a while before the two of you head over to the stickball demo," he says.

I grovel and plead that of course I was just kidding when I said I had no interest in covering the event and please, pretty please, can I go? Having grown up in the Bronx, being a Yankee fan as well as Italian-American, I am practically required to be there. I tell Howard. He instructs me to go over to the Sheraton Hotel on Sixth Avenue. I am given the room number where Joe D is staying. I will get a little one-on-one time with him before we ride in his limo to the stickball game. "There's only one ground rule," Howard said.

"Yes?"

"No questions about Marilyn Monroe."

"No problem."

At the appointed hour, I show up at the hotel room. I stop a moment before knocking. On the other side of this door is *the* Joe DiMaggio, and I'm going to meet him, *and* I'm not supposed to ask him any questions about Marilyn Monroe. Joe DiMaggio and Marilyn Monroe have become part of today's assignment! Is this really happening? How did I—Paul LaRosa, the shy kid from the projects—wind up in this spot, on this day, on the verge of meeting one of the greatest Yankees in their glorious history, a guy who was *married* to the legendary Marilyn Monroe? Fucking incredible! Then I do something I haven't done in a long while—I make the sign of the cross and knock.

An ordinary guy, not DiMaggio, appears. I wonder for a second if I've been tricked but then I step inside and see DiMaggio finishing up a phone call. He rises to greet me, and we begin chatting about everything. I ask him about baseball's free agency (he's in favor), his knees (ironically, after years of trouble when he was playing ball, they are the best part of his body now), whether he is truly shy (sometimes, he doesn't love all the attention but he's working on his natural reticence), his endorsement deals with Mr. Coffee and the Dime (he tells me proudly that he's no sellout and mentions how he's turned down $75,000 from a denture company "because I've got all my teeth").

I still can't believe I am speaking to the man himself but somehow I manage to take notes. Then comes the moment when we leave his room and walk through the hotel lobby. Every head in the place snaps his way. He is tall, good-looking and seemingly totally at ease, though I now know that is a ruse.

"Joe," says a cop, "I saw you on TV last night."

"How did I do? Did I look all right?"

"Joe, you looked great."

And he does. I feel like a midget next to the great DiMaggio. In the car, I hand Joe my notebook and ask if he wouldn't mind signing. He does, and hands it back. Soon, we get to the event and I watch as DiMaggio engages a few dozen kids in the finer points of stickball, even hitting a couple of Spaldeens himself. At the end, I thank him profusely and hustle back to the office to write a story.

The next day, I spot a package on my desk. I open it and inside is a baseball in a little plastic case. It is signed, "*To Paul LaRosa. Best wishes, Joe DiMaggio.*"

Validation

Gottlieb soon realizes that I have a special interest in housing and asks me about my background and where I grew up. I tell him about the projects and soon enough, I'm writing every housing story that appears in the section. As I move through that world, I hear a lot of so-called experts put down the projects as unlivable or crime-ridden. They are called a terrible mistake by analysts who, I'm sure, have never set foot inside one. But it doesn't stop them from bloviating about the way these large developments should never have been built, and the way they dehumanize people. I want to shout at them and tell them my truth, that, yes there are problems now, but that it wasn't always so. There was a time when the projects worked, and were one of the best things that ever happened to me. They gave me an immediate group of friends and helped make me the person I am today. They were very livable and could be again if the income mix of people were different, if working class folks were sprinkled in with welfare recipients. They could work if people were rewarded with a sense of pride and were not considered druggies merely for living there.

I even write a piece about the Housing Authority's 50th anniversary, with a sidebar on my life in the Monroe Houses. It's a little like coming out of the closet. A few reporters and editors tell me they had no idea I'd grown up in a public housing project, and listen with fascination when I tell them that for the first years I lived there, it was nearly idyllic.

My interest in housing extends in every direction. I grow interested in the movement to preserve some of the city's beautiful old buildings. Aghast that the elegant Penn Station was razed for the horrid Madison Square Garden, the city passes a new landmarks law. I begin writing about these topics and it puts me back into the orbit of Jacqueline Kennedy Onassis, who has thrown her support behind preservation. I go to press conferences and landmark hearings that are attended by Jackie O and am introduced to her so many times that she comes to nod in my direction every time we meet. Like everyone says, there is some unknowable quality surrounding her and I never feel comfortable enough to mention the summer that Caroline and I were copykids together.

Readers began sending me their own tales of housing woes and tips about special stories. Residents of the Belnord, a stately apartment building on W. 86th Street, tell me of an ongoing battle with their landlady who, they say, has nearly destroyed a building that was once thought to be on a par with the Dakota. I write about a lot of landlord-tenant battles and the gentrification that occurs when builders renovate old buildings and force out the older tenants. A revolution is going in the city as more and more rental units become cooperatives, and even SRO's (Standing Room

Occupancy hotels) are transformed into glittering new co-ops without regard for previous longtime tenants.

Gottlieb beams at my progress and tells me to keep it up, but in the next breath he tells me he's going to take a job with *The New York Times*. It's a sad day because, after all we've been through, I feel he is the one editor who really understands me and pushed me. What's more, he respected me.

I have to admit that Quinn's backhanded compliment has stuck in my psyche. It has never left. I hear his words as clear as if they were spoken yesterday: "I don't think it will last long."

Even though I am finally an established reporter at The News, I began to notice that newer and younger reporters are being hired from other papers and brought in from Columbia University's School of Journalism. It seems that the moment they arrive, they are anointed. They get the better assignments, the high-profile beats. I am afraid that I am overlooked because I started my life at *The Daily News* as a copy boy. While a lot of my old copyboy cronies are working as reporters, feature writers, photographers and copy desk people, none of us are in a position of power.

I decide that I need to do something to open up their eyes, to make them see me as something more than a blue collar reporter and more like a journalist. The best way to do that, I decide, is to enter a prestigious writing contest. The Pulitzer is out of the question but there is the Meyer Berger Award, a highly-regarded award given out by Columbia's School of Journalism. It is named after the famous *New York Times* reporter who invented the About New York column, the quintessential city feature. What I like about the award is that it's not given for deadline or investigative reporting—it is awarded for good writing.

Without telling anyone, I enter the contest, sending in five stories along with a brief biography.

And then I forget all about it until March 9, 1983 when I get a letter in my News mailbox marked CONFIDENTIAL from Columbia University. I open it and read on.

Dear Mr. LaRosa,

In 1960 a modest endowment was established at the Graduate School of Journalism to honor the memory and professional achievements of Meyer Berger with an award. The awards are made possible through the generosity of Louis Schweitzer, a New York industrialist, who knew and admired Mike Berger and his writings, and have been perpetuated each year with a gift from his widow, Lucille Lortel Schweitzer. They are given to New York area newspaper men and women "for distinguished reporting in the Mike Berger tradition."

The judges of the 1983 Mike Berger Award have selected the following two winners, in no special order of preference:

"To Anna Quindlen for her 'About New York' columns in the New York Times. Ms. Quindlen, a young writer of a new generation, observing a New York vastly changed from the lifetime of Mike Berger, sees its people with the same sensitive and compassionate spirit. She has the keen ear of someone who listens. She has the stole of one who cares deeply for the right word. In all those respects, she fulfills the essence of the Meyer Berger Award."

"To Paul LaRosa, for his stories in the Manhattan section of the Daily News. Many of Paul LaRosa's stories in the Daily News Manhattan section in 1982 probed into the lives

of New Yorkers who were battling back against the tribula-tions, challenges, and sometimes the tragedies of urban life. Witty or sardonic, Paul LaRosa's prose was always appro-priate to the human values on which he focused. His sto-ries have that particular New York flavor which marked the work of Meyer Berger."

You will each share a cash prize and each of you will receive a certificate from Columbia University. Presenta-tion will be made at a special luncheon commemorating the twenty-third anniversary of the Berger Awards. On this date, public announcement of the awards will be made. The luncheon is sponsored by the Faculty of the Graduate School of Journalism and will be held in the President's Room of Faculty House, 400 East 117th Street at Morningside Drive, on Thursday, April 14, at 12:30 p.m.

Meanwhile, our congratulations and our very best wishes.
Sincerely,
Osborn Elliott

I put the letter down and look out across the newsroom. The hustle and bustle, the ball-breaking, the cursing and all the rest of it is still going on, though less so. It's hard to see day to day to but there's no doubt that the newspaper is evolving. There are almost no more typewriters now. There are still a few of those big old Royals sprinkled around the newsroom but the workload of Nick the typewriter repair-man is dwindling by the day. *The Daily News* is changing. All of us work on big green-screened computers manufac-tured by the Mergenthaler Company, and that click-clacking that I loved so much is gone. Stories are measured now in inches, not takes. Remnants of the paper I experienced when

I walked into the city room are still present but we've made the switch from hot to cold type. There are no more vats of molten lead down in the pressroom, no more Linotype machines. Printers are no longer highly skilled workers. Now all they do is basically cut and paste cold type; the news stories come pouring out of machines looking more or less the way they will appear in the newspaper. There are so many superfluous printers that many of them are placed in the so-called "rubber room" where all they do all day is play cards and bet the races. The newspaper can't get rid of them but doesn't know what to do with them either.

Various press cards from my 16-year career at The Daily News

A lot has been lost with the changeover to computers, and it's not only jobs. *It's atmosphere.* The wire room and the reassuring hum of the AP and UPI wires are still. And it's not only the physical space that is changing. There are far fewer of the old guard reporters wishing for their next drink. The new guys, most of them anyway, could use a drink. They are aggressive, have college degrees, and all want to make their way in the world—before lunch if possible. *The Daily News* to them is a stepping stone to *The New York Times* or *The Washington Post.* Even Louie's is not as crowded as it once was.

But just as I'm thinking it's all so different, a reporter to my right screams out "copy" as loud as he can. On the bench behind me, a kid who's half-Asian jumps up, runs over and takes the library slip back to the morgue to pull the clips. All I can do is smile. It ain't that different, not yet. And, by the way, the globe in the lobby remains untouched, and I still walk by it every day and marvel at the way I did the first time. Throughout my life, it's been a witness.

I'm still holding the letter from Columbia University in my hand. I re-read it again and again and smile. Even though the letter says "confidential" I cannot help but call Gottlieb, and tell Mike Neill, who is now the editor of the Manhattan section. They're both very happy for me. Word spreads across the newsroom—*LaRosa won the Mike Berger Award.* People congratulate me all afternoon. It's not so much that someone from The News won the award, it's the idea that *I won it* that has them shaking their heads. They underestimated me. I see the incredulity in their eyes. I've surprised them, exactly my goal. Now I feel I have their respect.

Neill takes me out for a congratulatory lunch. And on

the way back, we stop for the light at the corner of 42nd Street and Third Avenue, right across from the last Horn & Hardardt luncheonette in New York. Incredibly, my old nemesis, Ed Quinn, winds up standing next to us.

He nods hello.

"Have you heard?" Neill asks him.

"What's that?" Quinn replies.

"Paul won the Meyer Berger Award."

Quinn's mouth falls open. He doesn't say a word.

"Isn't that great?" Neill says.

As we begin crossing the street, Quinn stands there. I consider what I want to say to him for all his "help" and "encouragement" over the years. I want to call him an ass-hole and lord it over him, I want to tell him "Looks like you were wrong about me, motherfucker." I want to say to him, "Looks like I lasted longer than you thought, huh?"

But I think better of it.

I don't say a word.

I give him a wink and keep on walking.

On April 14th, Mike Neill and my wife Susan accompany me to the journalism school at Columbia University to pick up the Meyer Berger Award and a check for $1,000. I'm almost afraid to walk into the room where the luncheon is being held. I know they like my work but will they like me? I step inside and meet a whirlwind of journalism students, Dean Osborn Elliott and *New York Times* Columnist Anna Quindlen, my co-winner. Also present is the woman who sponsors the award, Ms. Lucille Lortel. She's a charming senior citizen and I thank her.

Just before the formal luncheon begins, Anna Quindlen

whispers to me, asking if I've prepared a speech or anything. No, I tell her, I'm going to wing it, as is my way.

"Me too," she says.

So then they call my name and I wing it.

Then it is Anna's turn, and the first thing Miss Anna does is pull a prepared speech out of her bag and proceeds to read for about eight minutes. She's great, much better than me. But I have to laugh. At least I was honest.

After the luncheon, Mike and Susan and I mill around.

"We can't go back to work," Mike says.

I agree.

"Wanna get a drink?

Susan and I nod appreciatively. Just what we were thinking.

"Where to?"

And then I get an idea. "Let's go to the Oak Room at the Plaza."

Twenty minutes later, I am one of those guys in suits sitting at the bar of the Oak Room overlooking Central Park South next to an attractive woman—my wife. Through the window, I can see the horse-drawn carriages, but I'm looking for something else—the teenager who, years ago, wandered into the Plaza and stared open-mouthed at the grown-ups here in this room. I look over to where the maitre d' stands, and I can almost see that young boy. Almost.

Epilogue:
Fifty Years On

On June 5, 2011, a group of mostly overweight and aging men and a couple of women gather in a city park across from the projects and next to P.S. 100. It's been 50 years since my family moved into the Monroe Houses, and, thanks to Facebook, my old gang reassembles for a reunion. I've driven there by myself from Brooklyn where I now live. I park my car a couple of blocks away because I want to savor each approaching step. As I approach, I get more and more excited to see these childhood friends, most of whom I have not seen in person in more than 35 years. I am especially excited to see Frank who is now living in Florida.

I step into the park and walk over to the group. The years have been kinder to some than others. I spot Frank immediately even though he's no longer the skinny little freshman who ran on the Cardinal Hayes Track Team in the *sub-midget* category. A lot has changed for me as well. I left *The News* in 1991, taking a buyout after a long five-month strike and now I'm a producer at CBS News. I work with famous correspondents, travel the world and stay at the best hotels. I've hung out at the Playboy Mansion with Hugh Hefner and have been to London to work on the Royal Wedding. Sometimes I have to slap myself as a reminder that it's all real.

Project Reunion 2011, fifty years after most of us moved into Monroe

One thing I have held onto all these years is yoga. The panic attacks never reoccurred but I stuck with yoga and now practice four times a week. I don't know much about Frank's life since college when we drifted apart.

Frank gives me a big smile and we embrace. "Man you lost all your hair," he says.

"Yeah, well, I shave a lot of it. How are you?"

And then we do what comes naturally—sit on a bench as we had fifty years earlier and ease into a talk about the different paths life has taken us. Frank tells me that, back in the late '70s, he grew tired of New York after having a couple of motorcycles and a new car stolen. His way of coping was to get the hell out, and so began his journey around the country—he and his new bride, also from the Bronx. They travelled from Oklahoma City to Kansas and finally Florida.

"I can't believe you moved to Oklahoma City," I say.

"I know, right. I was a fish out of water with my accent and all."

"They must've thought you were in the Witness Protection Program."

We laugh and then John comes over to join the conversation. He sits down with us and suddenly the three of us—who've spent countless hours together playing sports and running around the lots—are back where we met, back on the benches. Between the projects and the copyboy bench at *The Daily News*, the richest conversations of my life have taken place on a bench of one kind or another.

The turnout is great and many other friends make it: Mike LaScala, Bobby Oliva and his brother Lefty, who married one of the Kathys; Fernando Santana, who joined the Army at the age of 32 and now lives in Texas; Eugene Duffy, who joined the Army during the Vietnam era but who luckily wound up being stationed in Hawaii. Even Tony is there. Tony has probably had the roughest time of any of us. He's lived on the streets for years although he's cleaned up and has his own apartment now. Those years were tough; Tony became estranged from his brother Billy who has also showed up. They haven't seen each other in nearly a decade but now they embrace and, as Tony later says on Facebook, "it was as though the years melted away." (It was great to

In June 2011, I stood in front of my project home,
1790 Story Avenue

see Tony that day but, just eight months later, he passed away from cancer.)

We all know the friends who are not at the reunion because they've died young. Good old Mary was the first to pass on, years before. Then my best bud Andrew succumbed to cancer in Chicago. Joe, a mainstay of our group, died only 18 months earlier, and Nancy, who eventually married Mike, died less than a year before.

We begin to walk back toward my old building which is smack dab right in the middle of the projects—1790 Story Avenue. And as we do, we keep talking about what we've been doing all these years as we bounce the Spaldeens that

Bobby has given each of us. Donald Kenneally has his own deli, Mike LaScala is an engineer, Duffy a "top mop" as he likes to call himself, a custodian at a public school. Phil Vassallo is a writing coach. Most of us are lucky enough to have long marriages. There are a couple of divorces. We talk about our children, all of them well past the age we were when we first met. Most of our kids seem well-adjusted but we all agree on one thing: none of them grew up as we had—with each other and not much adult supervision. We had no playdates, no videogames, no cell phones, very little money and of course we all agree that we are better off for it. We made our own fun, formed our own bonds, and had the time of our lives.

Author's Note

This book is based on my memory of events and, in some cases, I relied upon journals, newspaper stories and other people's recollections of tales often told and handed down over the years. It is entirely possible that someone might remember the same stories a different way. That's life.

In a few instances, I changed names but, for the most part, I did not.

I want to thank readers— Gail Hochman, Deb Keiser, Larry Celona, Michael Neill, Margaret Schankler and Nancy Cardozo—who looked at earlier versions and gave me tips, advice, and filled in some details.

As always, thanks to my wife Susan who also read an early version and is always enthusiastic about my writing; it's great to have a partner like her and I realize how lucky I am. Also thanks to my children Alexandra and Peter who do not know all these stories and may be surprised by a couple.

15076479R00184

Made in the USA
Lexington, KY
07 May 2012